BrainSMART®
60 Strategies
For Boosting Test Scores

Marcus Conyers

and

Donna Wilson, Ph.D.

First Edition 2000
Second Edition 2005

ISBN 1-58933-000-5

Layout Designer: Lorraine MacDonald
Cover Designers: Erika Amlund & Lorraine MacDonald
Interior Graphics: Rob Van Tol
Editors:
General – Dara Lee Howard
Content – Jeanne Zehr
Word Processor: Leslie Wilson

www.brainsmart.com

Contents

Introduction v

Chapter 1 1
BrainSMART Student Achievement

Chapter 2 15
Ten Key Facts About Your Brilliant Brain

Chapter 3 25
The BrainSMART Model™: The Synergy of Neuroscience and Common Sense

Chapter 4 29
State – The Power to Produce Results

Chapter 5 41
Meaning – How to Make Learning Meaningful in Your Classroom

Chapter 6 53
Attention – How to Gain and Sustain Focused Attention on the Real Work of Learning

Chapter 7 59
Retention – Teaching With Memory in Mind

Chapter 8 77
Transfer – A Toolbox of Strategies for Helping Students Transfer Learning From the Classroom to Success on the Test and Success in Life

Chapter 9 87
Sixty BrainSMART Strategies and Your Own BrainSMART Lesson Planning Guide

References and Resources for Further Learning 217

Appendix 229
Information About the Authors, Online Graduate Programs & Professional Development

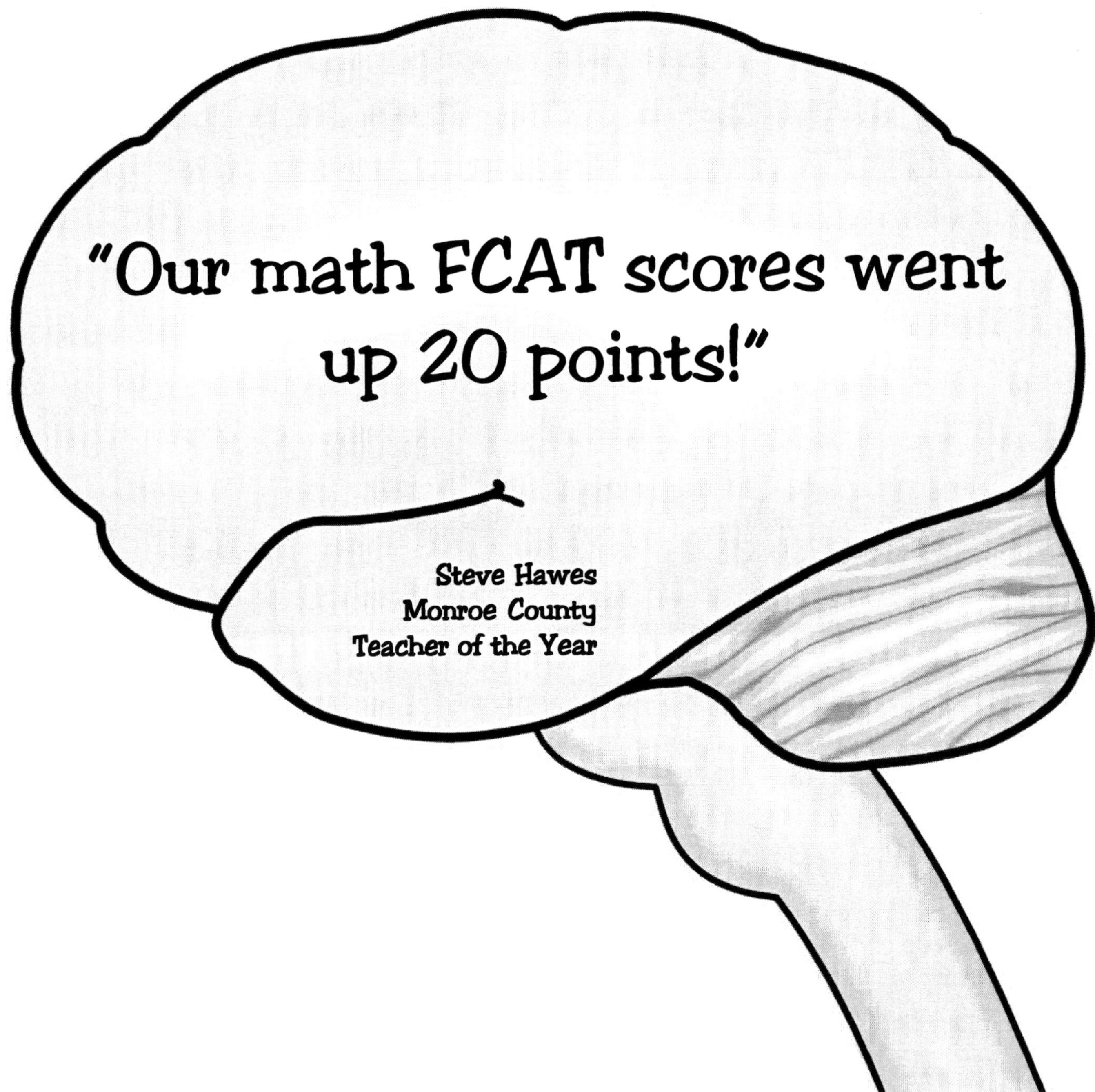
"Our math FCAT scores went up 20 points!"
Steve Hawes
Monroe County
Teacher of the Year

Introduction

What is BrainSMART?

BrainSMART is a systematic approach to boosting student achievement grounded in how cognitive research and neuroscience suggest human beings naturally learn. It is not a magic bullet nor a quick fix. It is a dynamic, systematic approach to teaching and learning that greatly increases the probability that students will learn successfully.

History

BrainSMART was researched and developed over a quarter of a century in 35 countries and refined through teaching 65,000 educators who reach more than 1 million students. It is being used as a state-wide initiative in Florida and in many of the largest school districts in North America. It concentrates on the core areas that have the greatest impact on raising student achievement:

- Understanding the **S**cience of how human beings learn.
- Mastering the **S**kills and **S**trategies of effective teaching.

During field research with thousands of teachers across the United States, the overwhelming desire of teachers was for the following:

- A clear understanding of how learning happens.
- A system for organizing their lesson plans in line with this knowledge.
- Practical tools that are quick to learn and easy to apply.

When observing teachers inspecting books on resource tables, we found that the usual response was to pick up a book on the brain and learning, flip through the pages, frown, and put the book back down again. From this, two other considerations became clear:

- Make the book extremely user-friendly and non-threatening.
- Make the book walk its talk, that is, model brain-compatible instruction in the structure of the book. That is why left-hand pages give the big picture for the right brain, and the right hand pages contain details for the left brain.

In response to these criteria, we focused on five fundamentals that brain research suggests are essential for effective learning. These became the basis of the BrainSMART Model™. They are as follows:

- Creating healthy, optimistic learning **S**tates.
- Making learning **M**eaningful in the mind of the learner.
- Engaging focused **A**ttention followed by downtime and feedback.
- Using skills and strategies to ensure **R**etention of knowledge and skills.
- Facilitating **T**ransfer and **T**ranscendence to academic and real world success.

The next stage was to focus on BrainSMART tools that were quick to learn, needed a minimum of preparation, and could be easily applied to get immediate positive results in the classroom. The outcome is this book, *BrainSMART: 60 Strategies for Boosting Test Scores*, which translates the implications of leading edge brain research into a system of practical strategies for facilitating learning and greater testing success by students.

How is BrainSMART Studied?

The BrainSMART approach is usually studied online through the accredited Master's Degree or Educational Specialist's Degree with BrainSMART specialization. It is also studied through a program of professional development personally conducted by authors Dr. Donna Wilson or Marcus Conyers in your district. See appendix for details for both online and live studies. You can also begin your studies right away by reading this book and starting to share some of the strategies with your students. Visit www.brainsmart.com for more information.

Chapter 1

BrainSMART Student Achievement

Our Math State Standardized Achievement Test Scores Went Up 20 Points!

Imagine the exhilaration of seeing your students' test scores go up. At the same time imagine the joy that flows from knowing that you have equipped your students with the optimism and the tools for thinking and learning they will be using to build healthy, productive, and joyful lives. This is the energizing power of balance we see effective teachers achieve time and time again when they teach smarter, not harder. Enjoyment is a core aspect of teaching when we teach for deep meaning and for test success. When great teaching translates into higher test scores a positive momentum starts to build. This was the case with Monroe County Teacher of the Year 1998 Steve Hawes.

"The Brain Guy and Doctor Donna"

One of the highlights of the year was to teach BrainSMART strategies to 750 students at Steve's school, Switlick Elementary in Monroe County, Florida, as "The Brain Guy and Doctor Donna." This was part of a statewide initiative with the Florida Department of Education to present the BrainSMART Model™ to a cadre of teachers and then follow up by modeling mini-lessons in classrooms throughout the state. Although we are delighted about the success at Switlick Elementary, we are not surprised. In our extensive review of the literature about what contributes to boosting student achievement, we discovered what we call the "Six MASTER Cylinders" that drive student achievement. In order to make these six factors memorable, we use the acronym M.A.S.T.E.R.

M.A.S.T.E.R. Teaching for High Achievement

Metacognition: Thinking About Thinking and Problem Solving
Application of Cognitive Strategies
States of Health and Optimism
Teaching Styles That Create Student Learning
Engaging and Relevant Instruction
Relationship With a Teacher

Six Cylinders that Drive Student Achievement

Metacognition – Thinking About Thinking

Application of Cognitive Strategies

States of Health and Optimism

Teaching Styles That Create Student Learning

Engaging and Relevant Instruction

Relationship With a Teacher

Research Supports M.A.S.T.E.R.

Current research in the area of student achievement creates a very important component of the framework for this book. Front and center is a meta-analysis of 91 studies on student achievement by Wang, Haertel, and Walberg (1993). Five important categories that emerged from this research are addressed in this book, in both the narrative and strategies sections. They are as follows: students' social relationship with their teacher, students' metacognitive skills, students' cognitive skills, classroom management, and parent involvement. Although this book was written with teachers in mind, we also worked with many parents who have enjoyed teaching the strategies to their children at home.

Many ideas and strategies in this book also come from a large and growing literature on learning, neuroscience, and cognition. A number of recently published resources from the fast-growing field of neuroscience are used throughout the book.

Metacognition: Thinking About Thinking

In the meta-analysis of 91 studies on student achievement by Wang, Haertel, and Walberg (1993), the use of metacognition emerged as the most important student characteristic for high student achievement. *Metacognition* is defined as thinking about thinking; an awareness and understanding of one's thought processes and behavior. This research is exciting because students can learn how to be metacognitive. Throughout the strategies section (Chapter 9), the left side of the page indicates possible questions teachers can pose to their students as they teach how to mindfully use the strategies to better their school lives and achieve at higher levels. When teachers habitually use questioning in this way, students become more independent as they regularly ask important questions of themselves as they learn.

Application of Cognitive Strategies

We include practices from the expanding area of cognitive psychology and education. Much of the cognitive work that we have included has been developed and refined during the past century. Highlighted are ideas based on the work of Feuerstein (1980), Sylwester (1995, 1998), and Amen (1998). The cognitive work by these researchers and practitioners, as well as others, is included because it holds the social and cultural

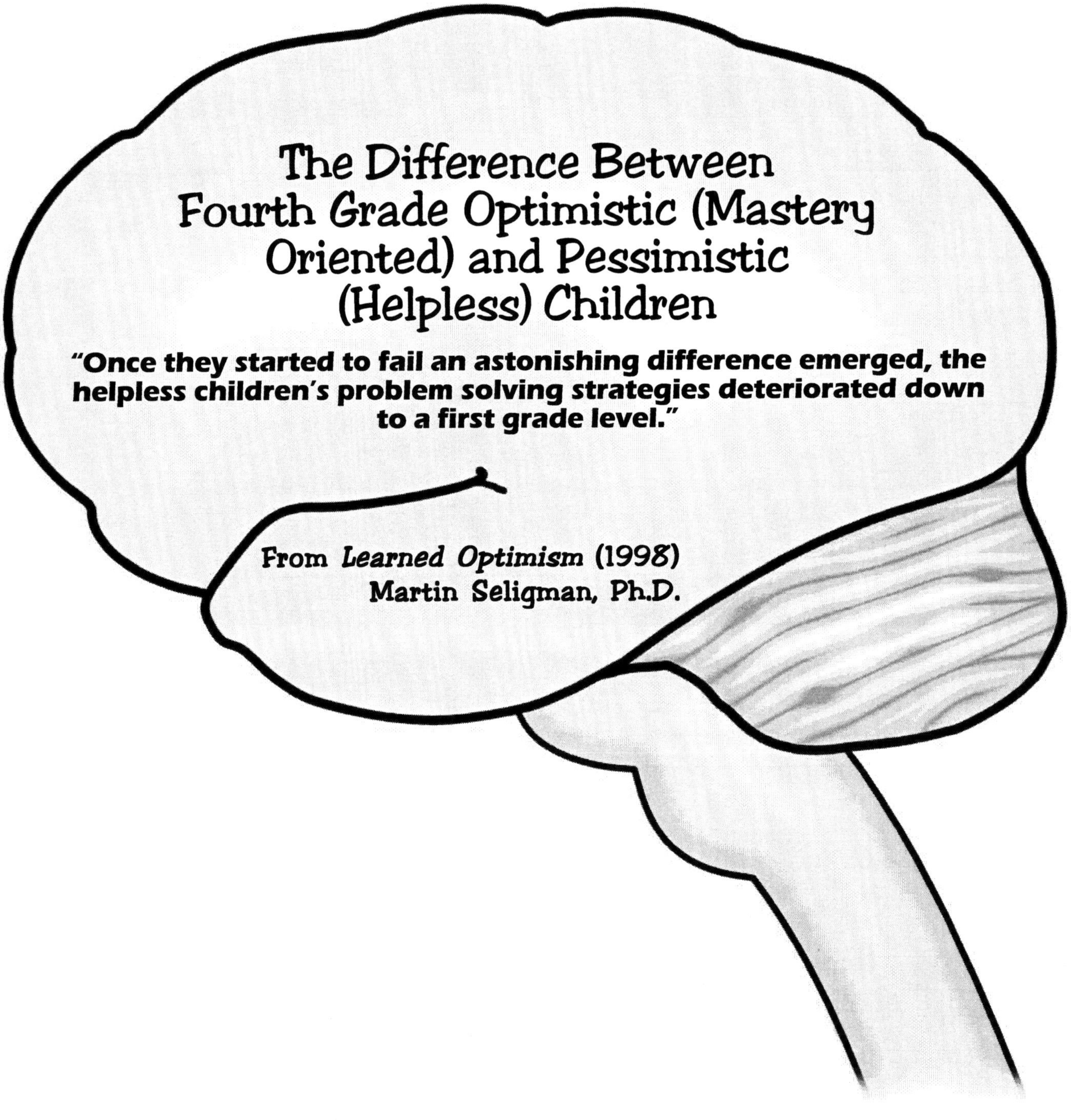

The Difference Between Fourth Grade Optimistic (Mastery Oriented) and Pessimistic (Helpless) Children

"Once they started to fail an astonishing difference emerged, the helpless children's problem solving strategies deteriorated down to a first grade level."

From *Learned Optimism* (1998)
Martin Seligman, Ph.D.

context of the learner, learner optimism, and thinking and memory strategies as central to student achievement.

We encourage you to join the many educators and parents who have helped "their" children learn how to be better learners in all aspects of their lives through the use of the strategies within this book. Research has shown that transfer in learning happens when strategies are applied in many different situations: at school, at home, and in social situations.

States of Health and Optimism

The work of Seligman (1998) indicates the importance of optimism in classrooms. Marilyn Elias (1999) from *U.S.A. Today* reported Kessler's results from his research at Harvard: approximately 23% of children and youth are clinically depressed. Additionally, we believe that optimism is key for all students today, including those who are not diagnosed with depression. Sapolsky's (1998) research indicates that stress is pervasive in American culture today and that no one in our society can escape it. In his book, *Timeless Healing*, Harvard researcher Benson (1997) suggests 75% to 90% of visits to a physician are stress related.

In Seligman's (1998) research, he examined fourth graders at work on tasks that were challenging for them. As the students struggled to complete the problems, two distinct groups emerged. One group appeared to be optimistic in the face of the challenge. That is, they asked questions and stayed with the task until it was completed. The other group gave up easily when the tasks become difficult. It was as if they did not think they could solve the problems, so they did not continue to try. Their cognitive ability dropped to that of first graders.

Teaching Styles That Create Student Learning

Over the past 20 years research and practice shows that learners come in many varieties. The different learner types include auditory, visual, and kinesthetic, as well as left and right hemispheric dominant. Education research (Hannaford, 1995) indicates that the typical classroom is usually a mismatch between the teaching style and 75% to 85% of learners. The teaching style is often lecture whereas the style of 85 of 100 students is more visual and kinesthetic and less auditory. With this in mind, the strategies included in this book are for all types of

The Big Picture

For Learning To Occur:

We must create a receptive state for learning.

We must make information meaningful.

We must get and maintain students' attention.

We must help students retain information.

We must help students transfer learning.

And:

Only 15% of students learn best through traditional instruction.

90% of books on the brain have been published in the past 10 years.

"Try harder" and "Do it again" haven't worked.

So:

Brain compatible techniques must be learned and applied to instruction.

BRAINSMART can provide strategies to use which are based on how the brain learns best.

learners in the classroom! Teachers who have used these tools report a high success rate with the visual, kinesthetic, and right hemispheric dominant learners in their classrooms. Often these students are those who have great difficulty in traditional classrooms.

Engaging and Relevant Instruction

Effective teachers create relevant, meaningful, and multisensory lesson plans that reach all learning styles. Haberman (1995) reports that star teachers describe the creation of meaningful work as their central important task. Research also suggests that meaningful, engaging lessons reduce considerably the probability of classroom discipline issues. This BrainSMART toolbox of strategies has been designed to reach all learning styles and to create sustained attention and feelings of competency.

Relationship With a Teacher

The research by Wang, Haertel, & Walberg (1993) and Sylwester (1998) is clear about the importance of positive relationships between teachers and students. There are two frameworks for this knowledge. One comes from neuroscientific research indicating that the brain is, first and foremost, social. The second is from cognitive psychology and indicates that language and thinking are learned best when positive relationships exist for learning. The strategies included here are those that offer fertile ground for optimistic relationships in classrooms where students are learning to be more effective thinkers and learners.

The BrainSMART Model: Translating Research to Results in the Classroom

It is through the important lens of these six critical factors that this book uses the following framework for focusing on these five fundamentals. Many of the teachers we have been privileged to work with have used BrainSMART strategies to translate these six factors into regular classroom practice. For example, Angel Cole was using these strategies during an observation for Teacher of the Year for Nassau County. She impressed the team so much that she was given that honor.

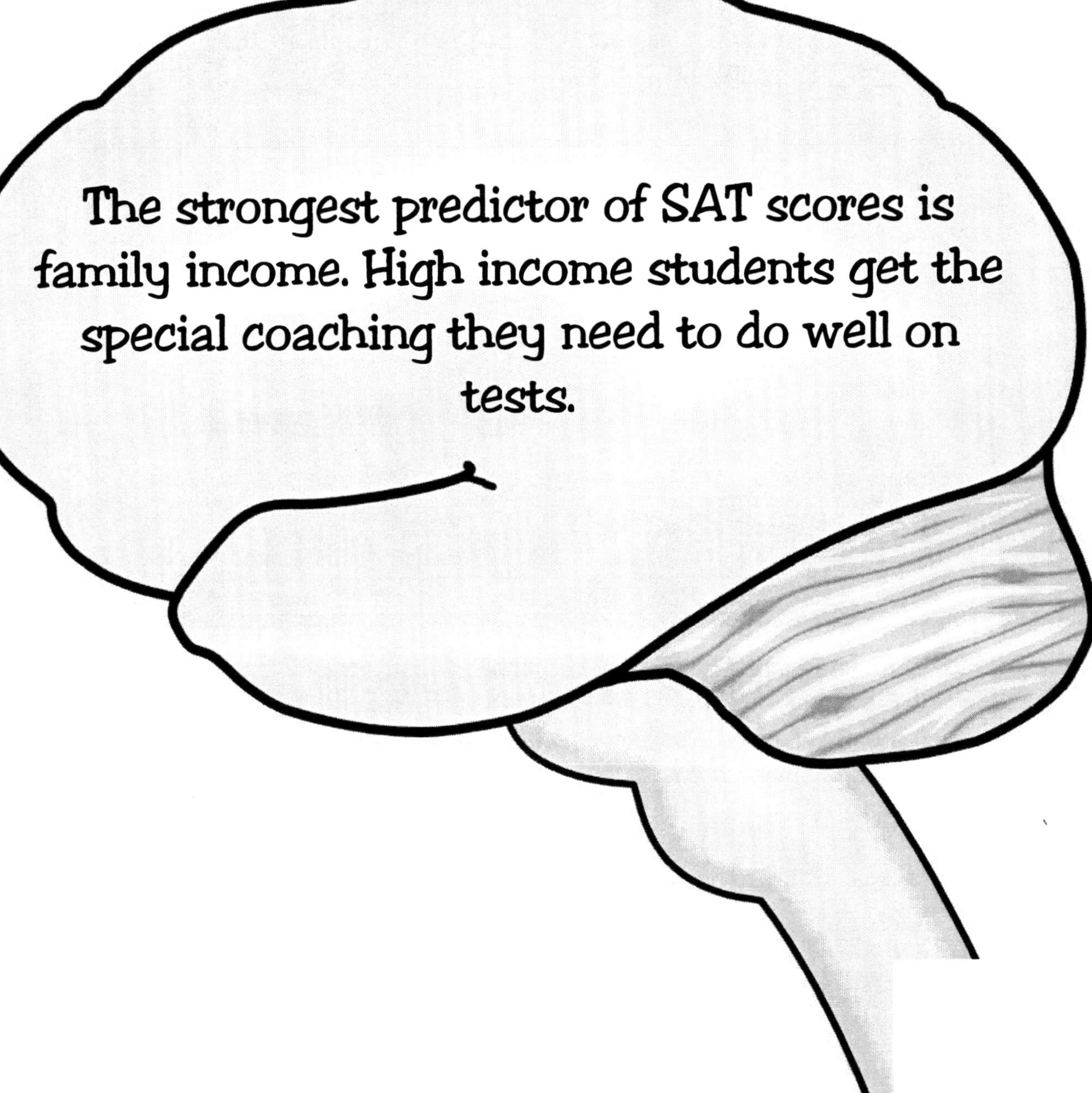
The strongest predictor of SAT scores is family income. High income students get the special coaching they need to do well on tests.

The following five components form the base of the BrainSMART model:

State: **Sustaining healthy optimistic states**

Meaning: **Relationship, styles, and experience**

Attention: **Interactive process and attention tools**

Retention: **Memorable lessons and retention tools**

Transfer: **Metacognition, strong original learning, and practice**

Systems of Effective Teaching for Student Achievement: Principles and Practice

Within the BrainSMART Model™, 12 leading principles have emerged as key to student achievement. The principles are both based on research and grounded in over 40 years of teaching and learning in education and business systems. These powerful principles lead to the BrainSMART toolbox of strategies ready for you to use in your classroom! They also form a foundation from which you can create your own strategies as many teachers we know have done.

State

1. **Optimism is a key predictor to academic achievement.**

   Effective teachers model and mediate an attitude of healthy optimism and teach the strategies that ensure that students internalize concrete experiences of success.

2. **Good nutrition and regular exercise are critical in improving student achievement and reducing stress and discipline challenges.**

   Effective teachers model and mediate healthy exercise and eating choices and encourage purposeful movement such as BrainObics.

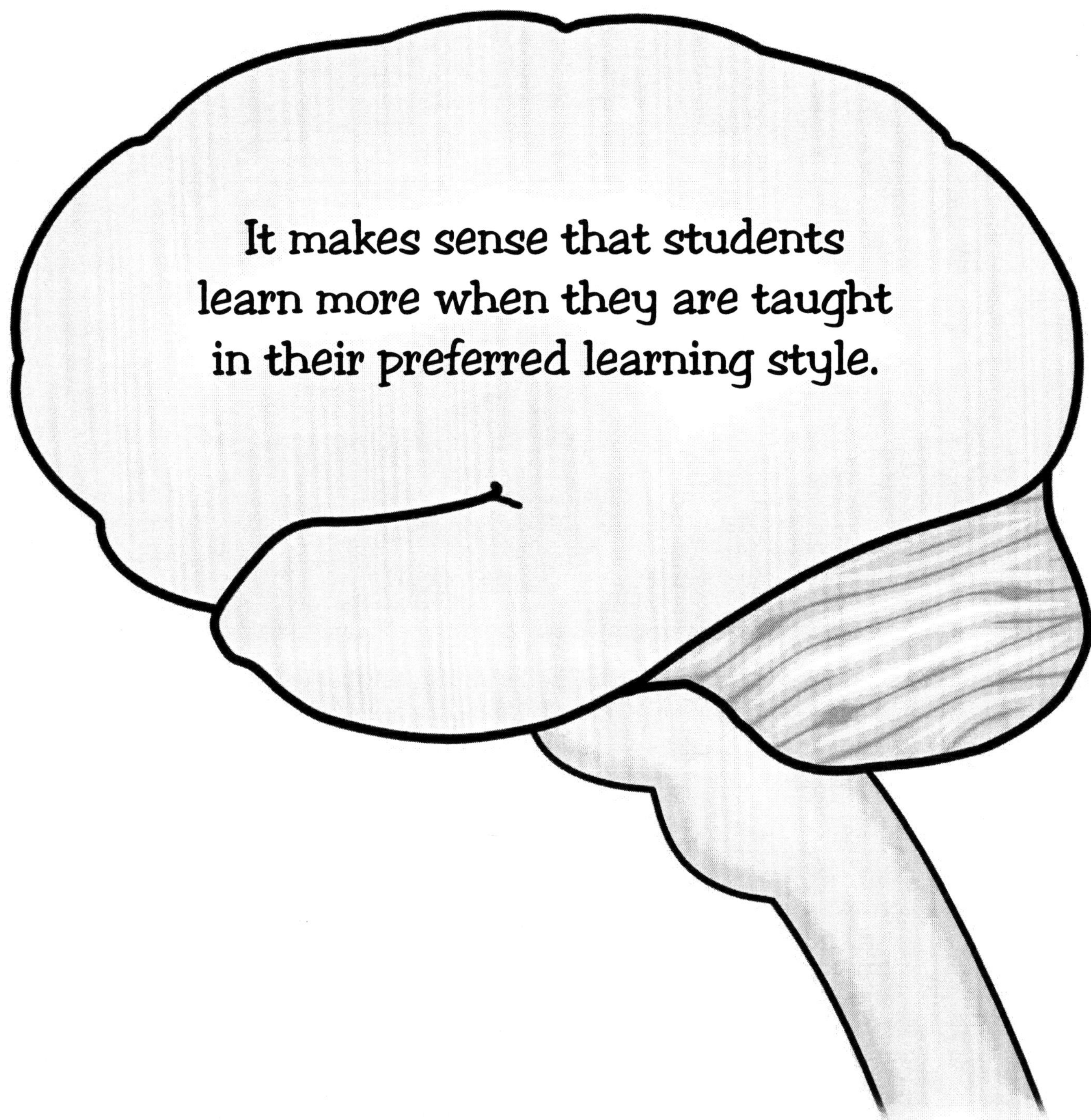
It makes sense that students
learn more when they are taught
in their preferred learning style.

Meaning

3. **Respectful relationships in a safe environment contribute to positive productive states and more on-task behavior.**

   Effective teachers relate positively to students without put downs or sarcasm.

4. **Students learn best in their own learning style.**

   Effective teachers teach in the learning styles of the students.

5. **Meaning is made in the mind of the learner by making connections to what is already known and through concrete learning experiences.**

   Effective teachers make learning meaningful by facilitating experiences that bring learning to life, and life to learning.

6. **The brain needs processing time for meaningful connections to be made.**

   Effective teachers give students time to process and create meaning.

Attention

7. **Emotion, variety, and interaction are primary engines of attention.**

   Effective teachers are enthusiastic, create curiosity, and use a variety of instructional methodologies to engage attention.

8. **Working at a level of appropriate challenge with regular feedback on interesting work sustains internal motivation and attention.**

   Effective teachers design lessons that engage intrinsic motivation and give regular feedback and downtime to process what is being studied.

Results of Instruction by Three Consecutive Highly Effective Teachers

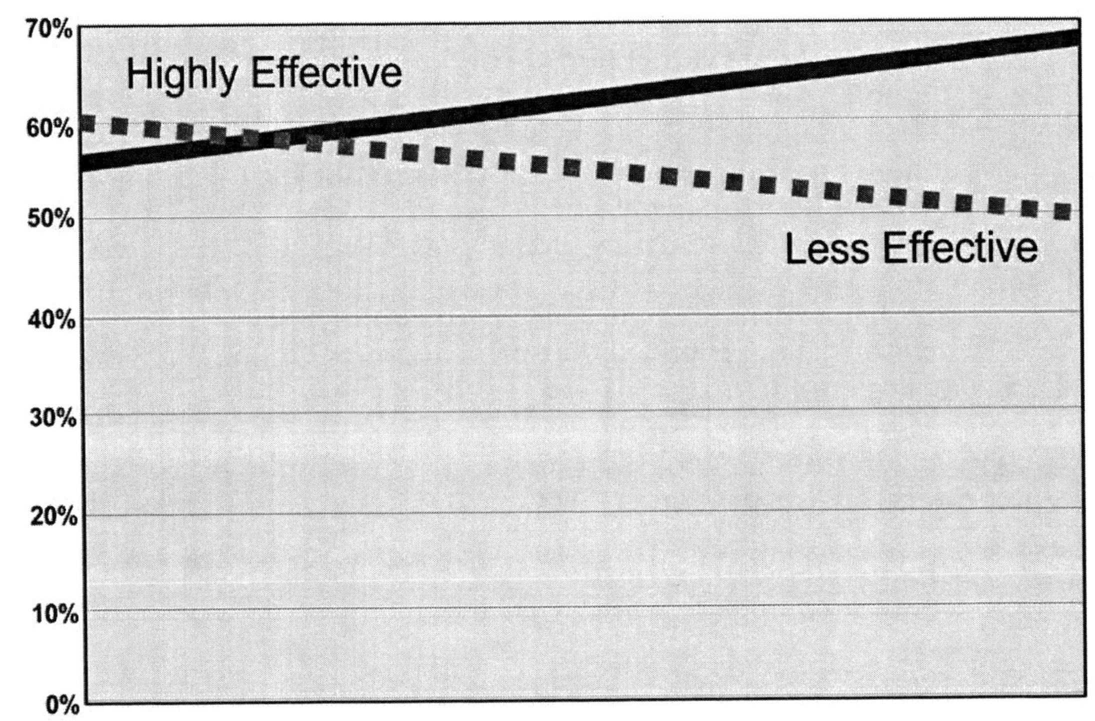

Sanders, W., & Rivers, J. (1996). Cumulative and residual effects of teachers on future student academic achievement. (Research Progress Report). Knoxville, TN: University of TN. Value-Added Research and Assessment Center.

www.brainsmart.com

Retention

9. **The brain is designed to SAVE what is useful and used and to delete what is not.**

   Effective teachers make lessons as useful and memorable as possible by using memory strategies and have their students use what they learn.

10. **"If the body doesn't move, then the brain doesn't learn!"**

    Effective teachers equip students with specific kinesthetic and interactive strategies for retaining and recalling important information.

Transfer

11. **Metacognition is the key to transfer: the ability to assess a situation, choose the right cognitive strategy, and execute the strategy well.**

    Effective teachers teach metacognition and facilitate many examples of transfer.

12. **Strong initial learning, regular review, and many examples increase probability that learning can be recalled and applied successfully.**

    Effective teachers create strong learning experiences and then review through regular mind mapping and student processing.

Our Experience with Teachers

As we have used the BrainSMART approach to professional development to train students and teachers in the use of these strategies, we have found teachers to be excited about this research based and lively way to teach. Across the United States at school sites and in state initiatives, teachers are energized and are eager to learn and use BrainSMART strategies. We applaud teachers for all that you give to the students you teach. We genuinely think that you will enjoy using the ideas and strategies included in this book designed especially for you!

Student Strengths

15% Are Left Hemispheric, Linear, and Auditory Processors Who Look at the Teacher

85% Learn Differently

Adapted from Hannaford, C. (1995). *Smart moves.* Arlington, VA: Great Ocean Publishers.

www.brainsmart.com

Chapter 2

Ten Key Facts About Your Brilliant Brain

In this section we introduce you to 10 key facts about the human brain. These are facts that we have found, in our workshops, to be most useful and immediately usable.

One

The brain has **one** hundred billion neurons, which, as Nobel-Prize winner Gerald Edelman (1992) calculates, have the potential for making more connections than there are atoms in the known universe. We have learned that it is not the size of the brain that is important in determining intelligence, but the number of connections. When examined, Einstein's brain was found to have a greater number of connections than the average person. Autopsies performed on students with advanced degrees revealed more dendritic growth and connections than for high-school dropouts. Marian Diamond's (1998) research revealed that the key to encouraging dendritic growth was to create stimulating environments.

Action: Create stimulating environments and believe in the incredible potential of the brain to learn.

Two

You have **two** hemispheres: left and right. Following the Nobel-Prize winning research by Sperry, reported in Springer and Deutsch (1998), we now know that each hemisphere of the brain has somewhat different functions. The left hemisphere is associated with more linear processing and logical thought, and works with words and numbers. The right hemisphere is particularly effective at visualization, movement, color, voice tone, and abstract thought. The German word *gestalt* has been used to explain the human need (especially the right hemisphere's) to create meaningful organized wholes. Recent research indicates that the right hemisphere is particularly adept at *recording* reality, whereas the left brain is good at *editing* reality to agree with patterns that already exist in our mental maps. Traditional education methods serve some left-brain learners well. In contrast, the vast majority of students labeled as having learning disabilities or difficulties are more right-brained.

Teacher Strengths

75% More Left and Logic Hemisphere Dominant

25% More Right and Gestalt Dominant

Adapted from Hannaford, C.(1995). Smart moves. Arlington, VA: Great Ocean Publishers.

www.brainsmart.com

Action: Harnessing the awesome synergy of the left and right hemispheres working in harmony to help all students learn more effectively.

Three

The brain weighs **three** pounds. Although it contributes only 2% of body weight, it consumes around 20% of the body's oxygen. Covering the brain like the thin peel of an orange is the neocortex. The neocortex makes up approximately 85% of the total neurons in the brain and burns 400 calories every day. The brain is able to process 1,000 new bits of information every second.

Action: Ensure that your students have plenty of purposeful movement to keep the oxygen flowing.

Four

There are **four** lobes of the brain.

1. The frontal lobe, which is excellent for planning, includes the pre-frontal region. This region is one of the last parts of the brain to develop and is critical for reading. Denmark, where reading is not formally taught until age eight or nine, has the highest literacy rate in the world.
2. The temporal lobe, center for speech and some memory.
3. The occipital lobe is the visual cortex. This part of the brain and other visual location sites, according to Nobel laureate Francis Crick (1994), are excellent for long-term memory.
4. The parietal lobe, involved in movement and touch, is crucial to kinesthetic memory.

Action: Use strategies that reach many different parts of the brain, and maximize the opportunity for attention, retention, and transfer of knowledge.

Five

The brain uses **five** senses. The eyes take in around one hundred million bits of data per second, the skin about ten million bits per second, and the ears, thirty thousand bits per second. The more senses we use in learning, the stronger the encoding, and the greater the ease of retention and recall. Research indicates that the traditional lecture format, which

Eye movements may
give clues to how
students learn best.

works primarily with the auditory system, works for only about 15% of students.

Action: Use multisensory experiences to ensure maximum learning among students.

Six

There are **six** eye positions. Research by Bandler (1985) and Grinder (1991) indicates that distinct functions of the human brain can be accessed by various eye positions. There are six primary configurations to focus on:

1. The occipital lobe and the visual system is accessed by eyes going up. Usually up left is for visual recall, and
2. Up right is for visual imagination.
3. The temporal lobe and auditory system is triggered by looking from side to side; looking left is for auditory recall, and
4. Right is for auditory imagination.
5. The kinesthetic aspects of the brain are triggered by looking down and to the right.
6. Self-talk and self-dialog is accessed by looking down to the left.

This pattern is true for some 95% of the population. Others, who are left-handed, may be reversed right to left.

Action: Observe eye movements of students to see how they are learning. For example, visual learners will often look up. Also, give students this information, so they can look up during tests in order to access visual information, rather than shutting down their memory by saying "keep your eyes on your own paper – look down."

Seven

The brain can focus on **seven** chunks of information at any one time. Research by George Miller included in David Sousa's (1995) book *How the Brain Learns* indicates that the brain learns best in chunks of seven. This number is very prevalent in our literature. Consider *The Seven Habits of Highly Effective People* (Covey, 1989), the seven seas, or the seven meninges of the brain. Essentially, the more items we ask someone to remember, the more likely they are to forget. These chunk sizes are smaller for younger students.

BrainSMART

Retention Probability Index

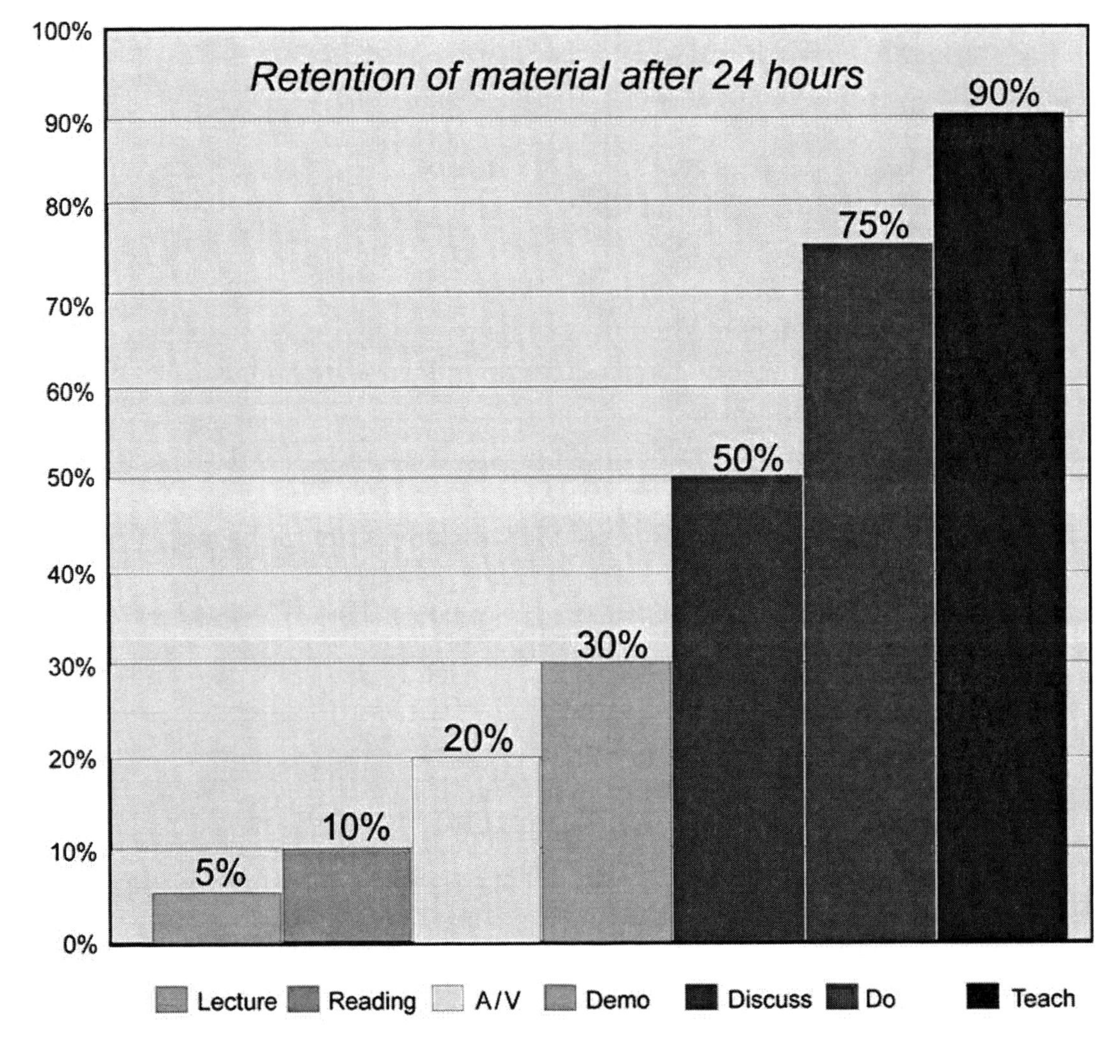

Adapted from Sousa, D. (1995.) *How the brain learns.* Reston, VA: National Association Secondary School Principals.

www.brainsmart.com

Action: Structure lessons in a maximum of seven chunks, remembering that less is more.

Eight

The human brain has an approximate eight minute attention span. If you look around the room, for example, during a lecture, you will find that people tend to tune in and out of what a speaker is saying after about eight minutes. We can count on attention span being less for some of our students, particularly students under eight years of age. Some keys for sustaining attention include:

1. Build curiosity. The neocortex of the brain is intensely curious and seeks novelty. Notice during the news introductions like, "When we get back, we'll tell you how to lose ten pounds, and never have another wrinkle."
2. Relevance in the mind of the learner will also increase the level of attention. In the television news example given earlier, that information would be relevant to many members of the viewing audience.
3. Ask questions. Another key to getting the brain to focus is to ask questions. For example, how is your left foot feeling right now? Gotcha!
4. Variety is the spice of attention. Researcher Howard (1994) describes the process of neuronal habituation. This happens when the brain hears the same signal over and over again. For example, what happens when you listen to a monotone voice?
5. Emotion. The brain is hardwired to focus on what is emotionally compelling. The stronger the emotion, the stronger the attention. Robert Sylwester's (1995) excellent book, *A Celebration of Neurons*, highlights the fact that it is biologically impossible for the brain to learn if it is not paying attention. We also know that emotion drives attention.

Action: Reduce the time you expect to keep attention to a maximum of twenty minutes for a lesson, and leave plenty of time for feedback and reflection. Use variety of voice tone and movement. Don't be fooled by looks of rapt attention, which is the first thing that students learn as a survival system.

Nine

The brain works in at least **nine** intelligences. Gardner (1983) from

FOR YOUR RIGHT HEMISPHERE	FOR YOUR LEFT HEMISPHERE
First Learn These Ten BrainSMART™ Pegs ...	**... Now Store These Facts**

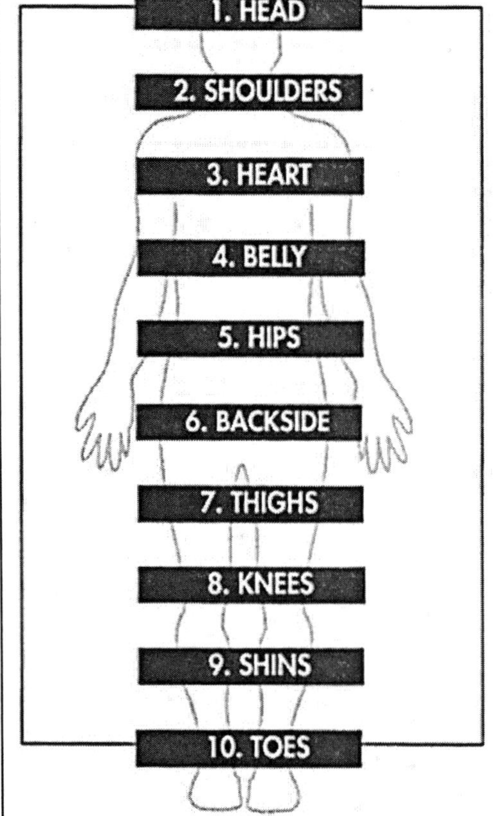

One	hundred billion brain cells
Two	hemispheres - left and right
Three	pounds of brain power
Four	lobes -frontal, temporal, occipital, parietal
Five	senses support learning
Six	eye positions
Seven	chunks of conscious thought
Eight	intelligences
Nine	second attention span
Ten	million books (storage capacity of the brain)

SEE IT! SAY IT! FEEL IT!

Congratulations! Now have fun sharing this system with teachers in your organization.

www.brainsmart.com

Harvard University proposed the theory of multiple intelligences. Originally, there were seven intelligences. Now there are nine. Students have a range of ability in each of these intelligences. Based on Gardner's work, the question is no longer "How smart am I?" but "How am I smart?" The intelligences include:

1. Interpersonal
2. Intrapersonal
3. Musical
4. Spatial
5. Bodily/Kinesthetic
6. Naturalistic
7. Mathematical
8. Verbal
9. Existentialist

Another possible intelligence defined by Gardner might be humor. Traditional education primarily works with just two of these intelligences, mathematical and verbal.

Action: Look for the unique ways in which students learn and utilize all nine of Gardner's intelligences in lessons.

Ten

Ten million books. Researcher Howard (1994), in his book, *An Owner's Manual for the Brain,* identified that the human brain has the capacity to store the equivalent of ten million books. Research at the National Training Laboratories (Sousa, 1995) indicated that, with traditional lecture format, 95% of information is lost within 24 hours. By using the retention systems highlighted in this book, you can move toward only a 10% loss after 24 hours. The brain has three primary retention systems;

1. Taxonal/semantic.
2. Procedural.
3. Episodic.

By focusing on the most efficient memory systems, we can boost student achievement. The chapter on memory addresses how we use these three systems.

Action: Learn to teach with memory in mind, using the strategies that are detailed in this book.

Teacher Readiness

4 of 5 Teachers Are Not Prepared to Teach in Today's Classrooms

Sanders, W., & Rivers, J. (1996). Cumulative and residual effects of teachers on future student academic achievement. (Research Progress Report). Knoxville, TN: University of TN. Value-Added Research and Assessment Center.

www.brainsmart.com

Chapter 3

The BrainSMART Model™ - The Synergy of Neuroscience and Common Sense

There is an explosion of information about the brain that is having a profound impact on education, business, and government. Many of the books written on the brain have been written during the past ten years. Membership in the Society of Neuroscience went up from about 500 people in 1969, to about 30,000 in 2000. It is critical that we translate this flood of information into simple, practical tools that can be used to help students right now. The BrainSMART Model™ distills critical components of this research into a structured focus on five fundamentals of effective learning:

1. State

Ensuring absence of threat and triggering high-challenge, low-stress states.

2. Meaning

Making learning meaningful in the mind of the learner. The brain operates on a *save-or-delete* system, in which meaningless data are automatically deleted.

3. Attention

It is biologically impossible for the brain to learn if it is not paying attention. Keys to generating attention are:

(a) Generate <u>C</u>uriosity using novelty
(b) Making information <u>R</u>elevant
(c) <u>A</u>sking questions
(d) Using <u>V</u>ariety
(e) Using <u>E</u>motion.

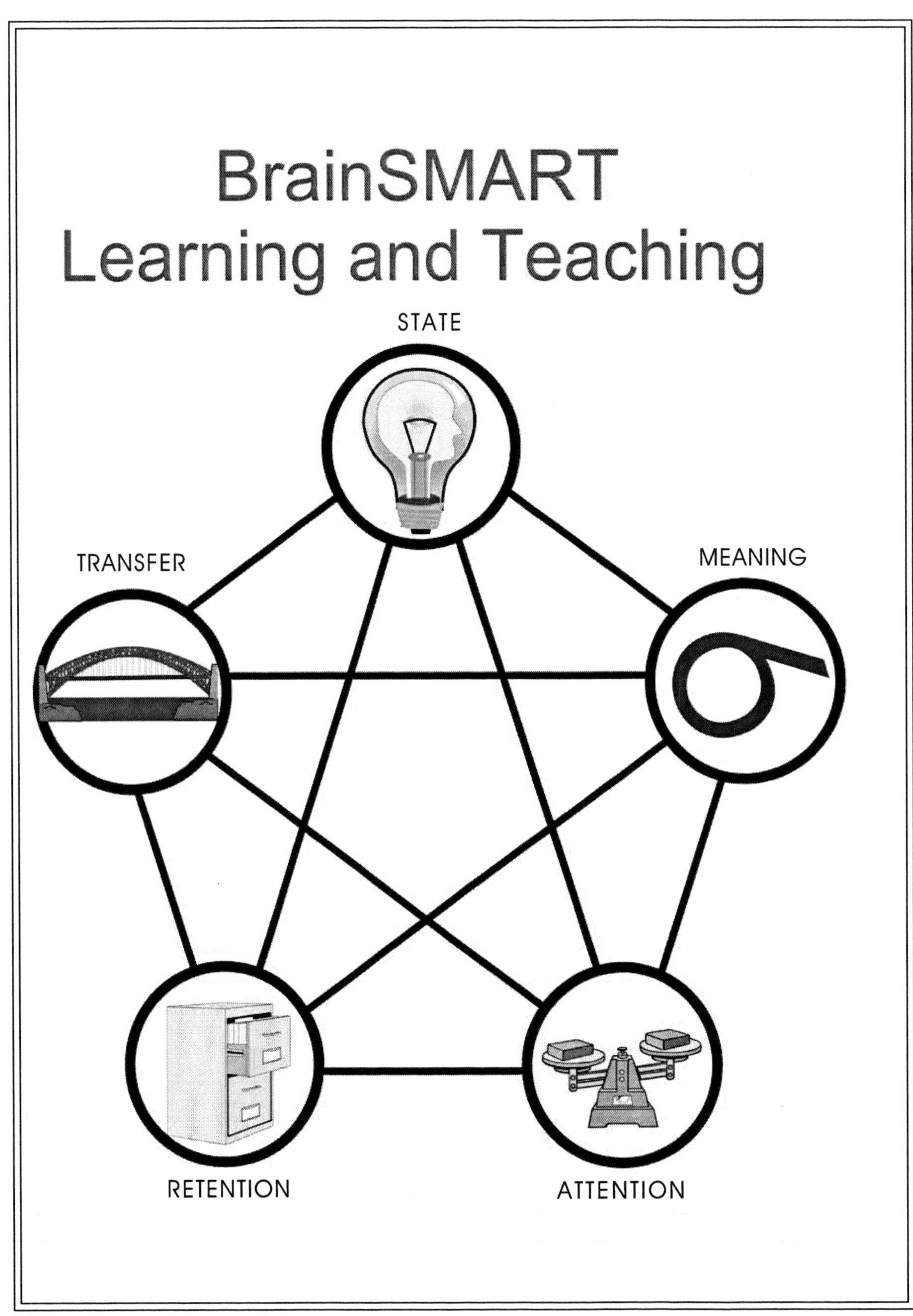
BrainSMART
Learning and Teaching
STATE
TRANSFER
MEANING
RETENTION
ATTENTION

4. Retention

The brain seemingly has a *save* key, to save data. We learn how to hit this button by using specific strategies.

5. Transfer

The bottom line of learning is transferring it from the classroom to the test and, more important, from the classroom to life. At the metacognitive level, transfer is encouraged by creating a meaning mechanism in the brain that allows us to apply knowledge in a variety of areas. For example, a question that can be taken into the classroom is "What's it like being taught by me?"

The BrainSMART Model™ integrates superbly with other learning systems including learning styles practices, accelerated learning, mediated learning, cognitive education and psychology, and neurolinguistic programming. The system also has been successfully tested with all manner of adult groups, from law enforcement officers, to fire fighters, to business professionals and educators. The key to BrainSMART is its simplicity and effectiveness.

Chapter 4

STATE - The Power to Produce Results

Helping students switch on positive, low stress \ high challenge states

Under Stress

Right Hemispheric and Usually Gestalt Learners

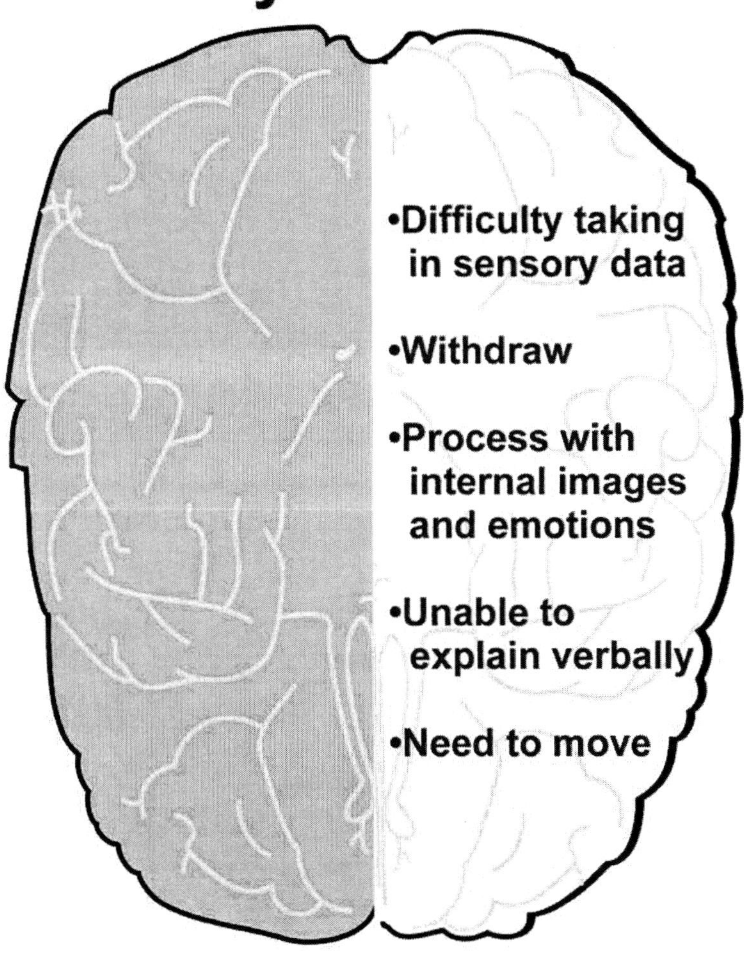

Adapted from Hannaford, C. (1997). *The Dominance Factor*. Arlington, VA: Great Ocean Publishers.

www.brainsmart.com

Chapter 4

State - The Power to Produce Results

BrainSMART Principles for Boosting Positive States 1-2

1. Optimism is a key predictor to academic achievement.

   Effective teachers model and mediate an attitude of healthy optimism and teach the strategies that ensure that students internalize concrete experiences of success.

2. Good nutrition and regular exercise are critical in improving student achievement and reducing stress and discipline challenges.

   Effective teachers model and mediate healthy exercise and eating choices and encourage purposeful movement such as BrainObics.

The first key to boosting student achievement is to systematically model and elicit healthy and optimistic states. This section gives facts about the importance of the state of our students. Powerful ideas for encouraging positive states in the classroom are shared. Additionally, the tools section contains many ideas for classroom use!

The Power of Purposeful Joy

Have you ever had a day when you were in a negative state? How quickly did your students detect that in you and how did they respond? Often, they are soon hitting your "hot buttons." How much learning happens? Very little. Think of a time when you were in a positive state. What happened to learning in your classroom? State is a central factor for ensuring effective learning. Goodlad's (1984) research in over 1,000 classrooms led him to describe the environments as "flat." The truth is that eliciting and sustaining healthy positive learning states are the first steps to boosting student achievement. In today's classrooms this may be difficult.

Keys to Positive States

Physiology

Movement, Posture,
BrainObics

Focus

What's Important Now?
What's Useful and Positive?

Food

Balanced Nutrition, Protein,
Healthy Essential Fatty Acids,
Vegetables and Fruits

"America is in the midst of an epidemic of pessimism and is suffering its' most serious consequence, depression."
— Martin Seligman (1998)

As mentioned in chapter 1, *U.S.A. Today*'s report (Elias, 1999) indicates that Harvard's School of Public Health identified depression as the fourth leading cause of disease burden in 1990 and predicts that by 2020 it will be the single leading cause. At the same time, 75% to 90% of all doctor visits are for stress-related disorders. In the same *U.S.A. Today* report, Harvard researcher Kessler suggests that 23% of students experience depression. Pessimism, a precursor to depression, is a learned theory of reality. Additionally, 60% to 80% of students with learning disabilities exhibit symptoms of depression.

Are we teaching children the tools they need to persist optimistically through failure and frustration until they succeed? When kids fail, their answers to these three questions determine their level of pessimism:
Is it personal?
Is it permanent?
Is it pervasive?
Martin Seligman, Ph.D. (1998)

How they answer these questions is a key determinant of their level of optimism or pessimism and academic achievement. If the child interprets failure as being caused by their lack of ability, which is a permanent statement of fact that affects their whole life, they may develop pessimism. Hence, the BrainSMART™ principle: **never question ability, always improve strategy**. By teaching students that failure is a temporary setback that can be overcome by learning effective strategies, we help students to build the sense of mastery that drives optimism and self-esteem. The key is to help students feel good by doing well and hitting the "save key" on their successes. In BrainSMART™ teaching we guide students in building a success file filled with concrete and authentic academic achievements.

Children learn pessimism from parents, teachers, coaches, and the media. They then become adults and recycle it to their children. Young people often develop what motivational researchers call "learned

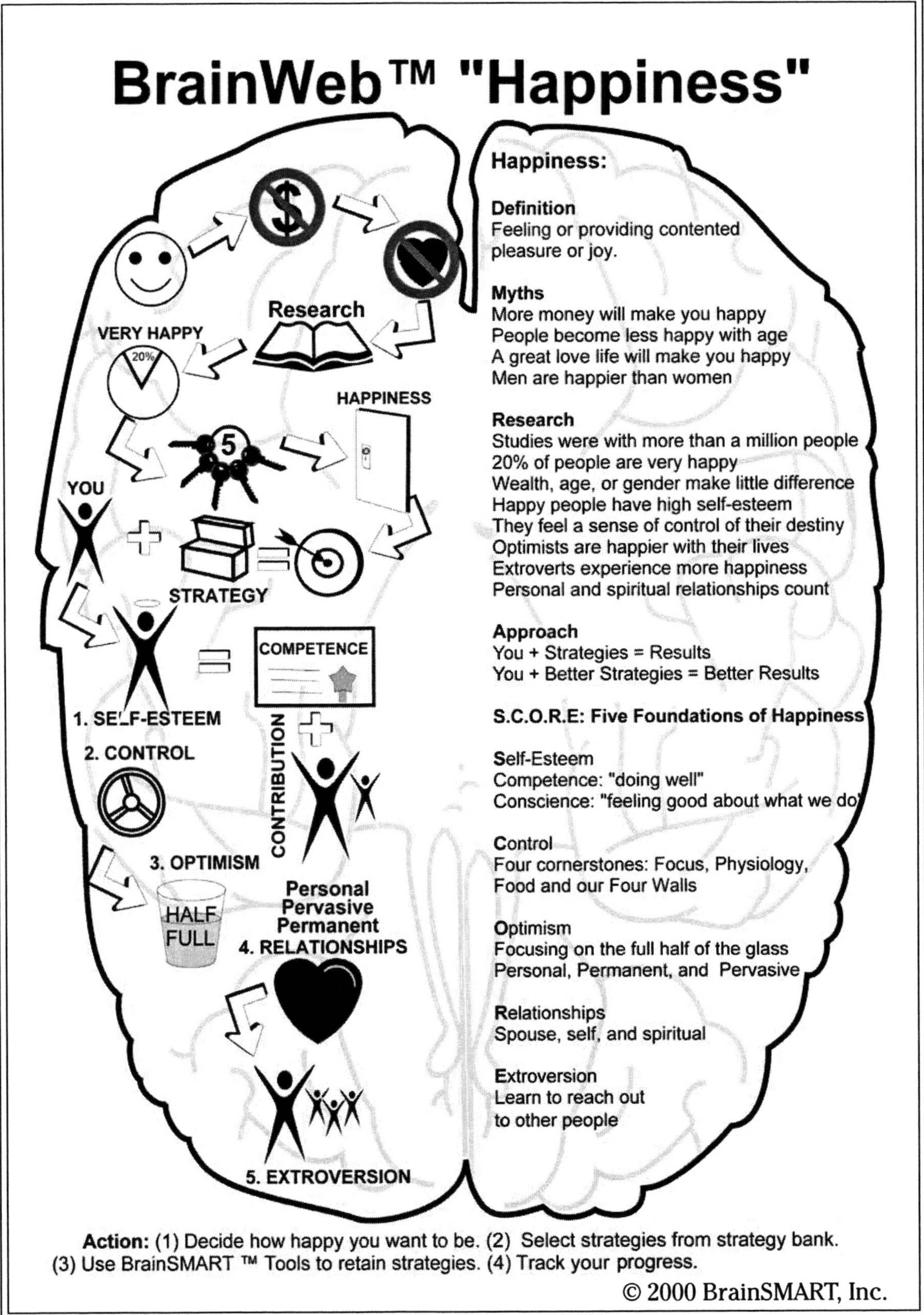
BrainWeb™ "Happiness"
Research
VERY HAPPY
20%
HAPPINESS
5
YOU
STRATEGY
COMPETENCE
1. SE_F-ESTEEM
2. CONTROL
CONTRIBUTION
3. OPTIMISM
HALF FULL
Personal
Pervasive
Permanent
4. RELATIONSHIPS
5. EXTROVERSION
Happiness:
Definition
Feeling or providing contented pleasure or joy.
Myths
More money will make you happy
People become less happy with age
A great love life will make you happy
Men are happier than women
Research
Studies were with more than a million people
20% of people are very happy
Wealth, age, or gender make little difference
Happy people have high self-esteem
They feel a sense of control of their destiny
Optimists are happier with their lives
Extroverts experience more happiness
Personal and spiritual relationships count
Approach
You + Strategies = Results
You + Better Strategies = Better Results
S.C.O.R.E: Five Foundations of Happiness
Self-Esteem
Competence: "doing well"
Conscience: "feeling good about what we do"
Control
Four cornerstones: Focus, Physiology, Food and our Four Walls
Optimism
Focusing on the full half of the glass
Personal, Permanent, and Pervasive
Relationships
Spouse, self, and spiritual
Extroversion
Learn to reach out to other people
Action: (1) Decide how happy you want to be. (2) Select strategies from strategy bank. (3) Use BrainSMART ™ Tools to retain strategies. (4) Track your progress.
© 2000 BrainSMART, Inc.

helplessness." After repeated failure, students who suffer from this problem decide they are not capable of performing well on academic tasks. Often, they are not motivated to even begin tasks at school, because they feel they won't succeed. These students may seem negative, pessimistic, or withdrawn. Eventually, they may drop out of school. Every two students who drop out cost their communities $1.5 million.

State mastery flows from systematically improving our skills at gathering information, interpreting accurately, and positively influencing the outcome.

The Impact of Stress on Learning

Hart (1983), in his book *Human Brain and Human Learning*, has highlighted the impact of stress on the learner. In high threat situations, researcher Hannaford (1995) suggests that students' nondominant hemisphere ceases to function effectively. Furthermore, the blood moves away from the cortical areas of the brain, which are essential to complex thought, into the survival areas of the brain, which are involved in the fight-or-flight response. This process makes learning virtually impossible.

Although avoiding unnecessary threat is important, the most effective learning happens when we move beyond the absence of threat to create a profoundly optimistic learning environment. Practical ways to do this include giving the learner choice. Choice, control, and experiences of success create *engaged* learners, the opposite of *helpless* learners.

The Pursuit of Happiness

Research suggests that there are five key components to achieving states of happiness: self-esteem, sense of control, optimism, relationships, and extroversion. Studies involving more than one million people indicate that we can move towards happiness by working on these components. (See the Happiness BrainWeb for more information.)

To help you track progress we have included a WinWeb that includes these five key components of happiness. The happiest teachers we have met seem to invest considerable energy at improving their skills in these five areas.

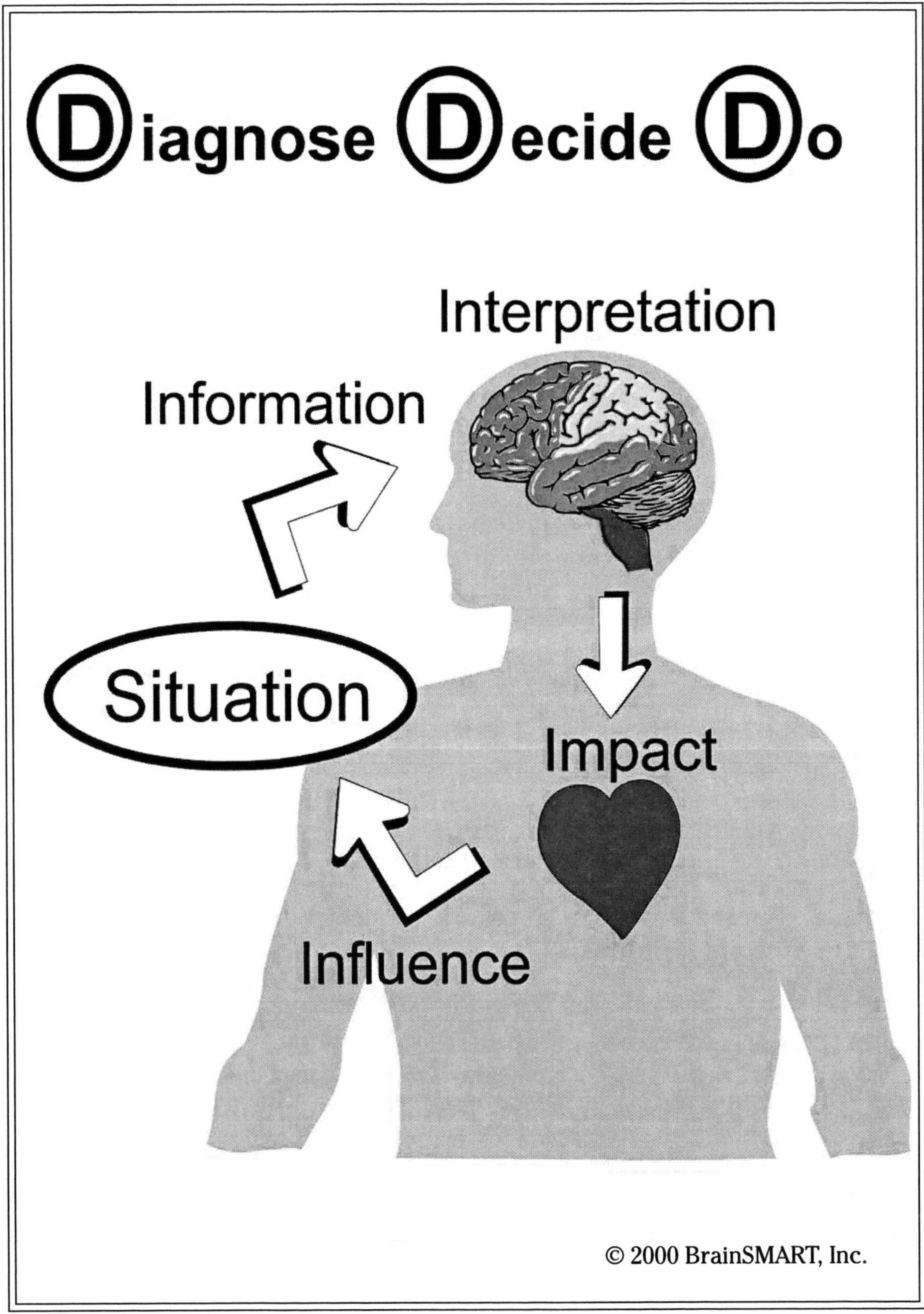
Diagnose Decide Do
Interpretation
Information
Situation
Impact
Influence
© 2000 BrainSMART, Inc.

Choosing Your Thoughts

We have approximately 4,000 thoughts per day. How we invest these thoughts determines the quality of much of our lives.

The Power of Flow

Remember a time when you were in the zone and your expertise was stretched to the max to achieve a task. You were experiencing the "FLOW" as described by Csikszentmihalyi (1990) in his book by the same name. Great teachers experience flow much of the time as they continuously improve their expertise and complete the important tasks of teaching. The following acronym will assist your memory for learning the steps in achieving a state of flow.

Select...

Task...

Assess, Adjust, Take Action, Get Feedback, and Balance...

Tasks You Take On With...

Experience You Are Developing...

Building reading strategies to a 98% to 99% comprehension level will assist this process. Comprehension for extended periods of time helps readers experience flow through the enjoyment that comes from understanding. For more about flow, read Flow by Csikszentmihalyi (1990).

The state of the teacher is also critical to learning as students will mirror the mood of the teacher. The use of music, movement, and color in the classroom are other powerful state motivators and movers. In BrainSMART we teach a system of strategies for supporting healthy optimistic states!

In the BrainSMART I-4 model, we focus on four parts of the process of thinking and state management.

Information:

What is happening in the world? We gather data through our five senses.

Interpretation:

What does this mean? We filter through our past history and explanatory style. Is it personal, pervasive, and/or permanent?

Impact:

How does this make me feel? We feel a biochemical response to our thoughts.

Influence:

What do I do about this? We choose and execute a strategy to influence the situation.

Key state creators for the classroom are as follows:

- I FEEL GOOD!! YES!!
- High five
- Humor
- Music
- Ask questions
- Use positive language
- Use positive body language
- Give learners choice
- Work in groups
- Tell success stories
- Catch students succeeding
- W.I.N. (What's Important Now)
- Use colorful posters
- Ball toss
- Sing
- Nutrition
- Water
- Breathing
- Neurobics
- Success seat
- Simon says
- Fragrance of the day
- Games
- Look up

Questions to ask ourselves:

- What do I need to do to consistently model a healthy optimistic state?
- What strategies will I systematically use to help my students use the same?

Chapter 5

Meaning -

How to Make Learning Meaningful in Your Classroom

Making learning relevant to the learner

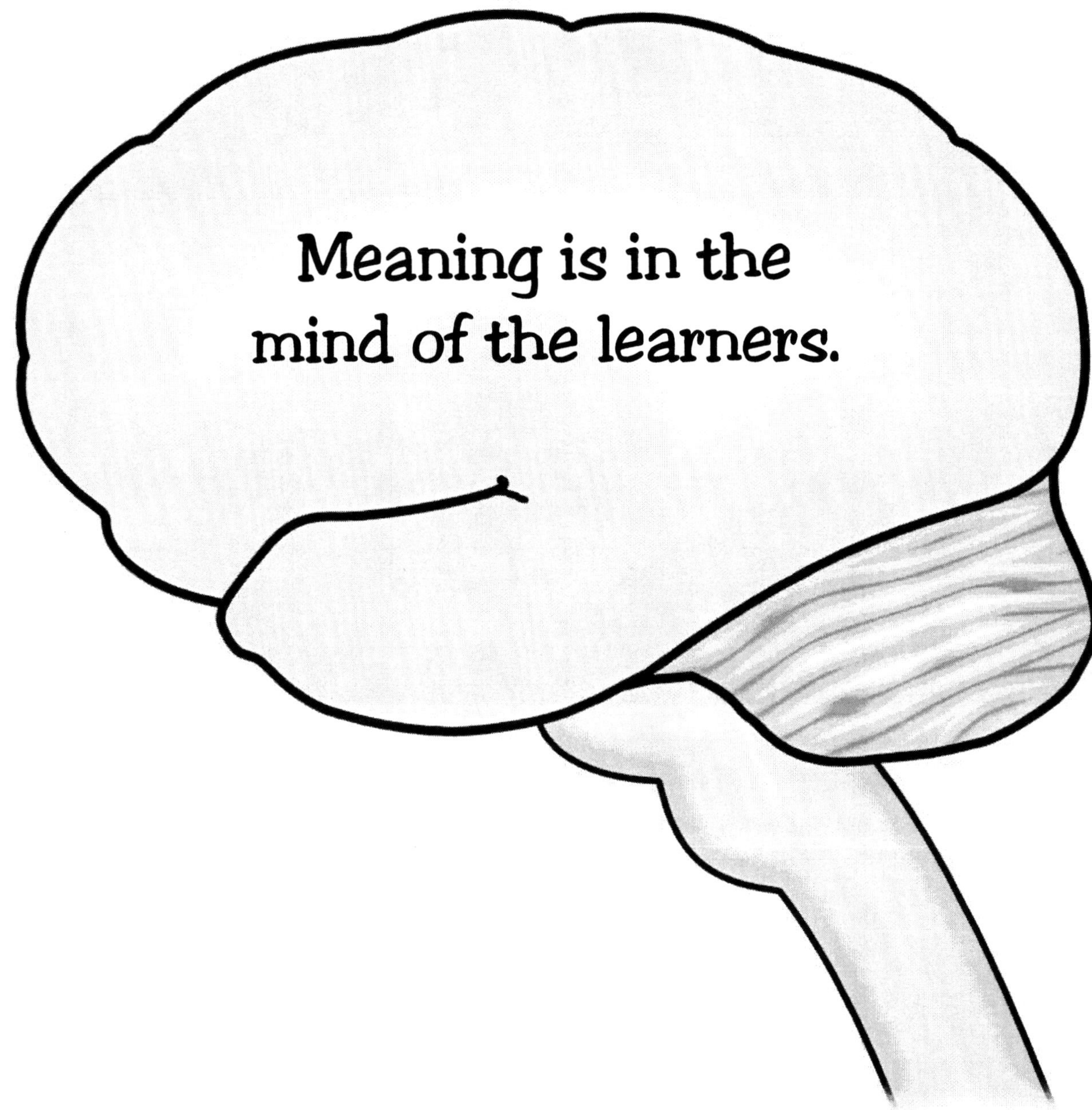
Meaning is in the
mind of the learners.

Chapter 5

Meaning - How to Make Learning Meaningful in Your Classroom

BrainSMART Principles for Making Learning Meaningful 3-6

3. **Respectful relationships in a safe environment contribute to a positive productive state and more on-task behavior.**

   Effective teachers relate positively to students without put downs or sarcasm.

4. **Students learn best in their own learning style.**

   Effective teachers teach to the learning styles of the students.

5. **Meaning is made in the mind of the learner by making connections to what is already known and through concrete learning experiences.**

   Effective teachers make learning meaningful by facilitating learning experiences that bring learning to life.

6. **The brain needs processing time for meaningful connections to be made.**

   Effective teachers give students time to process and create meaning.

The brain acts as if it has a *save* key and a *delete* key. It automatically deletes meaningless data – most of the data that it receives. To promote learning, we must make the information we teach meaningful. Meaning is in the mind of the learner and can be strongly generated by connecting to the real world of the student.

The brain learns best by using relevance, emotion, patterns, and context to create meaning. *Relevance* is how much the learner personally connects with the information. The stronger the emotion, the

Make Learning Meaningful

Make It R.E.A.L.

Relevant to Learner

Engage Learner in Active Learning

Associate New with Existing Knowledge

Learning in Students Styles

more meaningful it is. Strong emotional experience codes information as being important. The brain learns best when new information is connected to the big picture. Isolated information, on the other hand, is often meaningless and easily forgotten.

Students learn in a variety of styles. Some are visual, some auditory, and some kinesthetic. Presenting information in a manner suited to a student's preferred learning style is an important part of making it meaningful to that student. Use of strategies aligned with Gardner's (1983, 1992) nine intelligences (see Chapter 2) will also make learning

R.E.A.D.

Kinesthetic Learners

Rate:	**Slow Speech**
Eyes:	**Down to Right**
Action:	**Relive Events, Gestures Towards Body**
Dialogue:	**Feel, Grasp, Concrete, and Tough**

Auditory Learners

Rate:	**Medium**
Eyes:	**Left and Right**
Action:	**Few Gestures Point to Ears**
Dialogue:	**Say, Talk, Tell, Loud, Quiet, Hear, and Listen**

Visual Learners

Rate:	**Fast (to keep up with pictures)**
Eyes:	**Up**
Action:	**Paints pictures with hands**
Dialogue:	**See, Watch, Show, Bright, Picture**

Learning Preferences and Student Achievement

- 90% + of students at-risk of dropping out of school before high school completion have a kinesthetic or visual preference in modality.
- Preference or style often has a neurological base so students are unlikely to change their preference in style.
- 85% of students are learners who prefer the gestalt style.
- 15% of teachers have a gestalt preference in style.
- 7% of students are able to switch easily and automatically to nondominant preference.
- The classroom instruction, environment, and relating must be in alignment with ways students can be successful.

meaningful. The R.E.A.D. model is a diagnostic tool to help educators understand students' modality preferences.

Meaningful learning creates energized youth. A large body of cognitive research based on the work of Feuerstein (1991) indicates that teachers have a very powerful role in guiding students to experience learning as meaningful.

In fact, without a specific kind of guidance that we call "Coaching for Learning" from an experienced adult who feels a caring connection, students do not experience learning as meaningful and energizing. After teachers have coached students to experience profound meaning in learning, students then have the skills necessary to discover meaning in learning for themselves, without a guide. However, meaning first occurs in the mind of the learner as it is energized by good teachers!

Key to creating meaningful learning in schools is to develop classrooms that respect and honor all people who make their home there — the students and teachers. The following acronym illuminates important points about meaning that energize learning and thinking.

PRE-Cognition

Partnership in Learning

Relationships Around Learning

Energy Through Synergy

Culture of Belonging

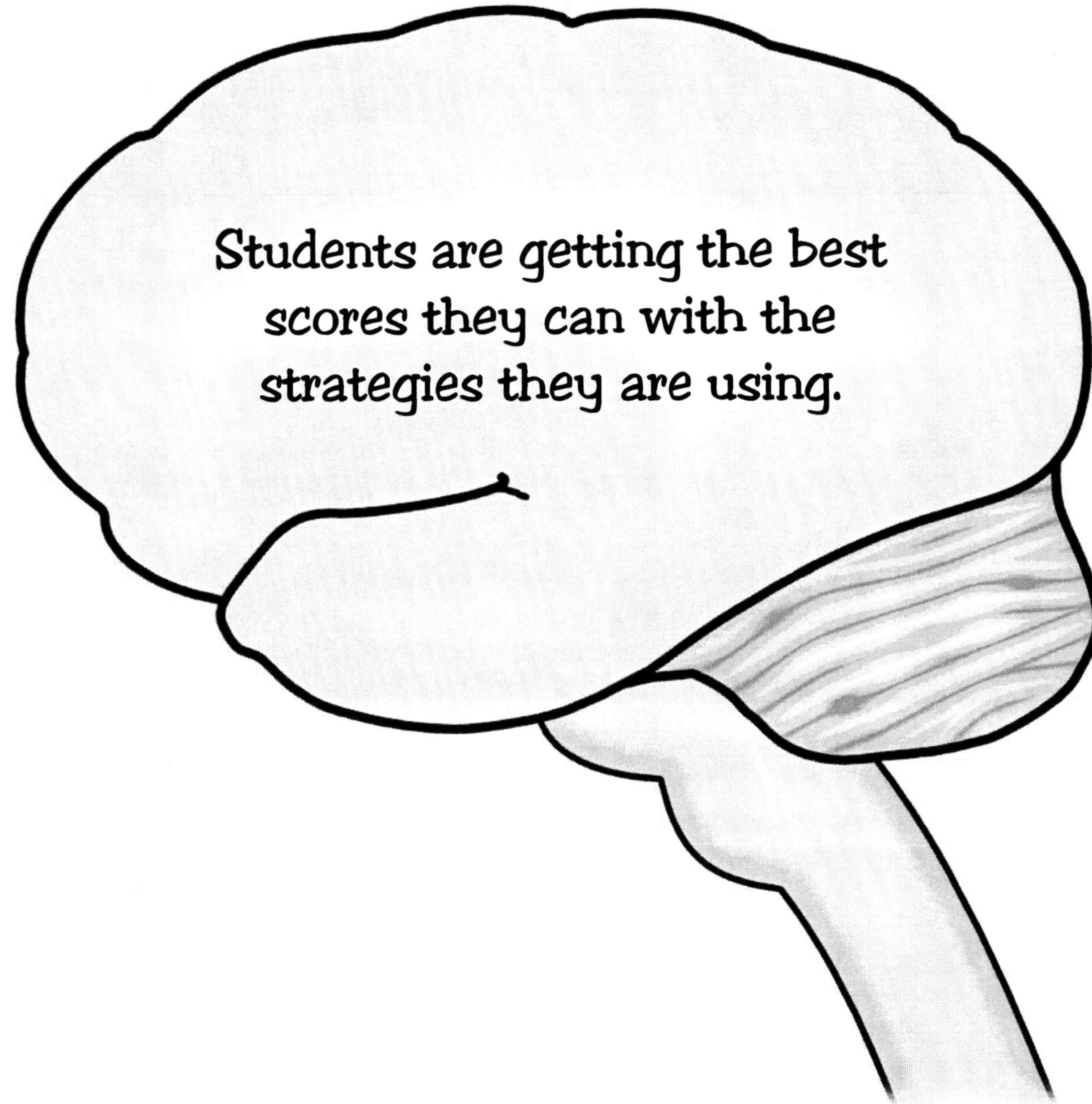
Students are getting the best
scores they can with the
strategies they are using.

BrainSMART Thinking:

Strategies for Reaching A-V-K Learners

Research in the learning styles literature suggest that at least three primary modalities are used in thinking: auditory (A), visual (V), and kinesthetic (K). The following ideas for including these three modalities have been shown to increase student learning.

Auditory Modality

- Developing metacognition, some also V-K
- Naming and using cognitive strategies, some also V-K
- Using H.E.A.R. strategy, also V-K
- Questioning strategies to engage
- Awareness of tone and verbal cues as well as other BrainSMART Tools

Visual Modality

- Mind Mapping and Brain Webbing
- Using other graphic organizers such as the fishbone and Venn diagrams
- Eye movements
- Sketching the problem during instruction and test taking
- Many of the BrainSMART Tools include Visual Modality

Kinesthetic Modality

- BrainObics for thinking and learning
- Story-scape for reading and language arts
- Memory-scape for social studies and language arts
- Many of the BrainSMART Tools include kinesthetic modality

BrainSMART is successful with at-risk students because the science and practice that reinforce the model include the kinesthetic and visual modalities that comprise between 80% and 90% of learners today. Research shows that most at-risk learners have kinesthetic and visual strengths.

Relating in the Classroom: A Necessary Framework for Learning

Current research is clear about the importance of positive relationships between teachers and students. There are two frameworks for this knowledge. One is recent understandings from brain research indicating that the brain is, first and foremost, social. The second is from cognitive psychology and indicates that language and thinking are learned best when positive relationships exist for learning.

Frameworks have been established and used in schools across the world to enhance relationships between teachers and students that will in turn enhance learning and thinking. Many schools use a specific framework, developed by Israeli psychologist Reuven Feuerstein, known as mediated learning.

This approach has been used with many different populations of students, ranging from gifted to special education students. For example, it has been used with students who have Down's Syndrome and students who have suffered depression, including those who have had the loss of family and friends. Most often, the mediated approach has been used with at-risk students. In fact, it was originally developed to prepare survivors of the Holocaust for life and work in the late 1940s and 1950s.

Pre-C stands for Partnership in Learning, Relationships Around Learning, Energy Through Synergy, and Culture of Belonging.

This approach for developing students who experience meaning in learning has been tested with students having great difficulty, as well as with students who are succeeding, in school and life. For example, many students at the Feuerstein institute were victims of the Holocaust. Many of them had lost family members to death or had lost contact with other survivors. Many did not even have pictures of their loved ones and former communities. Caring teachers had the privilege of being with these children and hearing stories about how they did not want to rise in the mornings because they had so little for which to live. For them, creating new meaning for learning in relationships with their teachers and other youth probably contributed to their very survival, as well as future ability to love and work.

Here are some BrainSMART tools for creating meaning:

- Field trips
- Student-generated questions
- Build a model
- Auditory teaching
- Kinesthetic teaching
- Debates
- Cartoons
- Journal writing
- Encourage peer teaching
- Implement in your personal life
- Videos
- Exhibition
- Music and songs
- Experiments
- Role playing
- Coach for meaning
- Enjoy community mentors or volunteers in your classrooms

An Important Suggestion:

Include plays, stories, music, and other means of collecting wisdom from all the cultures represented by the students.

Questions to ask ourselves:

- Is this interaction, lesson, or process meaningful to me?
- How can I make this meaningful to my students?

<u>You</u> Control the Save and Delete Keys of Your Life

S.A.V.E. - Success

Deal - With Problems

Delete - Negatives

The Next Time - I Will!

Chapter 6

Attention -

How to Gain and Sustain Focused Attention on the Real Work of Learning

Sustaining focused learner attention followed by downtime and feedback

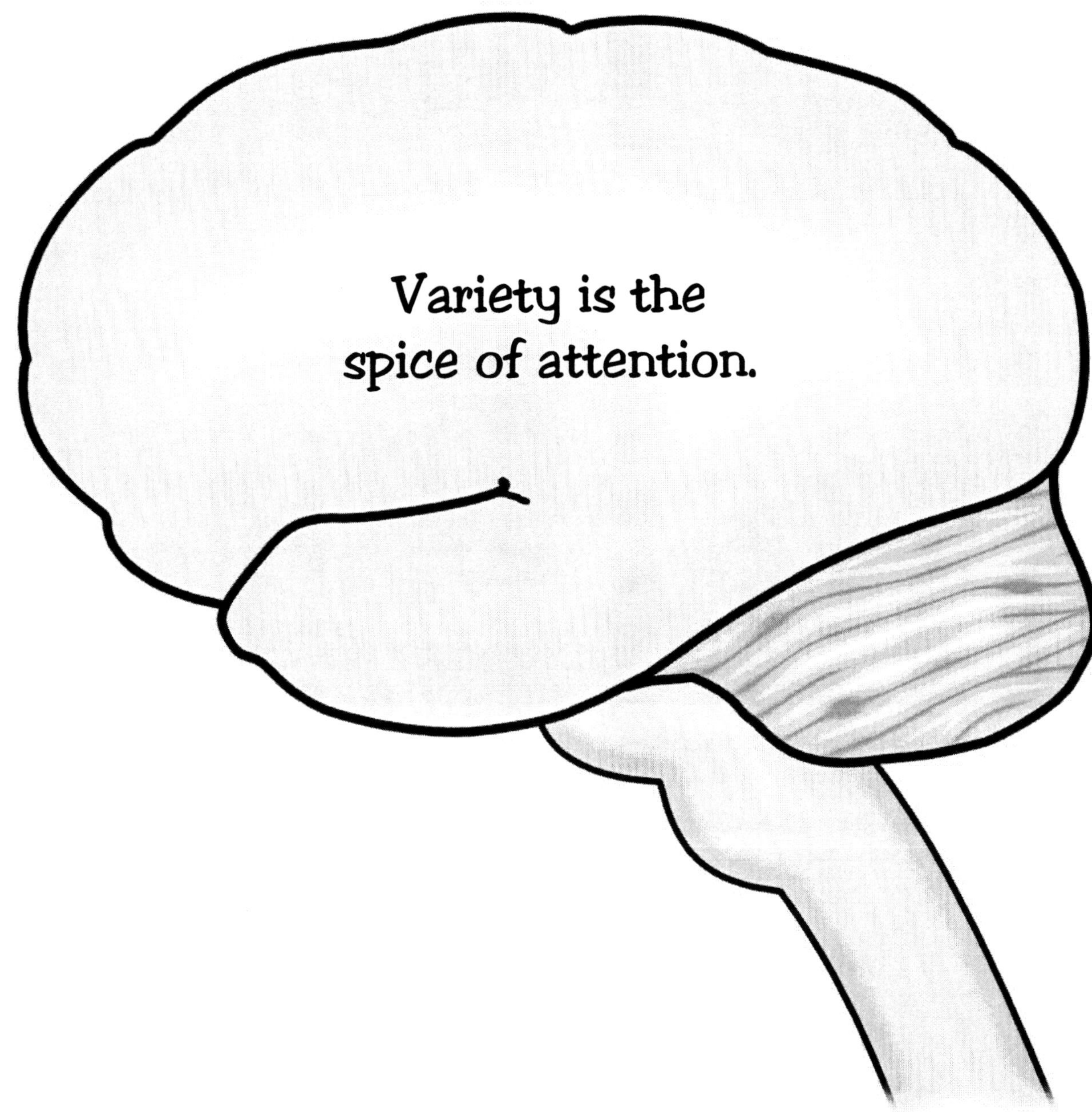
Variety is the
spice of attention.

Chapter 6

Attention – How to Gain and Sustain Focused Attention on the Real Work of Learning

BrainSMART Principles for Sustaining Focused Learner Attention 7-8

7. **Emotion, variety, and interaction are primary engines of attention.**

   Effective teachers are enthusiastic, create curiosity, and use a variety of instructional methodologies to engage attention.

8. **Working at a level of appropriate challenge with regular feedback on interesting work sustains internal motivation and attention.**

   Effective teachers design lessons that engage intrinsic motivation and give regular feedback and downtime so that students may process what is being studied.

It is biologically impossible to learn without paying attention. The brain pays attention to a specific hierarchy of needs, which is unique to each student. In *Completing the Puzzle*, Jensen (1996) reports that research by Cloniger shows that the three different parts of the brain respond to different stimuli. The reptilian brain is engaged in activities that involve avoiding pain or danger. The limbic system is involved in stimuli that offer the promise of pleasure. The neocortex craves novelty and curiosity.

Research shows that the attention span for an adult audience is around nine seconds, and the brain causes a series of shifts in and out of present attention. It is important to allow for this when presenting information.

Another on-again off-again feature of the brain's activity is an attention cycle about 20 minutes long, with the highest attention level being at the beginning and at the end. These are known as primacy and recency, respectively. In order to boost learning, it is important to organize material in chunks of time of approximately 20 minutes, and to present the most important information first or last, when attention is naturally greatest.

<u>Never</u>

Question
Ability

<u>Always</u>

Improve
Strategy

Marcus Conyers
Co-Founder, BrainSMART Professional Development

One of the keys to effective learning is to have a balance between focused attention on content versus downtime and feedback. This ensures that the brain has the opportunity it needs to receive new information and also time to process it.

The opposite of attention is neuronal habituation. This happens when the brain is getting too much of one signal which will shut off the brain, such as a monotone, which is one tone, or a monochrome, which is one color, or a monologue, which is a one-way conversation. With a monotone, monochrome, or monologue, the brain shuts down and can drift off to sleep.

Here are some BrainSMART tools for generating attention:

- Guest speakers
- Mind mapping
- Simulations
- Dramatic story telling
- Unique visuals
- Discussions
- Use graphic organizers
- Halt, Engage, Anticipate, Respect, and Replay
- Coach breathing techniques for stress reduction and focus
- Games
- Attention Bingo
- Walks
- Dramatic demonstrations
- Teamwork
- Interviews
- Student presentations
- Model attentive and engaged learning
- Teach mind-body exercises such as BrainObics

A question to ask ourselves and our students:

- What do you think is important here?

Three Brain Questions That Drive Attention

Shall I:

Run from it?
Eat it?
Mate with it?

The Brain Focuses on:

Avoiding Danger	Pursuing Opportunities

Chapter 7

Retention -

Teaching with Memory in Mind

Using multiple strategies for facilitating natural memory

Three Memory Systems

Motor

Episodic

Taxon

Chapter 7

Retention – Teaching With Memory in Mind

BrainSMART Principles for Facilitating Natural Memory 9-10

9. **The brain is designed to SAVE what is useful and used and to delete what is not.**

   Effective teachers make lessons as useful and memorable as possible by using memory strategies and having their students use what they learn.

10. **"If the body doesn't move then the brain doesn't learn!"**

    Effective teachers equip students with specific kinesthetic and interactive strategies for retaining and recalling important information.

Teaching With Memory in Mind

One of the most exhilarating opportunities for enhancing student performance and boosting their self-esteem is to teach in ways that trigger long-term retention and recall. In learning how to do this, we have found that the brain acts as though it has a secret code for deciding what to remember and what to forget. The brain seems to operate like a computer. Bombarded with billions of bits of data each day, it decides to hit the "*save* key" on only a tiny fraction of this and to automatically "delete" everything else.

In spite of this auto-delete feature, the potential of the brain to save information is immense. Consider the example highlighted in the following quote from Nobel Prize winner Francis Crick (1994), which demonstrates the awesome power of successfully hitting the *save* key:

"A subject shown about 2500 different color slides for about 10 seconds each, could still recognize about 90% of them after ten days."

– Francis Crick, Ph.D.

Compare this with the findings of the National Training Laboratories, reported by Sousa (1995). This research shows that, using traditional

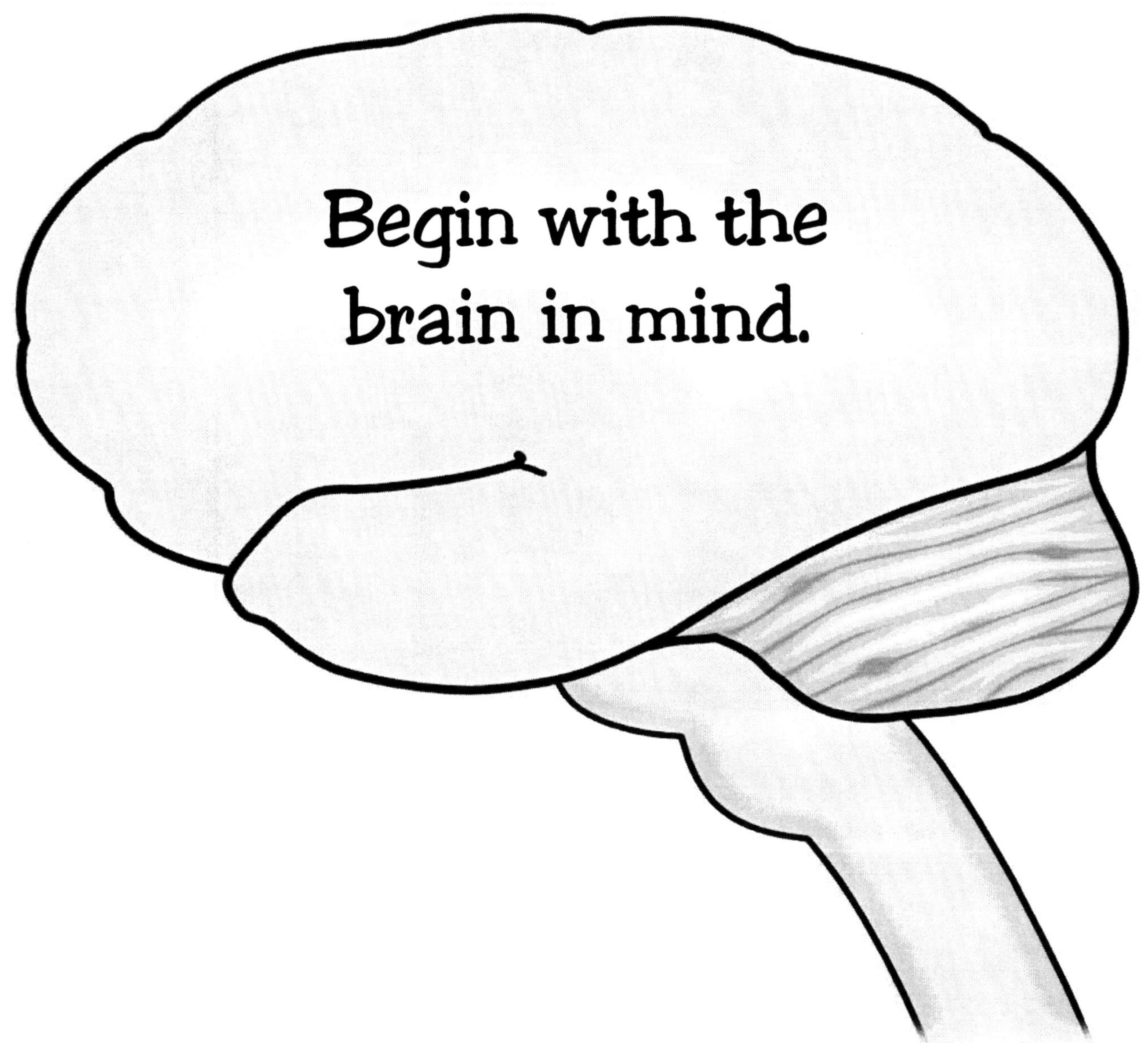
Begin with the
brain in mind.

lecture style teaching, *only 5%* of information is remembered after only 24 hours! This shows the effectiveness of the *delete* key.

In this chapter, we review a process we call "teaching with memory in mind," which gives you tools for translating the enormous potential for student retention into actual performance — in the classroom, in taking tests, and in life. This process not only boosts students achievement, it has an incredibly positive impact on their self-esteem and their ongoing desire to learn.

First, let's look at the three different memory systems that the brain uses to store data. For ease of recall we will call them the MET, which stands for:

Motor Memory

Have you noticed that, after you learn how to drive, ride a bicycle, tie your shoelaces, or type, that you have this memory forever? These functions flow from what researchers describe as *motor* memory. In this system, information is processed primarily in the cerebellum area of the brain. After information is learned, it often lasts a lifetime. In life, we naturally take advantage of this highly effective memory system. For example, much childhood learning is naturally facilitated by running, climbing, jumping, and experiencing firsthand through the senses. In the BrainSMART process, we also utilize the power of motor memory, in tools such as the "Ten Pegs" we learned in Chapter 2.

Episodic Memory

Episodic memory is also called location/spatial memory. For example, what did you have for lunch last Saturday? Notice that the first thing your brain had to do was remember where you were at that time. It was using its episodic, or location, memory. With this system,

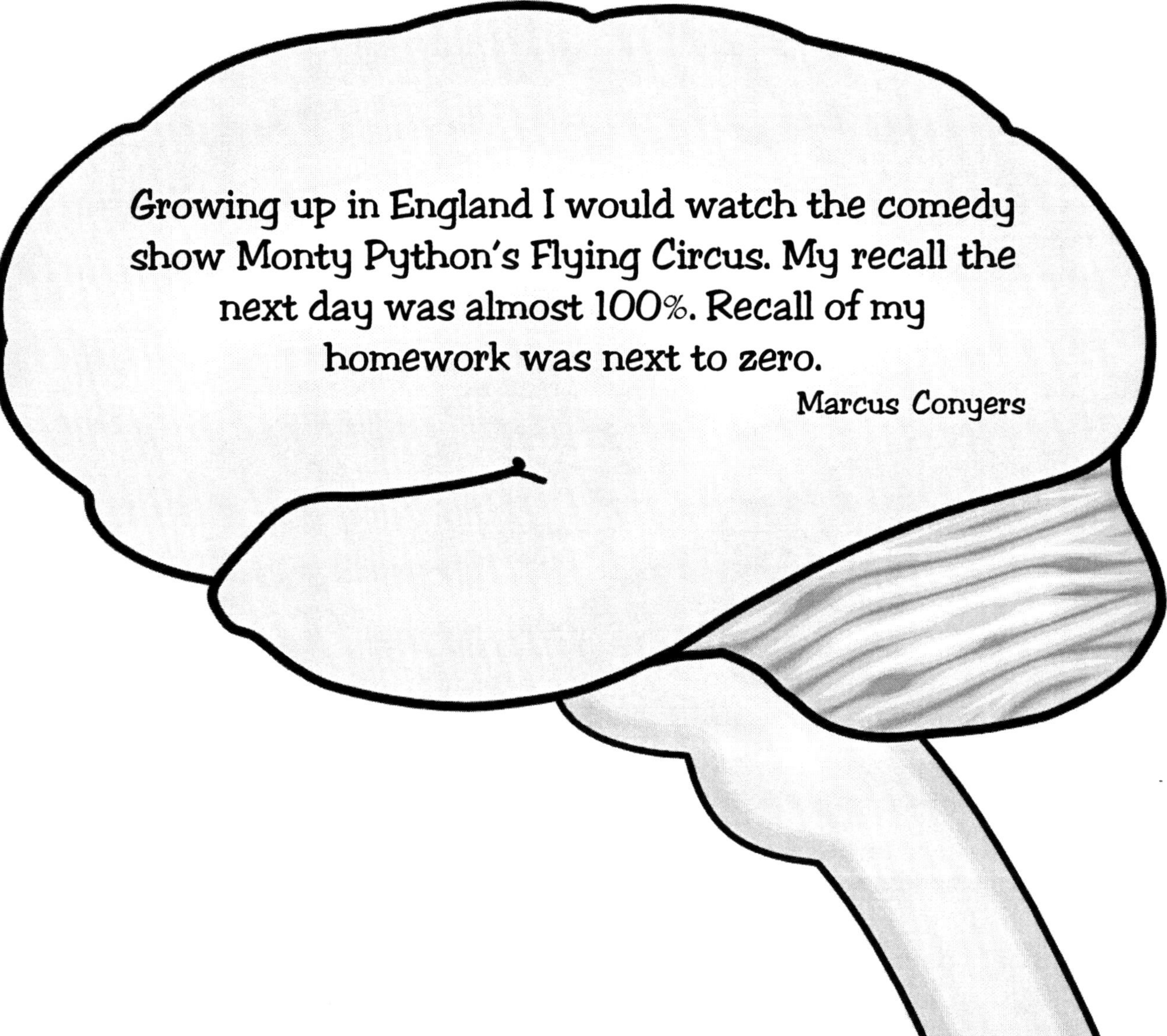
Growing up in England I would watch the comedy show Monty Python's Flying Circus. My recall the next day was almost 100%. Recall of my homework was next to zero.
Marcus Conyers

the key to successful retention is similar to that of successful real estate: location, location, location. Our episodic memory has a limitless capacity, is quickly updated, and is used naturally by people all the time. This memory is encoded when students are in a state of high curiosity and when educators use novelty. It is amplified by using a variety of sensory input — the more senses used, the stronger the encoding. This is also the system used to remember important life events. For example, where were you when you heard about the Challenger disaster, or the death of Princess Diana?

You can maximize the use of this system in the classroom by encouraging students to change seats, by ensuring that you move around the room, by using props, guest speakers, and anything that makes episodes of learning unique.

Taxon Memory

The third and least effective memory system is taxon memory (semantic/categorical). Have you ever met someone in a grocery store that you have known for ten years, and when you go to say hi, their name just drops out of your mind? Have you ever been reading a book and when someone asks you, "What are you reading?" you can't even remember the author? Have you ever sat down to take a test and found it difficult to recall the information you had studied in books, or from your lecture notes? You were relying on taxon or semantic memory. The brain is not designed to easily remember print, text copy, or isolated facts. This is one of the reasons why, after 24 hours, typically only 5% of a lecture is remembered. Taxon memory generally lacks the power to overcome the brain's tendency to automatically delete information. In fact, using this process to remember any information at all requires constant practice, rehearsal, and a high level of motivation on the part of the student.

The taxon system has a "working memory" part that lasts for approximately 15 seconds. Hence, when you look up a telephone number, you have about 15 seconds until it drops out of your mind. This "working memory" can focus on a maximum of seven chunks of information at any one time for people over fifteen years of age. By comparison, a seven-year-old can store around three chunks and a five-year-old, just two chunks.

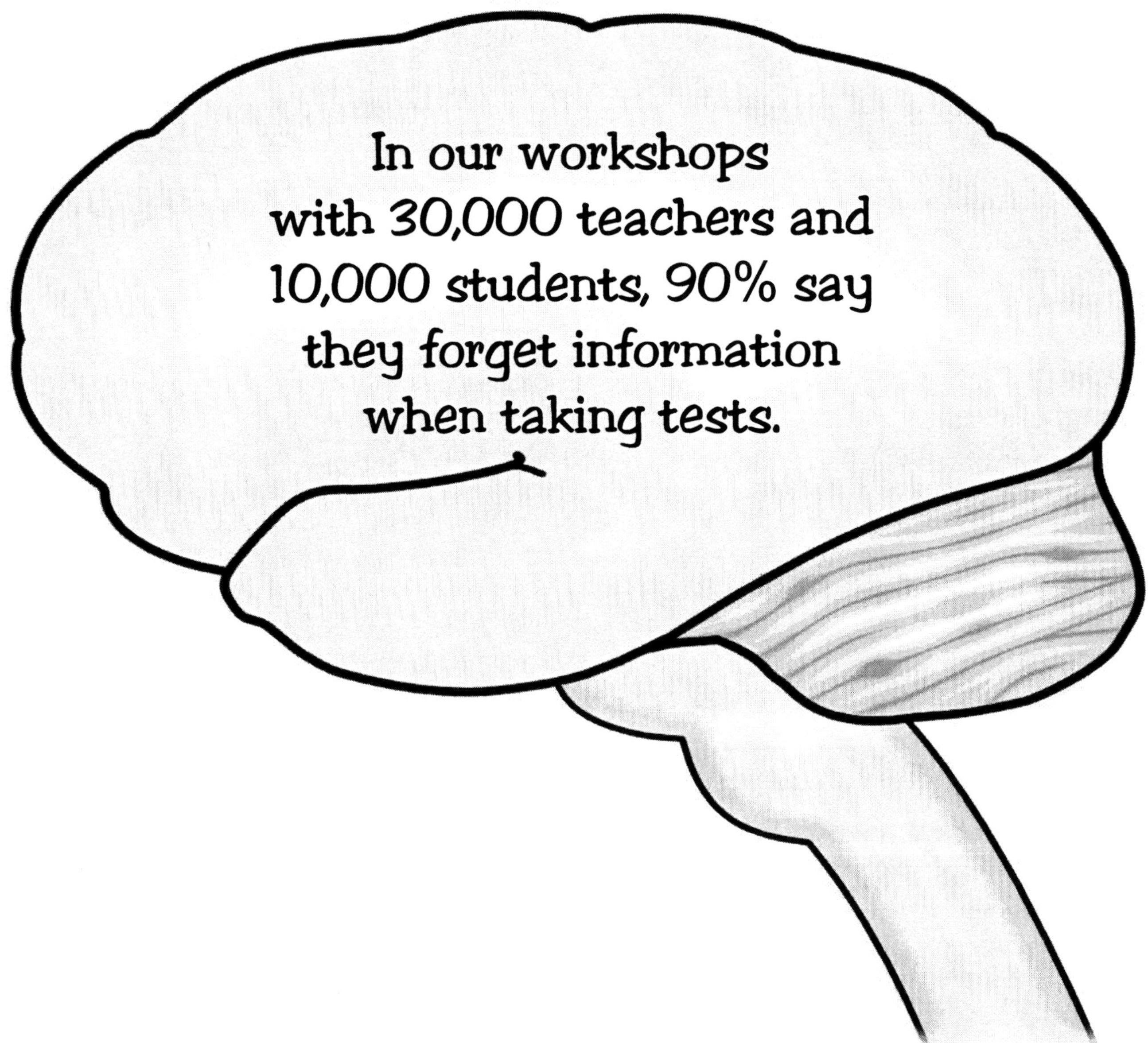
In our workshops
with 30,000 teachers and
10,000 students, 90% say
they forget information
when taking tests.

Although taxon memory is the least effective system of the three, it is the one most commonly used in education today. However, by using the BrainSMART tools in this chapter, you will be able to transform taxon information into a format that allows the brain to readily retain and recall it.

Memory-Scaping

Marcus developed this process to use the power of location memory to map out an event that we want students to remember. He began testing this with the battle of Waterloo, first teaching it in the taxon/semantic way, which got an audience response of groans and yawns. Then, he memory-scaped the battle. Marcus tells about this powerful teaching tool!

"I began on the right side of the room, describing the red English uniforms, and how they held their muskets and bayonets in front of them as they moved across the field. I then physically moved to the left side of the room to describe the French, dressed in blue, with their black hats, aiming their cannon at the approaching troops. After this, I moved to the back of the room to describe the Russian cavalry dressed in gray, riding down the hill, and then to the front of the room to describe the rockets bursting up above. When I presented the battle of Waterloo this way, the students had a lot more fun during the presentation, and could easily recall all the details afterward."

Imagine creating a giant memory-scape in the gymnasium, using string to mark out different countries. Imagine then getting a student to be the ruler of each country, and to learn five key facts about that country. Now imagine each child going for a voyage around the world, learning information from each ruler. This system uses motor and episodic memory systems, and involves all of the senses, in order to facilitate retention and recall.

One of the most thrilling benefits of applying such BrainSMART tools is to see students who are brimming with confidence that they have retained the information. When they cannot wait to take a test in order to show off their knowledge, the "test torture seat" is transformed into the "success seat."

Hit the SAVE key in your memory

SEE

ASSOCIATE

VIVIDLY

EXPERIENCE

Here's a story from Marcus' life that illustrates the difference in effectiveness between memory systems. "While growing up in England, I used to watch a comedy show called *Monty Python's Flying Circus.* I would spend three hours a night doing my homework and twenty-five minutes watching the show. The next day, my retention for my homework was near zero, but my recall of the television show was almost 100%. You may have had a similar experience of easily remembering a favorite comedy show. Why the difference between homework and *Monty Python*? My homework, of course, was accessing taxon memory. The TV show, on the other hand, was effectively engaging episodic memory."

Marcus encourages us to enjoy another example from his youth. "My classmates and I studied French for twelve years and, for most of us, a dismal amount of the language was retained. They would put us into language labs with hot, heavy headphones, where the most boring voice you ever heard would say, "The word 'bonjour' means 'hello'." Pretty soon, our brains started saying *delete, delete, delete.* That's taxon memory for you! By contrast, when I went to Paris to celebrate a friend's birthday during my late teens, we all learned a lot of French, like 'mademoiselle', 'beaujolais', etc. This event accessed episodic and motor memory to store the information."

Getting through school by laborious use of taxon memory was an unpleasant experience for Marcus. Perhaps it was for you, as well. Marcus continues with his story. Even more frustrating was the fact that, come test time, I would know the information right up until I sat down to take the test. The act of sitting down seemed to hit the *delete* button in my brain and I couldn't remember anything. Then, when I walked out of the room after the test, all the information suddenly came back, just in the nick of too late. Have you experienced this too? You're not alone; 90% of students and educators in our workshops have had experiences like this."

When you look back at your own experiences, and at what you remember about your own schooling, you will be very aware of the *delete* key having worked very consistently throughout your education with very little being saved.

Imagine what it would be like if you could help your students hit the *save* key instead, so they instantly remember key information and can

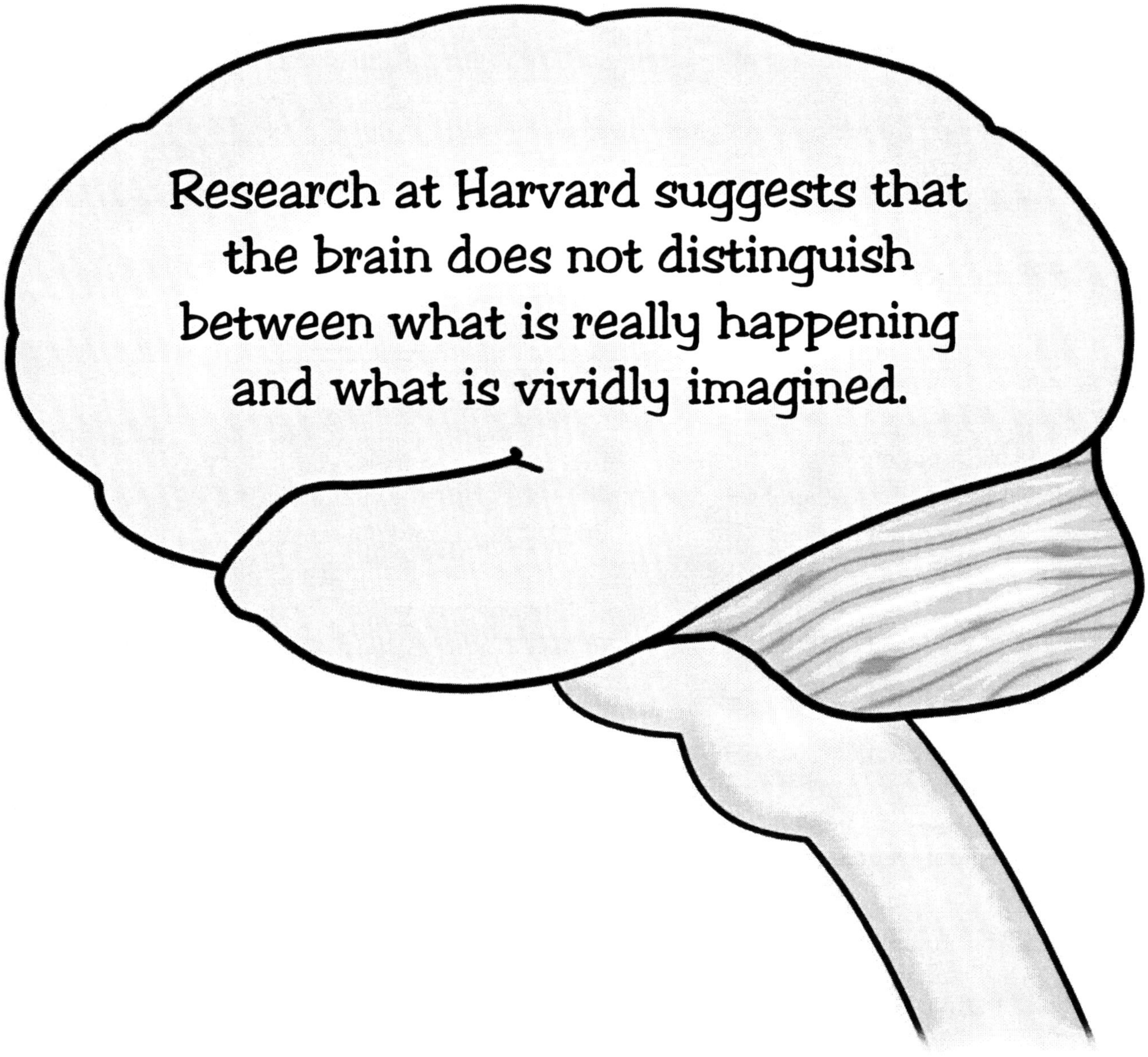

Research at Harvard suggests that the brain does not distinguish between what is really happening and what is vividly imagined.

recall it when they need it. All it takes is to switch from low-retention teaching methods like lecturing and reading, that use taxon memory, to high-retention methods that draw on the power of episodic and motor memory. There are dozens of simple tools in this book to help you make this switch easily and quickly.

Let's look at the essential elements for accessing motor and episodic memory, so that your students can hit the *save* key, and store information successfully. We will use a BrainSMART tool for this purpose based on the acronym SAVE. This acronym represents four key elements in learning retention:

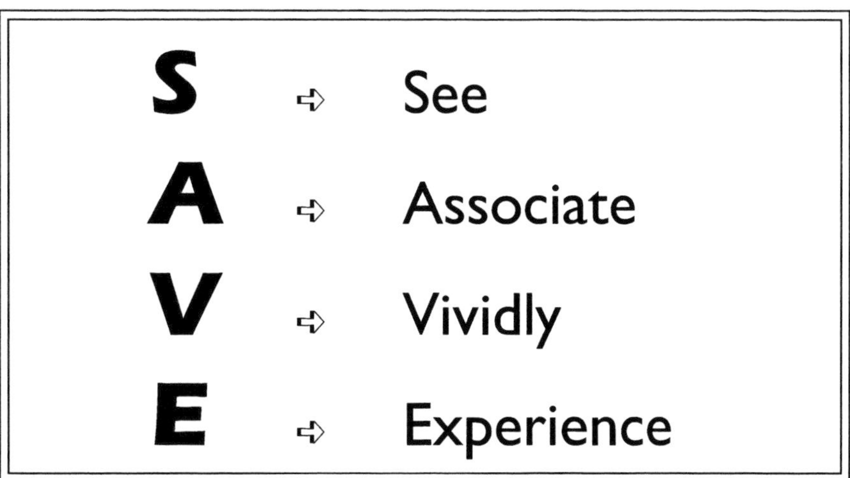

Let's examine each of these elements in more depth:

S

See

Recall the research on visual memory mentioned earlier in this chapter and highlighted by Nobel Prize winner Francis Crick (1994) from the Salk Institute, in his book *The Astonishing Hypothesis*. In that study, some 2,500 pictures were shown to a group of test subjects. When interviewed days later, they had 90% recognition. The implications are that the occipital lobe in the brain can help store virtually limitless amounts of information visually. Consider evidence from your own life. Which do you usually remember – the face or the name – when you meet someone? Most people remember the face. One of the reasons for this is that visual information is much more easily received, retained, and recalled.

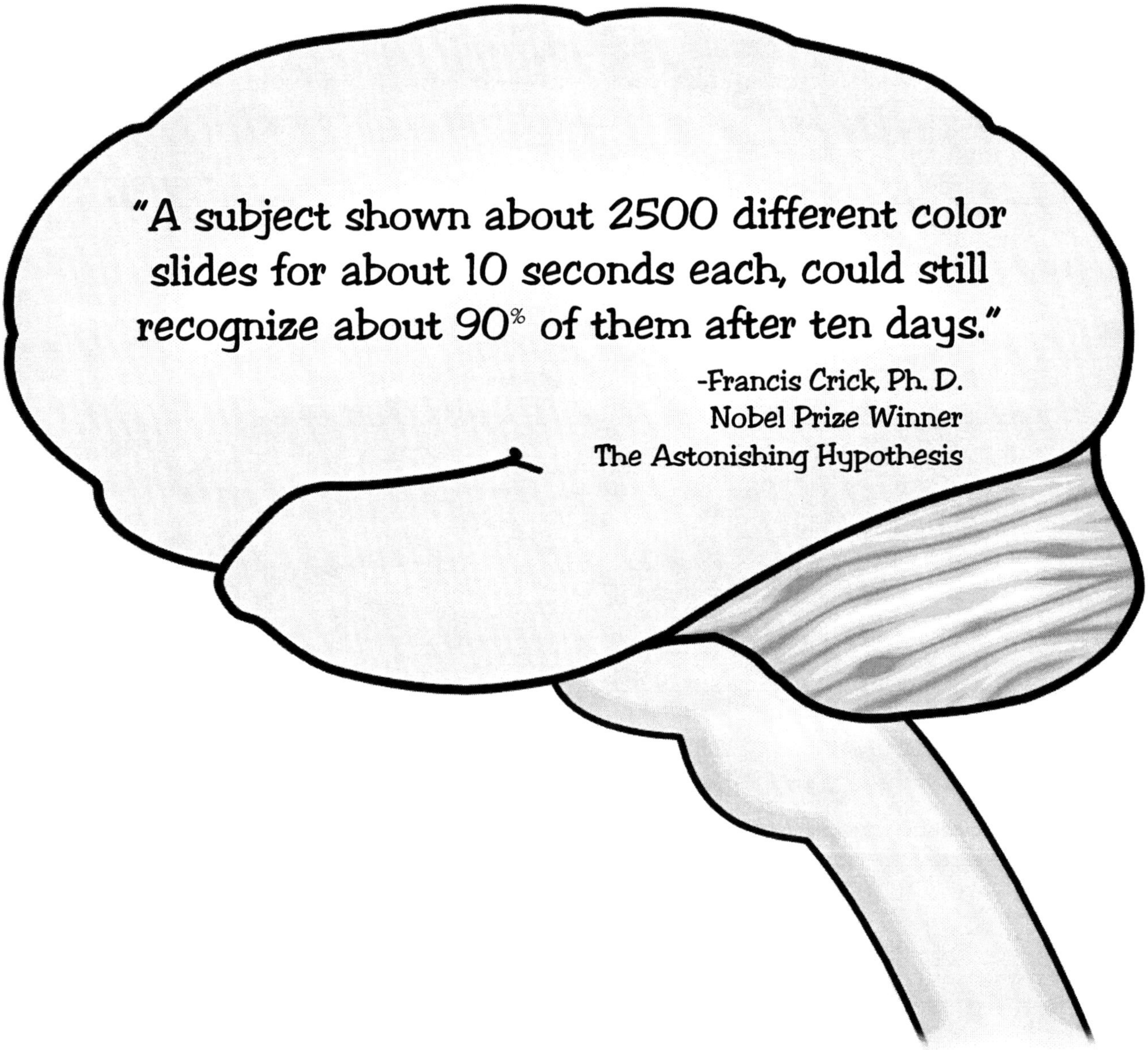

"A subject shown about 2500 different color slides for about 10 seconds each, could still recognize about 90% of them after ten days."

-Francis Crick, Ph. D.
Nobel Prize Winner
The Astonishing Hypothesis

Several of the BrainSMART tools presented here will tap into the amazing power of visual memory.

Associate

The brain, to make sense of information, needs to attach new data to existing information. For example, in a lecture where the speaker was giving information that you really did not understand, what did your brain do? Did it go *save* or *delete*? Usually, such data will be automatically deleted.

We will be sharing with you a wide variety of BrainSMART tools to help you use the power of association to remember information. For example, to remember names, you can associate a visual picture with the name in a very direct way. Suppose you want to remember that someone's name is Frank. You can stick a *frank*furter through his neck, so he looks like *Frank*enstein. This combines two factors; the power of the visual brain and the power of association.

Some of the BrainSMART tools associate on a kinesthetic level, so you can help those hard-to-reach kinesthetic learners.

Vividly

Research suggests that the brain does not know the difference between what is really happening and what is vividly imagined. For example, Herbert Benson (1997), in his book *Timeless Healing*, reports in his research that during showings of *Lawrence of Arabia*, sales of drinks skyrocketed. You have experienced the same thing in your own life. If you went to see the movie *Jaws*, did your own pulse race? Did you feel afraid? Did you see the audience jump? There was no shark in the theatre, yet your body reacted *as if* there was.

We will share with you BrainSMART tools for making your experience vivid.

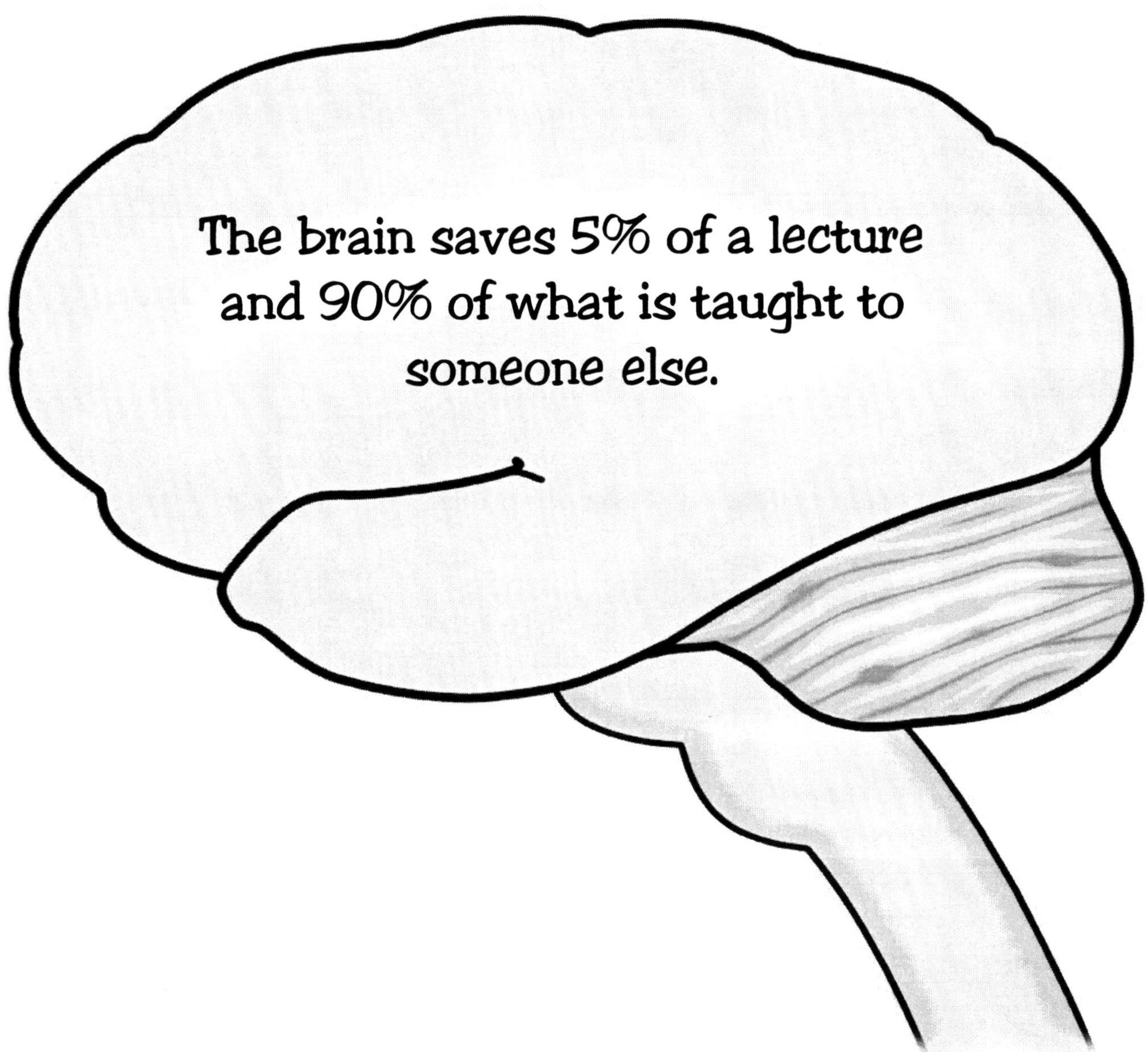
The brain saves 5% of a lecture
and 90% of what is taught to
someone else.

E

Experience

It is an adage that the brain learns best from experience. By combining the previous three components of making it visual, associating it, and then creating vivid sensory experience, we can build strongly encoded memories.

One way we do this during BrainSMART workshops is by performing many physical exercises, so that the whole body experiences the learning. An example of this is the "I Feel Good!" exercise. When I meet up with participants years later, their memory of vivid experiences is much stronger than of the information given auditorially.

In the retention tools section, we will examine ways you can translate all this theory into practice in your classroom, so that you, too, can experience the thrill of seeing your students hit the *save* key, instead of the *delete* key.

Besides the obvious benefits of remembering more information more easily, there is an interesting, highly positive side effect. The brain learns by installing new information into the context of what it already knows. This means that the more knowledge you have, the faster and more easily you can acquire additional knowledge. The bigger your database, the easier it is to add to it. Better retention, therefore, has a *compound effect* on learning speed.

A question to ask ourselves:

- Have I taught this lesson in a memorable way?

Chapter 8

Transfer -

Helping Students Transfer Learning from the Classroom to Success on the Test and Success in Life

Facilitating transfer of learned information to real life and test taking

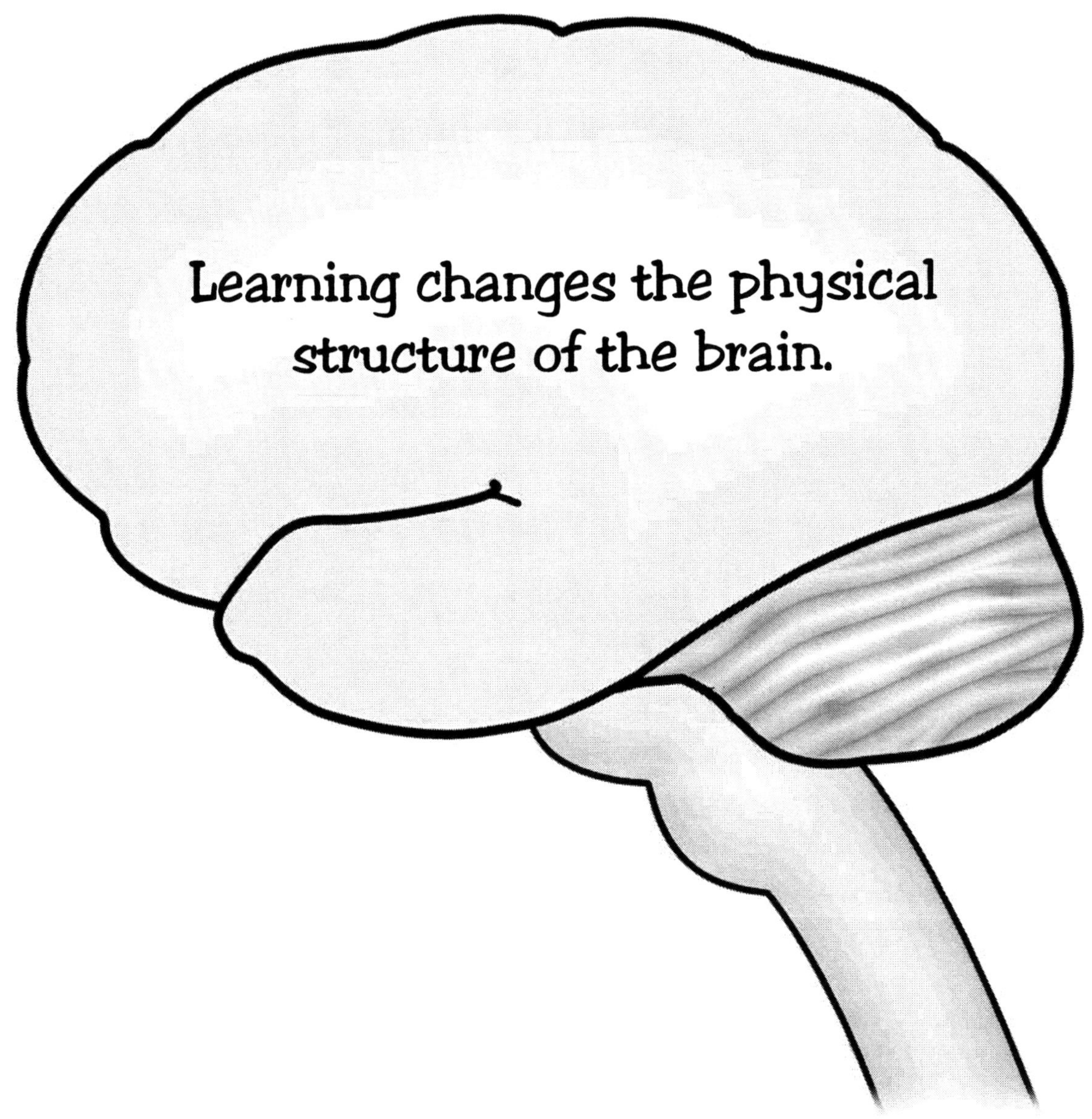
Learning changes the physical structure of the brain.

Chapter 8

Helping Students Transfer Learning From the Classroom to Success on the Test and Success in Life

BrainSMART Principles for Facilitating Transfer of Information to Test Taking and Real Life

11. **Metacognition is the key to transfer: the ability to assess a situation, choose the right cognitive strategy, and execute the strategy well.**

    Effective teachers teach metacognition and facilitate many examples of transfer.

12. **Strong original learning and regular review increase probability that learning can be recalled and applied successfully.**

    Effective teachers create strong learning experiences and then review through regular mind mapping and student processing.

Transfer is the bottom line for learning. Being able to take information from the classroom and to remember it and use it during the test is one important factor. To this day, college graduates earn 80% more during their lifetimes than high school graduates. Perhaps the most important transfer of information is from the classroom to life. Notice that transfer of skills is often stronger than the transfer of knowledge. Many students report that typing, or how to drive, was the most important thing they learned in school.

A meta-concept in transfer is to ensure that what is being taught is initially useful. The more useful it is and the wider the variety of contexts in which it can be applied, the stronger the transfer that will take place. Hunter (1982) suggested that transfer is the basis of all creativity, problem-solving, and the making of satisfying decisions.

Sousa, (1995) describes transfer as a two-part process: one, the effect that past processing has on new learning and two, the degree to which

Question and Develop Metacognition

Think aloud with your students – Include questions

Example – As a part of the lesson take opportunities to talk the problem through. Include any difficulties that come up. When we talk through problems we illustrate that teachers make mistakes too and good problem solvers persist and "fix-it."

How can we solve this subtraction problem (on board)? Well, let's see! Hum.... What will happen if I borrow from this column here? Is this correct? Is there another way to get the correct answer?

Bridge to real life as well as academic issues

Studies such as those at Research for Better Schools (Presseisen, 1988) have shown that students who have difficulty at school need many opportunities to think aloud and bridge to real life situations that interest them. This is often the motivational hook to capture their interest, given that these students may well be very good problem solvers in life!

Example – (With the above math example we can process with the class after the problem completed.) So, when in our lives is there more than one way to solve a problem? For example, when your family takes a vacation, are there alternative plans (any age student)? How can we "save face" if a peer is having a party on the weekend that we don't really want to attend (older students)?

the new learning will be useful to the learner in the future. Whenever new learning moves into working memory, then the long-term memory (most likely stimulated by a signal from the hippocampus) searches the long-term storage sites for any past learning that is relevant or similar.

Guide Students to Develop Principles

To guide students to greater transfer of knowledge and wisdom, it is important to use several ideas in our teaching practice. The first is to guide the students to develop principles that will change the course of their lives and schooling if they use them. The following example is from Donna's practice as a teacher at the middle school level.

Students are involved in a discussion of the directions for an exercise that the teacher has asked them to do in groups. There is considerable debate about what is required on the page. *The principle is that cues are important in many situations.* Students might be involved in lessons, test taking, or job interviews where it is necessary to observe cues in order to succeed at the task. In the case of lessons or practicing for tests or job interviews, the teacher might guide student understanding of this important principle by posing questions: How did you know what was asked of you in this situation? (Students will answer in various ways.) Then did they use cues? (Maybe the students mentioned it first and the teacher capitalizes on this learning opportunity.) Meaningful discussion follows as the students discuss the cues as hints that detectives use to find the answers when they solve problems. They begin to discuss that some clues are given in words. The teacher labels these as *explicit* cues. The students then mention that directions do not always tell you everything. For example, directions do not often tell you how long it might take to do the task, or if you are to write in pencil or pen. The teacher labels them as *implicit* cues, those that are not given in words, but that you might infer from past practice or imagine as being correct.

After a discussion of cues, explicit and implicit, students are guided by the teacher as they develop meaningful examples of the use of cues at school. They discuss how important it is to gather information about what teachers expect in each of their classes, as teachers' rules are often different from class to class. In math it is important to watch for the operational signs to tell you what to do in the problem. With dating it is important to watch for how someone treats you on a date. If they don't

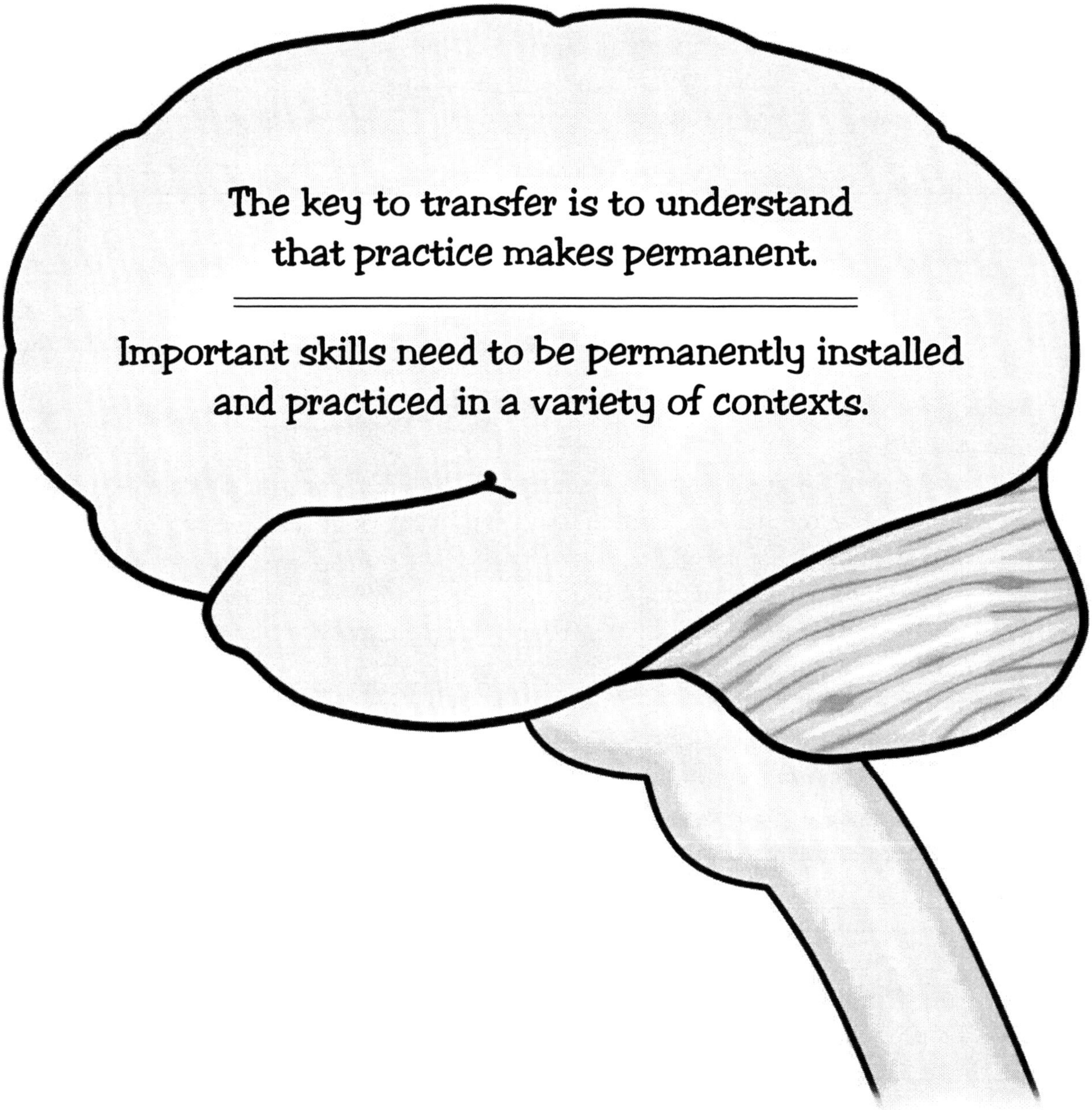

The key to transfer is to understand that practice makes permanent.

Important skills need to be permanently installed and practiced in a variety of contexts.

treat you well, this is a big cue. In job hunting, check cues for how to dress and what is expected in the interview ahead of time.

The teacher also asks for examples of what might happen if cues are not observed. Examples from the students are as follows: Some people might go ahead and date the wrong person and get into a lot of trouble. In math you miss a lot of problems on a test, even though you might know how to do them. You could not get a job, not because of your skill, or what you know, but because you did not know how to dress for the interview.

This is one of many examples from our teaching practice that highlights the need for explicit teaching of principles of good thinking practice. When students are guided to develop, understand, and practice using principles of good thinking, they transfer the principles to become good at scoring on tests, as well as lifelong learners. Consider only the example given, which is one of over 25 that we teach. What if our students all knew how to gather both implicit and explicit information as they consider problems on tests and in life? What a difference it makes!

Memory for Learning

It is essential that teachers use students' life experiences and memories as the foundation upon which new learning is built. For example, when we encourage students to work in cooperative groups at school, we guide them to remember how they cooperate with others at home. They are encouraged to use this knowledge and practice with others at school as they further develop skills for cooperation.

A useful question students might ask to guide their thinking is "What in my life experiences will help me solve this problem?"

Metacognition - Most Important for School Success

Perhaps the most important student characteristic for ensuring high student achievement and life success is metacognition. *Metacognition*, the skill of thinking about one's own thinking, is often not a characteristic of students in difficulty at school. In fact, many of the teachers that we have worked with across the United States are concerned that students today do not exhibit metacognition in their classrooms.

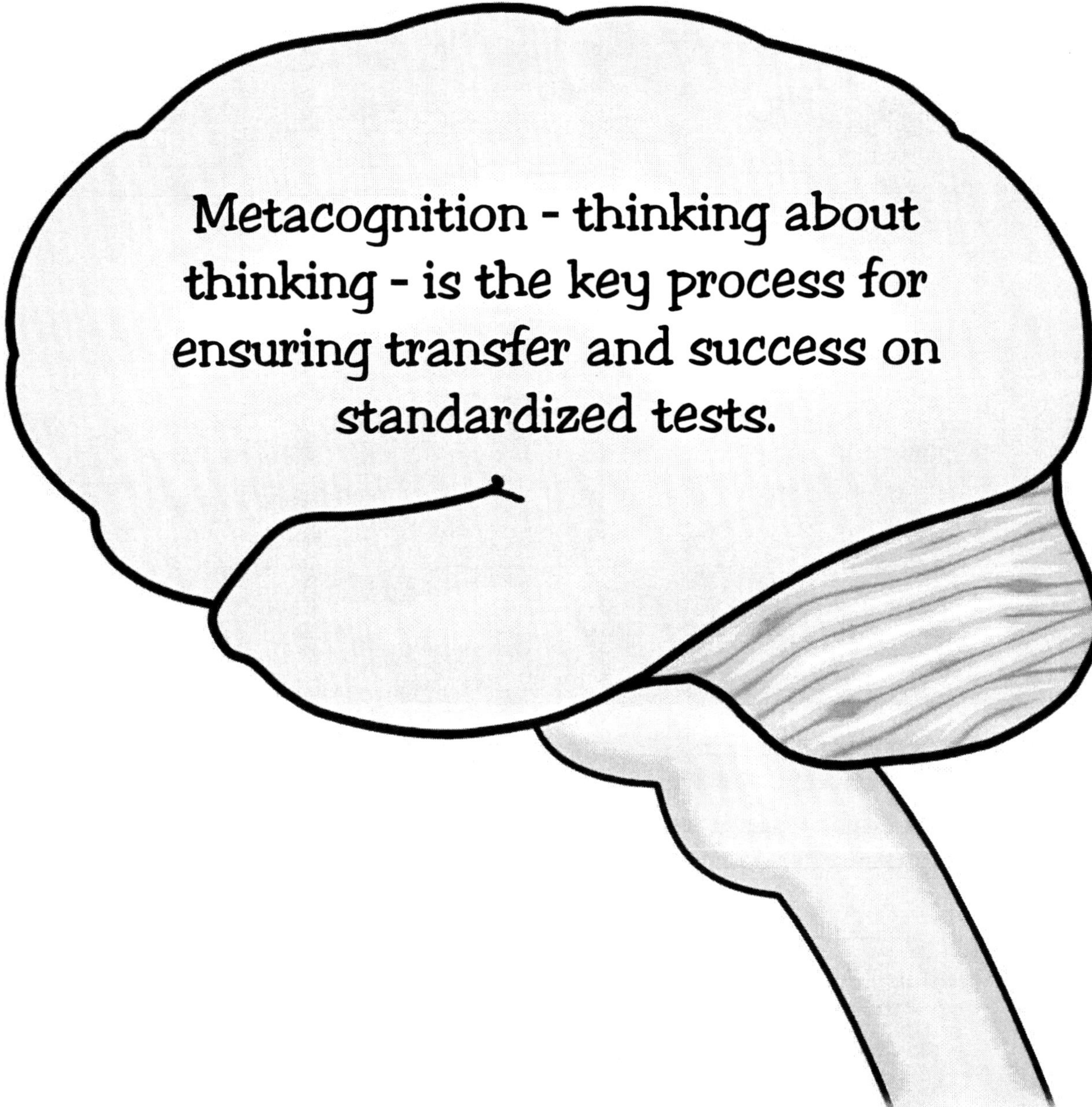
Metacognition - thinking about thinking - is the key process for ensuring transfer and success on standardized tests.

A point that we passionately want to share is that metacognition is a learnable skill that can be taught and here is how! Model problem solving out loud so that students hear your thinking process and can learn how to do the same as they listen. As a part of this process, make mistakes aloud and check yourself so this is experienced as a part of problem solving. Encourage your students to do the same.

Ask guiding questions that engage students in thinking about their thinking. For example, in the next chapter we share 60 strategies to increase student learning and achievement. You will find most of these strategies on the right hand side of the pages. On the left hand pages we have included sample questions that you can begin to ask your students so that they begin to think about ways they might use these strategies to help them learn more effectively.

An important point here is that we teachers pose critical questions as a way to guide students to become metacognitive in their orientation. The questions that we ask are meant to be *catalysts for students to begin to question themselves* as they problem solve. As you use the questions that we have given as examples, consider others that you want your students to ask themselves as well.

Here are some BrainSMART tools for triggering transfer:

- Metaphors
- Teaching other students
- Success simulation
- Make the learning useful
- Senior grade teach lower grade
- Make video or audio tape
- Physical reminder token/artifact
- Generate meaningful examples
- Teach in reference to real life lessons
- Amplify the principle to be transferred
- Use mental models and schemas
- Role playing
- Link with previous learning
- Rehearsing different states
- Journal writing
- Create a story about information covered during context
- Ask students questions that guide them to explore how they will use what they are learning in their lives

Questions to ask ourselves:

- Is this something that my students must be able to transfer?
- If not, is it worth teaching?
- If so, how have I created opportunities for transfer?

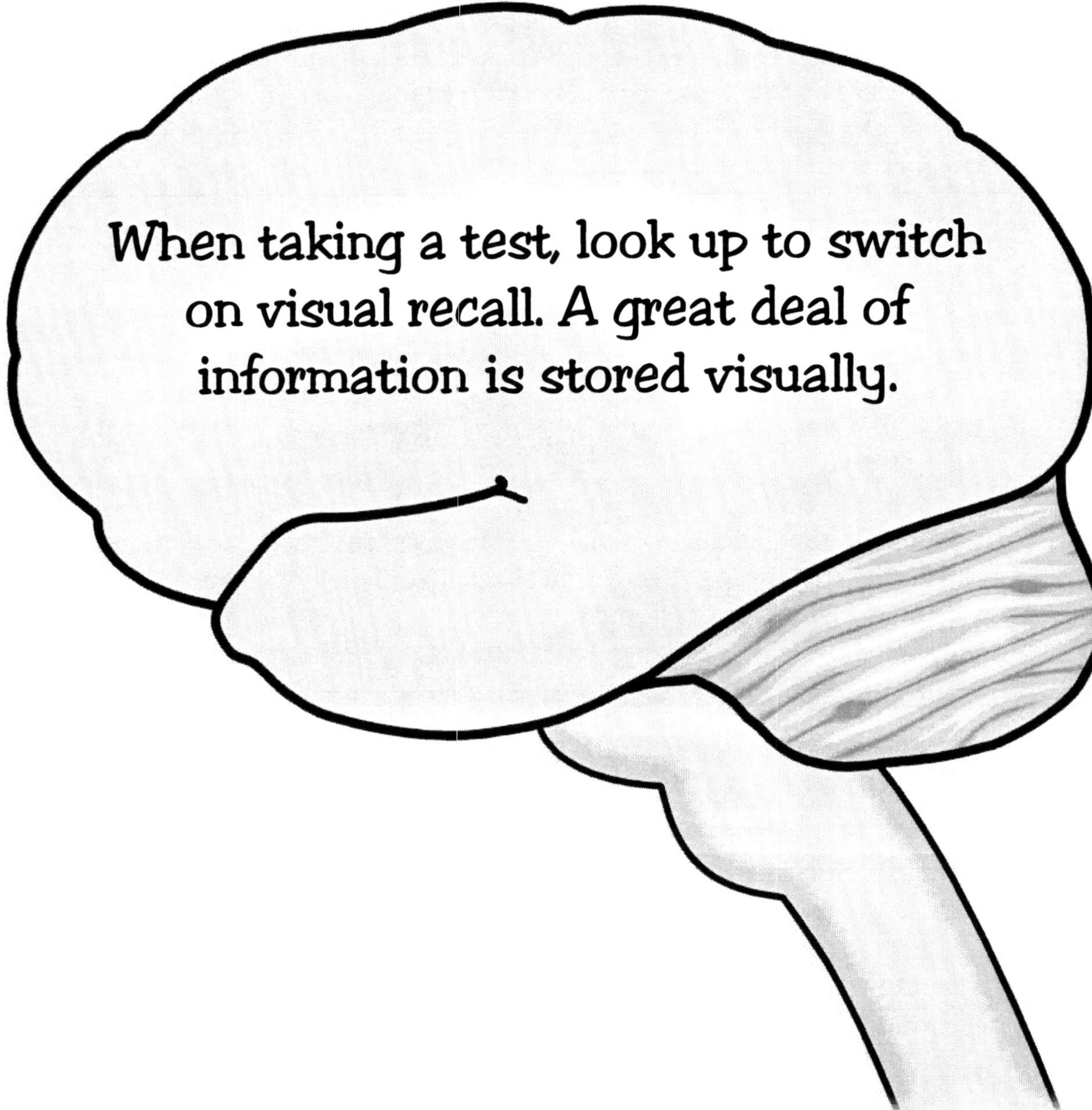
When taking a test, look up to switch
on visual recall. A great deal of
information is stored visually.

Chapter 9

Sixty BrainSMART Strategies and Your Own BrainSMART Lesson Planning Guide

Guide your students to become more effective learners. As you use these powerful strategies in your classroom teach your students to use the strategies independently. The left side of the page has questions that are guides to help you create a classroom of independent and high-achieving students.

Fill your Toolbox with 60 BrainSMART Tools you can use on Monday

10 BrainSMART Tools For State

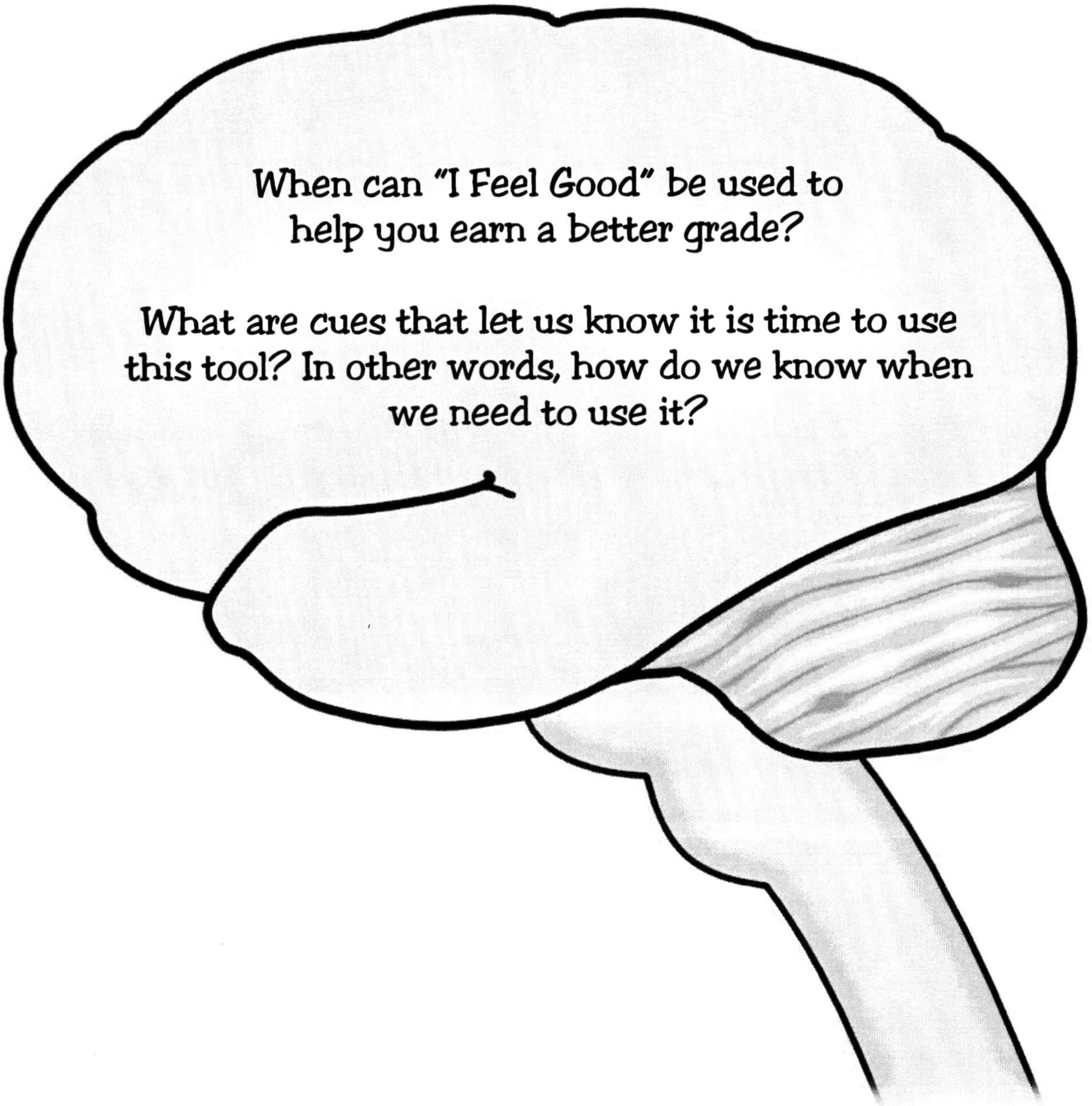

When can "I Feel Good" be used to help you earn a better grade?

What are cues that let us know it is time to use this tool? In other words, how do we know when we need to use it?

"I Feel Good!!"

Purpose: Creating a positive mental state, creating enthusiasm, rewarding individual and group achievements, fostering a positive self-image.

- **Step 1:** Ask the question, "Do you have any friends that are miserable?"
- **Step 2:** Ask participants to stand the way a miserable person would stand (for example, shoulders slouched, eyes down, shallow breathing, etc.).
- **Step 3:** Ask, "How do you feel?"
- **Step 4:** "Now rub your hands together."
- **Step 5:** "Reach your hands up towards the ceiling."
- **Step 6:** "Smile, and try to feel bad!"
- **Step 7:** "Now, rub your hands together, reach toward the ceiling, and say: "I Feel Good!"
- **Step 8:** Ask, "How would you like to be able to trigger this state at will?"
- **Step 9:** "To do this we will make a switch."
- **Step 10:** Say and demonstrate, "Hold your arm straight out and make a fist."
- **Step 11:** "Quickly draw your arm back toward your body and say, YES!"
- **Step 12:** "Now, put it all together."
- **Step 13:** "Arms straight up, say "I FEEL GOOD!!," fist straight out, draw it back quickly and say, "YES!".

NOTE: I FEEL GOOD! And YES! tools may be used together or by themselves. Students can use YES! to reward themselves or others for a job well done. Teachers can use YES! to recognize individual or group achievements.

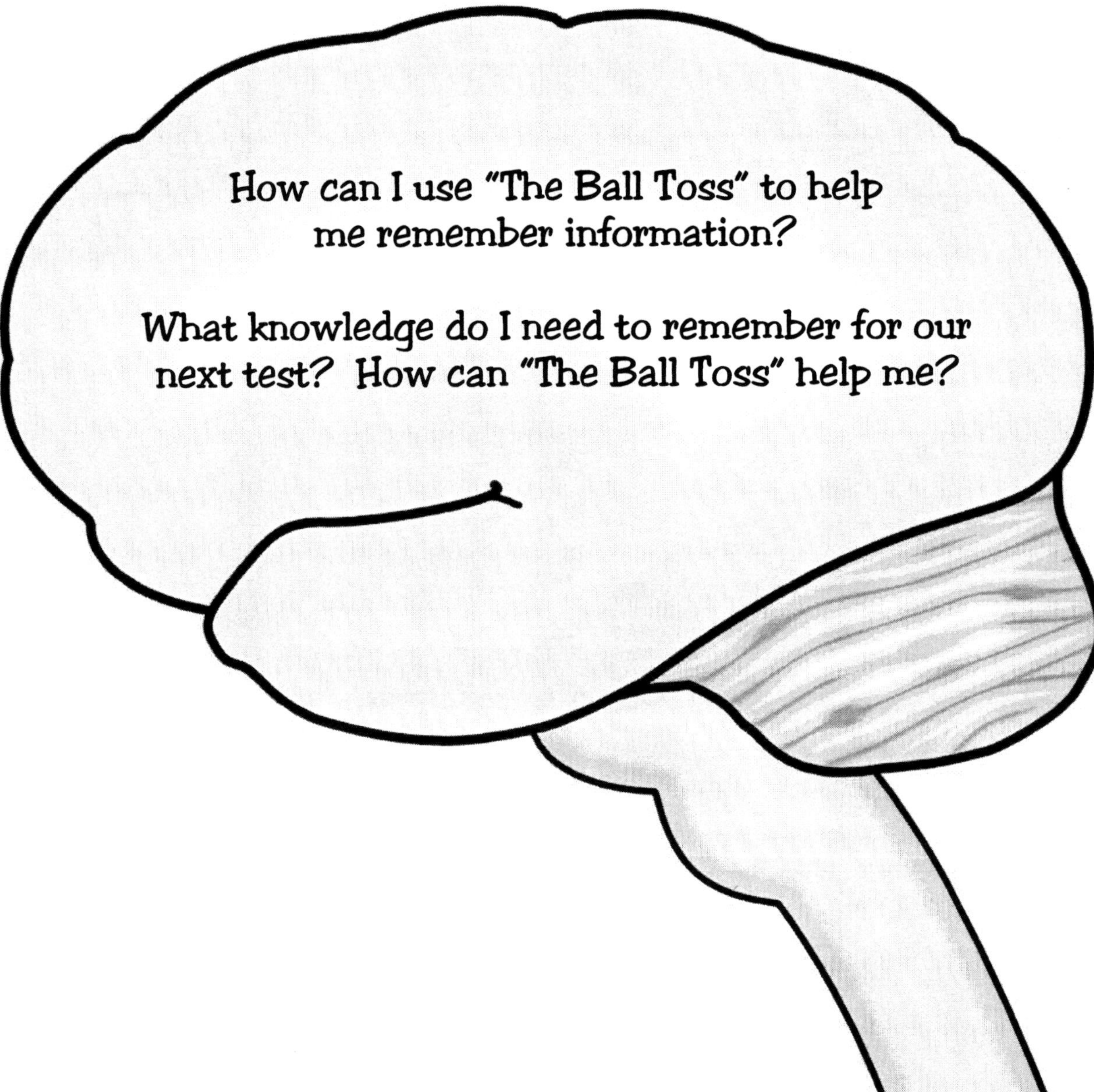
How can I use "The Ball Toss" to help
me remember information?
What knowledge do I need to remember for our
next test? How can "The Ball Toss" help me?

The Ball Toss

Purpose: To help students get re-energized and re-focused on positive learning.

- **Step 1:** Present information to your students in a positive and powerful way.
- **Step 2:** Insure that there is a good level of retention and recall of the material by asking questions and asking students to create a mind map, and so forth.
- **Step 3:** After you feel there is an adequate level of knowledge, begin the ball toss game.
- **Step 4:** Ask students to pass the ball to another student. Whenever a student picks up the ball, they must say just one thing known about the topic. Often a student catches the ball, he or she nominates who to throw the ball to and that person has to remember something about the subject.
- **Step 5:** At the end of the exercise, congratulate everybody, get them to do an "I feel good!" and get ready for the next stage of learning.

NOTE: This exercise can quickly get students back into a positive learning state. It allows them to demonstrate what they know and also to get some practice at remembering information under stress.

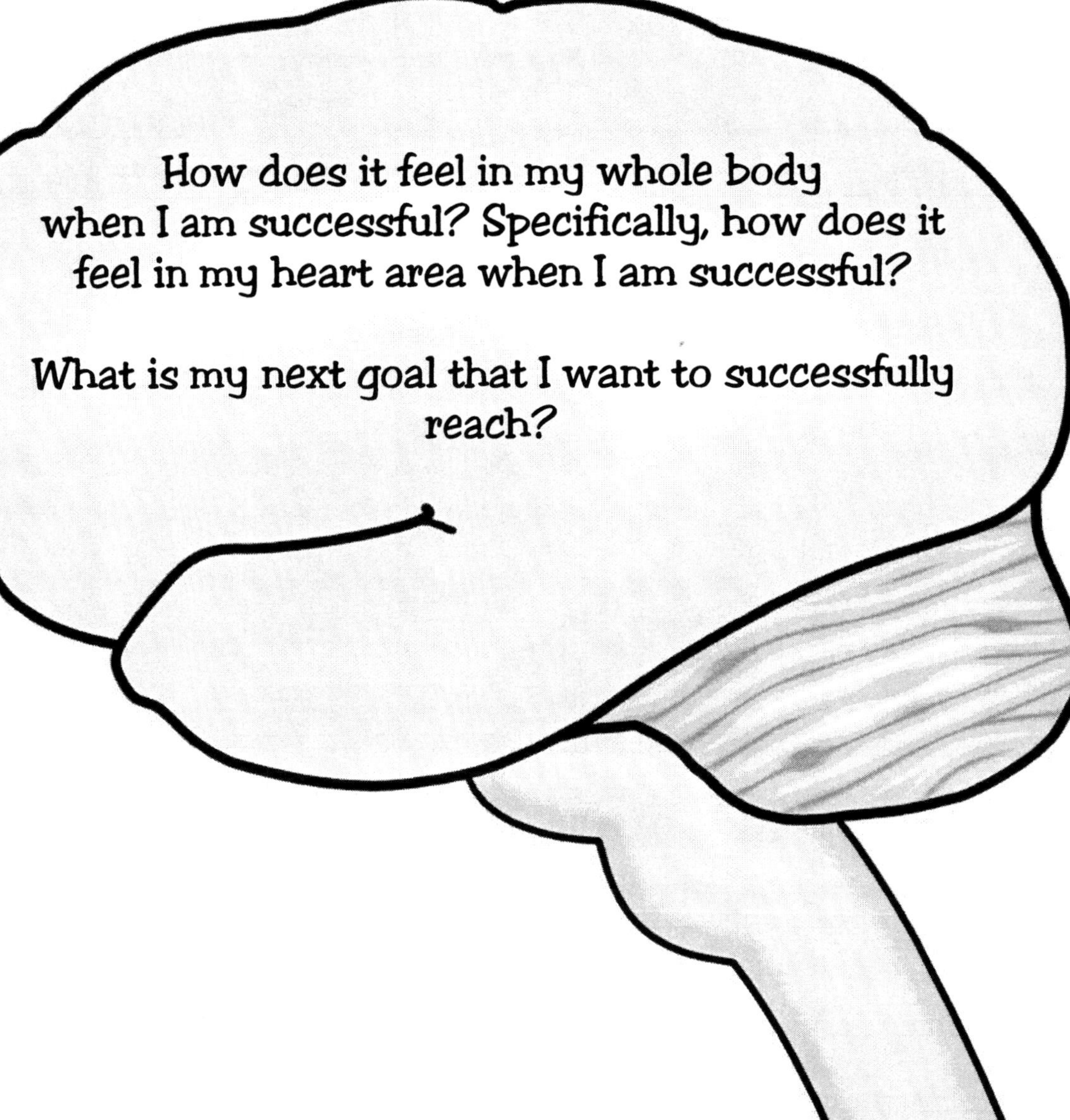
How does it feel in my whole body
when I am successful? Specifically, how does it
feel in my heart area when I am successful?
What is my next goal that I want to successfully
reach?

Success Mapping

Purpose: To help students build a positive, concrete feeling of success in a consistent and systematic manner.

- **Step 1:** Give every student a bright yellow success file.
- **Step 2:** Explain the reason you have a yellow file is that it is one of the colors that the brain likes and remembers best.
- **Step 3:** Ask students to write the word *success* on their file (if they are able; if not, draw a picture of a smiley face or a representation of success).
- **Step 4:** Every day while you work with students help them draw a mind map of each success that they have.
- **Step 5:** The definition of success in this context is that they completed something.
- **Step 6:** Each day get students to complete their success map and store it in their success file.
- **Step 7:** Each morning when you start with your students, get them to review their success map from before and start the process over again.

NOTE: The more students can re-connect to previous successes they have, the more successful they'll be in the long run. The definition of success here is completing a project rather than an abstract score. For example, success could be turning up at school and being there until the end of class or remembering some key information that you've helped them learn using some of the retention tools.

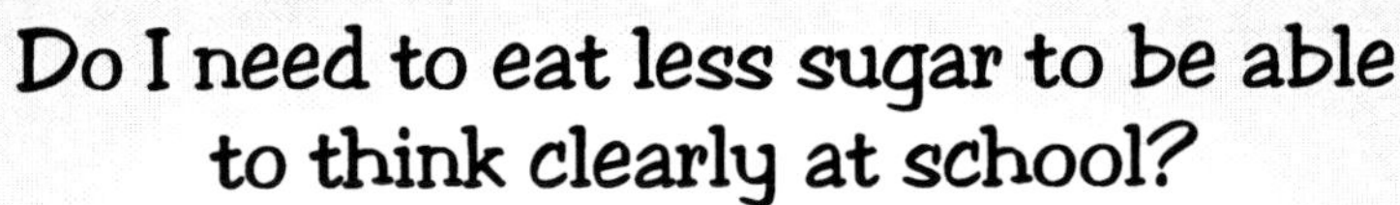

Do I need to eat less sugar to be able to think clearly at school?

Is there a particular time of day when I usually "crash"? Is it when I have eaten too much sugar earlier in the day?

The Power of Nutrition

Purpose: To help students understand the impact of nutrition on their ability to learn and stay focused.

- **Step 1:** Tell students that the average American consumes 150 pounds of sugar a year.
- **Step 2:** Ask students what the impact of this sugar might be on the health of Americans.
- **Step 3:** Ask students where they can find sugar in the different foods they eat.
- **Step 4:** Explain to students the impact of sugar in terms of (a) giving a lot of energy and then (b) having too much sugar in the body so the sugar gets pushed into the fat cells, and the brain gets tired.
- **Step 5:** Explain to students that by eating less sugar and a little bit of protein with their meals they can increase their attention and energy levels.
- **Step 6:** Suggest students read the sugar content on labels and that they understand that carbohydrate equals sugar.

NOTE: There is an increasing epidemic of obesity in the United States and the average young adult in America is 10 pounds heavier than 7 years ago. One important step is simply helping students to understand how much sugar they are actually consuming.

When is it most important to think positive thoughts to help me make good grades?
Who in my life can benefit greatly if I teach them this tool?

Arm Test Tool

Purpose: To help students experience the concrete, physical power of their positive or negative thoughts.

- **Step 1:** Ask students to stand up.
- **Step 2:** Get students spaced evenly around the room with enough room to swing one arm back behind them without hitting another student or the wall or furniture.
- **Step 3:** Ask students to point straight ahead of them and swing their arm as far as they can behind them.
- **Step 4:** Ask them to notice how far they got.
- **Step 5:** Now ask students to close their eyes and see themselves going farther still and then to turn or swing their finger as far as they can behind them and then open their eyes and notice how far they got.
- **Step 6:** This time get students to close their eyes and imagine themselves going farther and this time to tell themselves, "I can go farther." The students then swing their finger as far as they can get, open their eyes, and see how far they got.
- **Step 7:** This time get students to see themselves going farther, tell themselves they're going farther still, and feel in their gut, "I feel good," and swing and see how far they got.
- **Step 8:** Ask students by a show of hands to see who went farther.
- **Step 9:** Discuss with students why they went so much farther than last time.

NOTE: This exercise can be life-changing in that after students understand that they constantly underestimate themselves, they can begin to change perceptions and change performance. This is a great exercise to do at the start of the year.

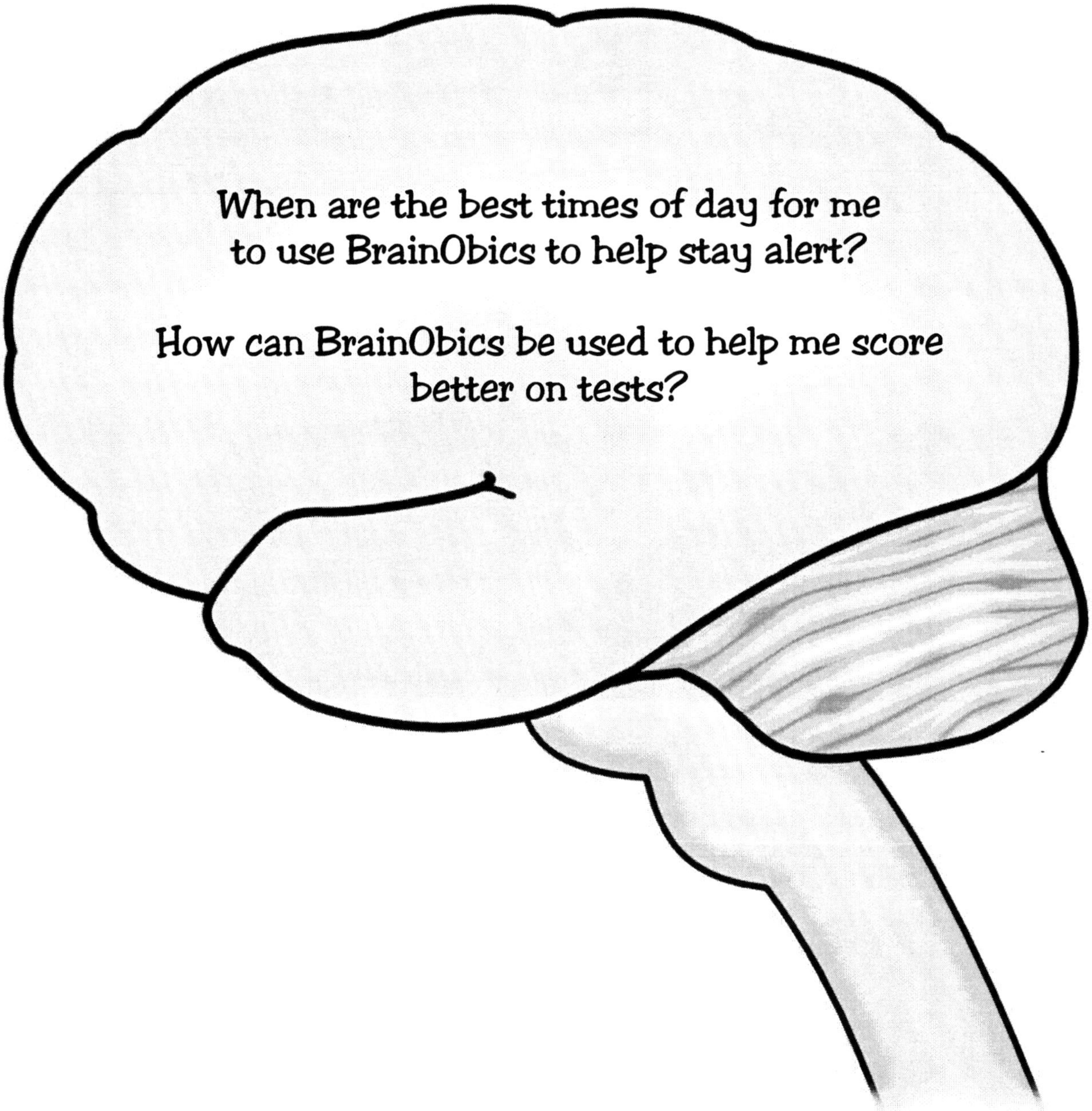

When are the best times of day for me to use BrainObics to help stay alert?

How can BrainObics be used to help me score better on tests?

The Power of BrainObics

Purpose: To wake up the brain-body system so that it is alert, refreshed, and ready to absorb information and participate in active learning.

- **Step 1:** Ask students to stand up.
- **Step 2:** Ask students to model you as you slowly reach over your shoulder and touch alternate shoulder blades. Keep going for around 60 seconds.
- **Step 3:** Then start to pat alternate knees, keeping it rhythmic and slow.
- **Step 4:** Start to tap alternate heels.
- **Step 5:** Repeat the process.

NOTE: This simple exercise can do a great deal to activate both hemispheres and integrate them in a way that will maximize learning.

When can LinkUps help me?
Do I know someone who could benefit from knowing how to do a LinkUp to keep out of trouble at school? If so, I can teach it to them.

The Power of LinkUps

Purpose: To allow students to calm down and achieve a clear, focused state. This is particularly useful after lunch or after any negative incident.

- **Step 1:** Get the students to stand up.
- **Step 2:** Cross arms and legs.
- **Step 3:** Put tongue to the roof of the mouth
- **Step 4:** Breathe deeply 3 times.
- **Step 5:** Keep breathing deeply for about 60 seconds and then unlock arms and legs and put finger tips together.
- **Step 6:** Drop arms to the side and notice how clear and focused the mind is.

NOTE: After a fight situation we will often ask students to do this for around 2 to 4 minutes before we talk to them. The impact is that it moves blood up from the reptilian area of the brain to the frontal lobes where reasoning resides.

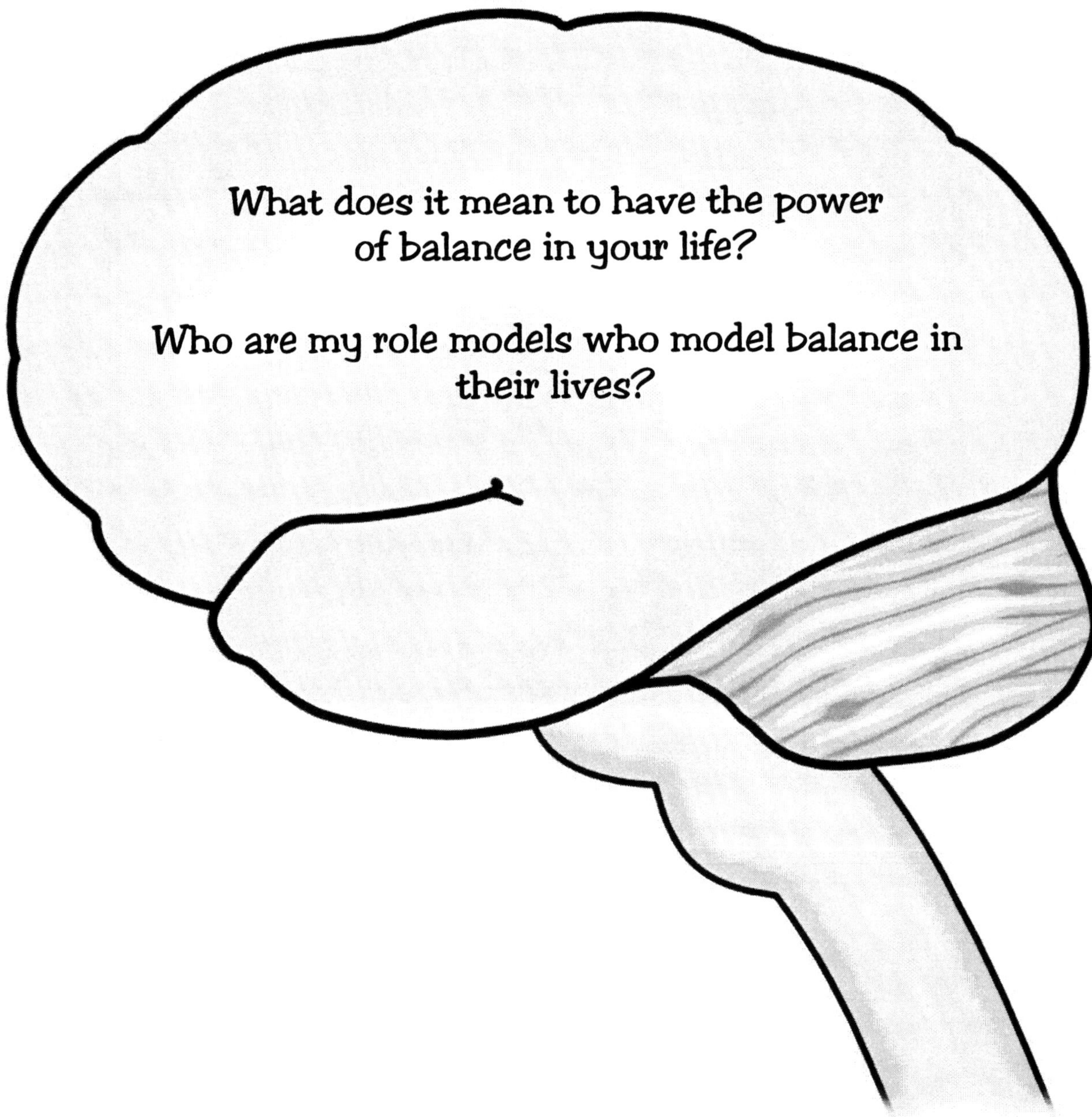
What does it mean to have the power
of balance in your life?
Who are my role models who model balance in
their lives?

The Power of Balance

Purpose: To help students understand that when they are balanced they are strong and that in a balanced state they can achieve more.

- **Step 1:** Get students to stand up.
- **Step 2:** Work with one student in the class to demonstrate this technique.
- **Step 3:** Ask the student to stand facing you, feet slightly apart.
- **Step 4:** Lightly push the student at the top of the chest and notice how they will rock back.
- **Step 5:** Now ask the students to focus their attention around the belly button area and to feel very balanced and to take a full breath.
- **Step 6:** Now push partner once again and notice how rock-solid and balanced they are.
- **Step 7:** Discuss and dialogue with your class why balance is important.

NOTE: When students physically experience the power of balance it is a lesson they will always remember. It is also a great metaphor for maintaining a balanced view, sustaining a balance between novelty and challenge, and for living a balanced life.

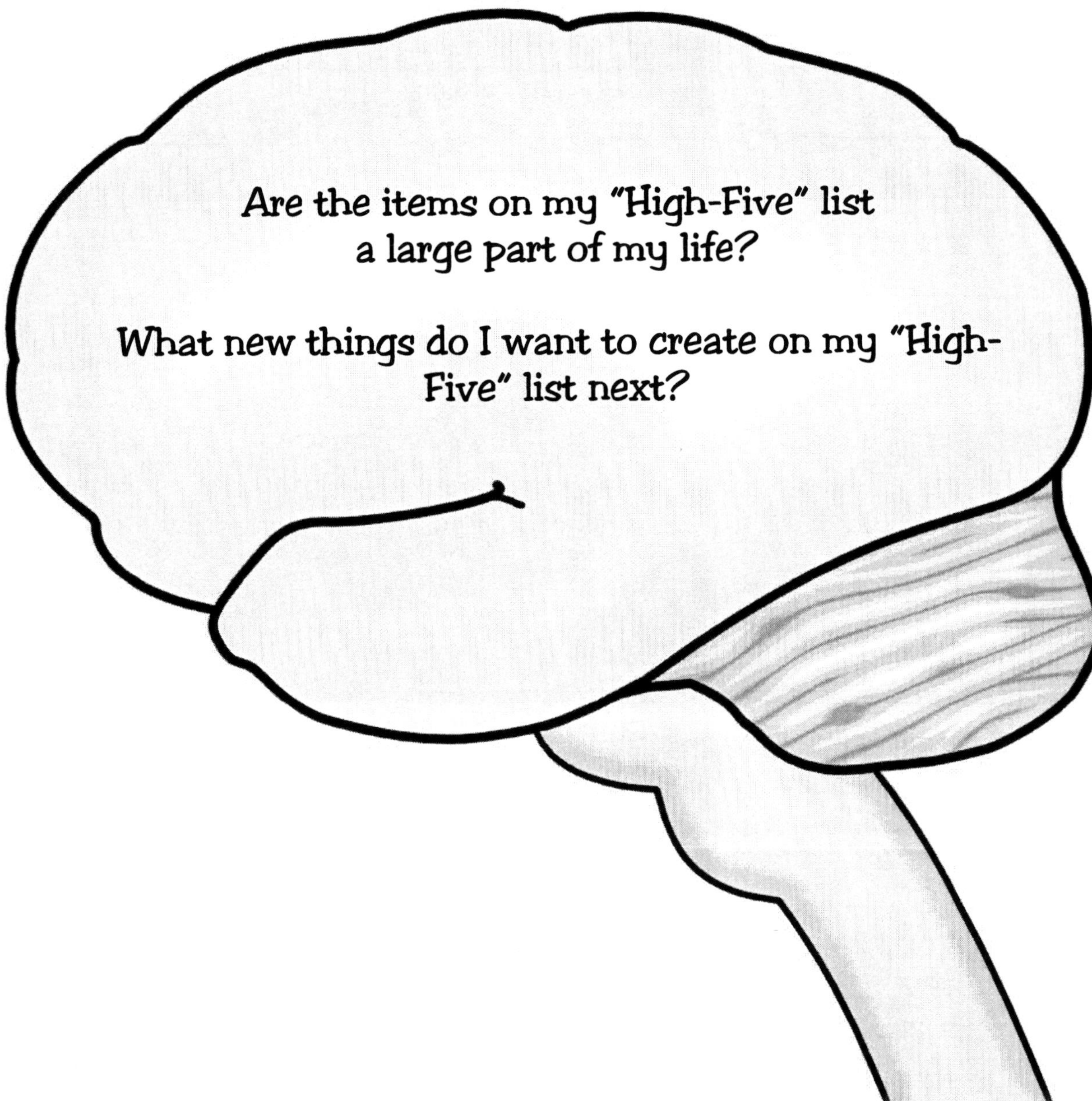
Are the items on my "High-Five" list
a large part of my life?
What new things do I want to create on my "High-
Five" list next?

High-Five

Purpose: To help students to develop the habit of consistently focusing on what's useful and positive in their lives.

- **Step 1:** Ask students if they would like to learn a way to more consistently sustain positive learning states.
- **Step 2:** Read aloud the attached story about Treasure Hunters and Trash Collectors.
- **Step 3:** Ask your students if they would like a simple way to become more of a treasure hunter.
- **Step 4:** Ask students to think of five things that they could feel good about, five things in their life that they like. Note: Make it very simple for them to think of five good things. Then when they have completed the five things, go to the next step.
- **Step 5:** Ask your students to draw a mind map or write or draw what their five things are.
- **Step 6:** Then get students to go to five other people, give them a high-five, and read to them what their high-five things are.
- **Step 7:** Continue to use this process once a week or once a month and encourage students to find more and new things to put into their high-five list.

NOTE: This simple technique is a wonderful way to get students to begin to focus on what's useful and positive. The true power of this comes when teachers model it on a weekly, monthly, or (ideally) daily basis.

Treasure Hunters and Trash Collectors

Attachment to High-Five Step 2

It seems that in life there are two types of people. The first are treasure hunters. Every day they seek out what is useful and positive and focus on it, talk about it, think about it and treasure it. Each of these moments is treasured like a bright, shining jewel that they store in their treasure chest forever.

And then there are trash collectors who spend their lives looking for what is wrong, unfair, what isn't working and they focus their energy and their time and their thoughts on the trash and every day they put that trash into a big old trash can.

Now every day the treasure hunters proudly carry their treasure into the future and every day the trash collectors drag their big, heavy, smelly trash can from one day to the next. The question is when they get to the end of the year, what does each person have? A treasure chest full of useful, positive memories or a trash can full of things they didn't like.

The choice is yours.

You get to decide.

10 BrainSMART Tools For Meaning

Meaning -

How to Make Learning Meaningful in Your Classroom

Making learning relevant to the learner

The Power of Cartoons

Purpose: To illustrate to students that to communicate meaningfully we need first to understand the other person's point of view.

- **Step 1:** Show the attached cartoon to your class.
- **Step 2:** Ask the students, "What does the figure look like to the man?"
- **Step 3:** Ask students, "What does the figure in the middle of the table look like to the woman?"
- **Step 4:** Then ask, "Who is right?"
- **Step 5:** Explain to students that the idea for this cartoon came from an old Middle Eastern legend in which two princes were at war for many years. One prince looked at the image on the table and said it was a six while the other prince said it was a nine. For years the battle raged and then one day when the princes were seated at the table a young boy turned the tablecloth around and for the first time they could see the other's point of view. The war came to an end and the princes became firm friends.
- **Step 6:** Illustrate with an example from your own life in which something similar has happened in terms of you arguing with somebody simply because they had a different point of view.
- **Step 7:** Get students to work in small groups discussing how important it is to understand that many people disagree with us simply because they have a different point of view.
- **Step 8:** Debrief the student comments.
- **Step 9:** On a regular basis refer back to the six and nine on the cartoon.

NOTE: This simple cartoon can help students and teachers alike make a quantum leap in remembering that everyone has the right to have a different point of view from us.

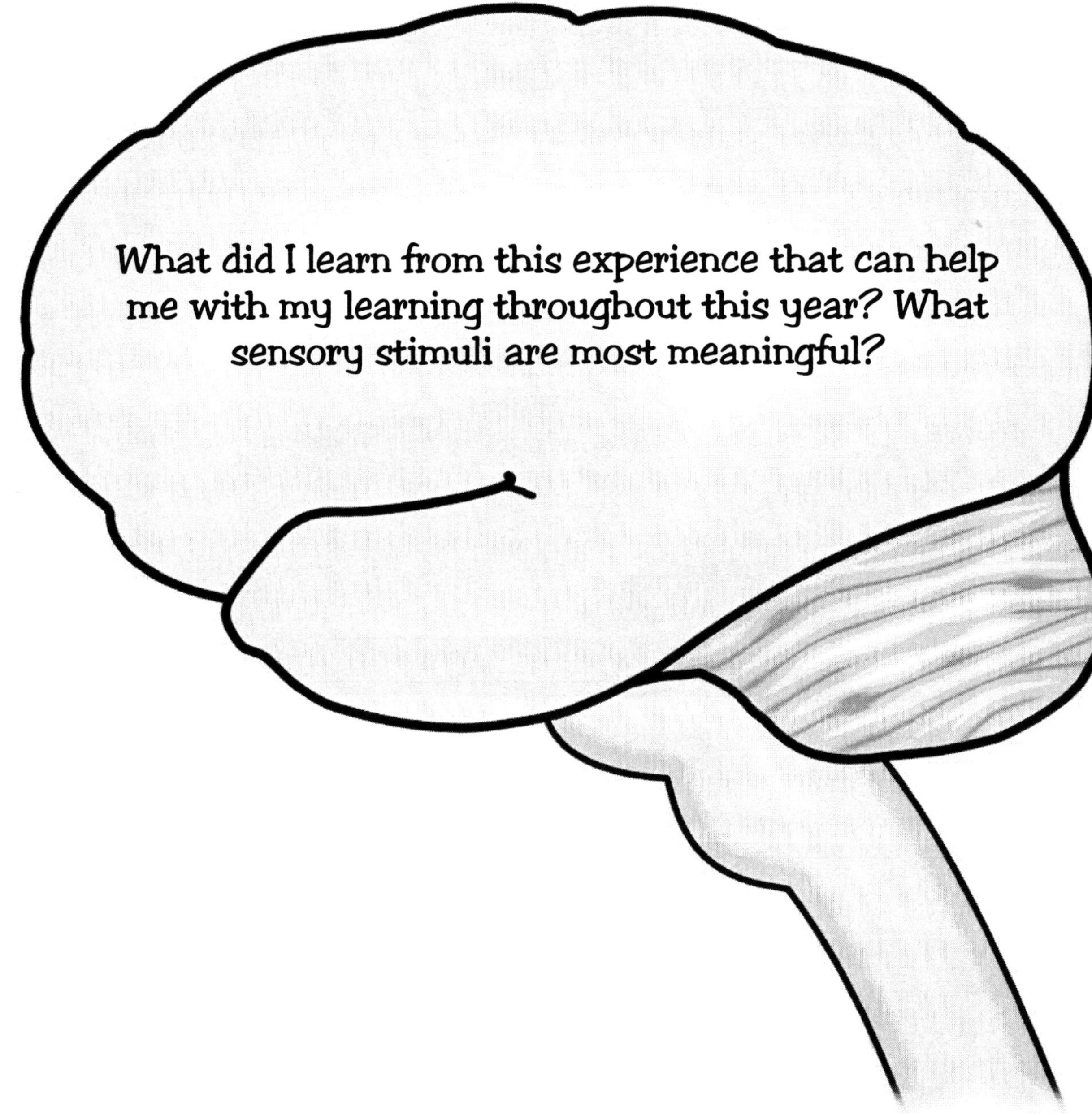
What did I learn from this experience that can help me with my learning throughout this year? What sensory stimuli are most meaningful?

Effective Field Trips

Purpose: To help students gain true personal meaning from experiences outside the classroom.

- **Step 1:** Review with students a field trip that you would like the class to take. (Ideally if you have a range of opportunities you may wish to dialog these with your students.)

- **Step 2:** Take some time to see what links can be made from this field trip to your content area.

- **Step 3:** Take the trip as early as possible as you can in the year. (Many field trips are organized as a perk at the end of the year thereby losing a whole year's worth of meaningful connection to your content.)

- **Step 4:** During the field trip encourage children to engage fully in all activities using all the senses.

- **Step 5:** After the field trip get students to put together mind maps of everything that they learned individually.

- **Step 6:** Allow students to then work in groups to build a mind map of what they experienced and to present mind maps to the rest of the class.

- **Step 7:** Throughout the rest of the year connect your material to the meaningful experience of the field trip.

NOTE: When we ask teachers what they remember about their school days, field trips come out as the most powerful memory that they have. Field trips are worth the effort. They will create a long-lasting, memorable impact on your students.

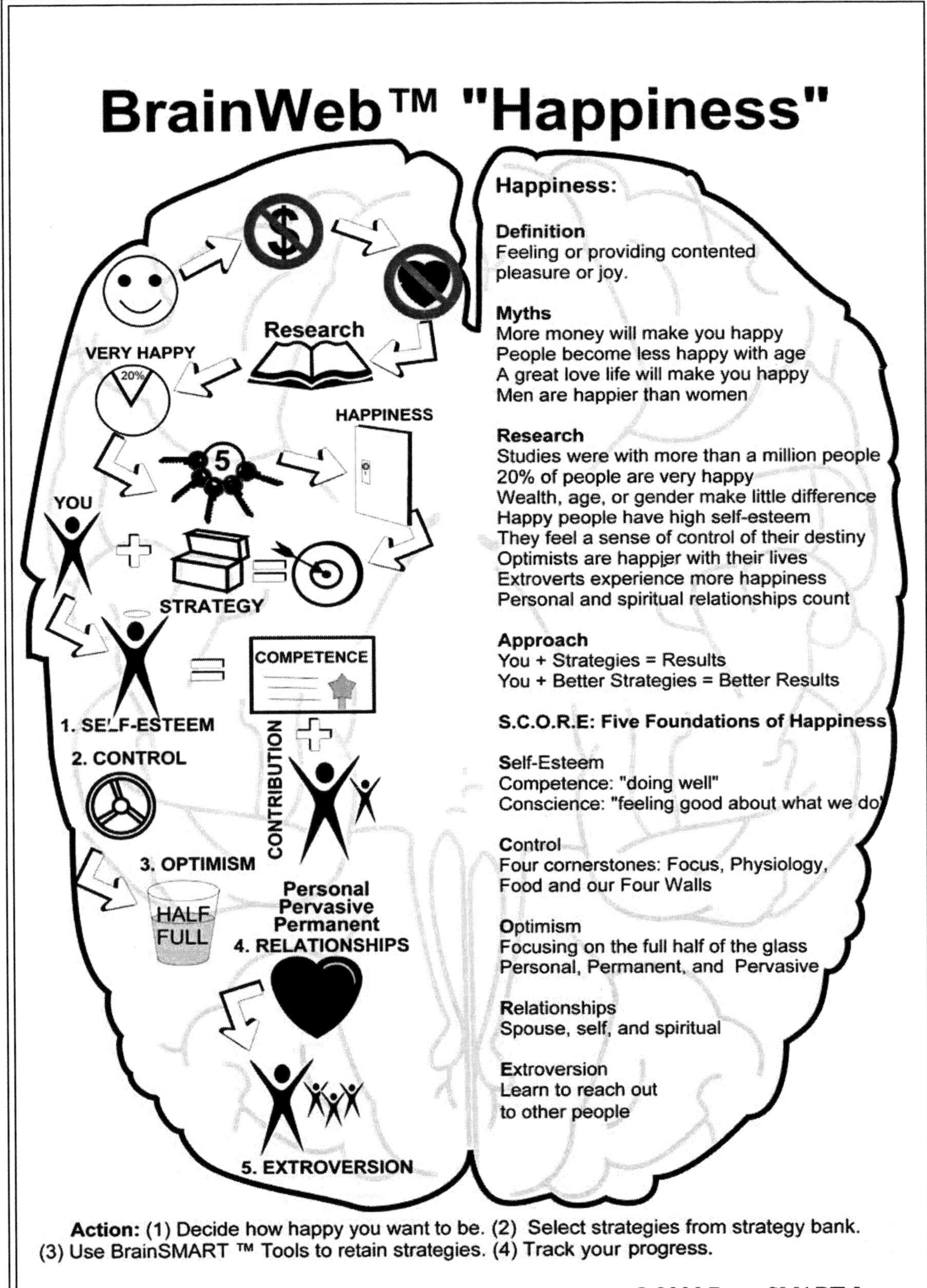
BrainWeb™ "Happiness"
Research
VERY HAPPY
20%
HAPPINESS
5
YOU
STRATEGY
COMPETENCE
1. SELF-ESTEEM
2. CONTROL
CONTRIBUTION
3. OPTIMISM
HALF FULL
Personal
Pervasive
Permanent
4. RELATIONSHIPS
5. EXTROVERSION
Happiness:
Definition
Feeling or providing contented pleasure or joy.
Myths
More money will make you happy
People become less happy with age
A great love life will make you happy
Men are happier than women
Research
Studies were with more than a million people
20% of people are very happy
Wealth, age, or gender make little difference
Happy people have high self-esteem
They feel a sense of control of their destiny
Optimists are happier with their lives
Extroverts experience more happiness
Personal and spiritual relationships count
Approach
You + Strategies = Results
You + Better Strategies = Better Results
S.C.O.R.E: Five Foundations of Happiness
Self-Esteem
Competence: "doing well"
Conscience: "feeling good about what we do"
Control
Four cornerstones: Focus, Physiology, Food and our Four Walls
Optimism
Focusing on the full half of the glass
Personal, Permanent, and Pervasive
Relationships
Spouse, self, and spiritual
Extroversion
Learn to reach out to other people
Action: (1) Decide how happy you want to be. (2) Select strategies from strategy bank. (3) Use BrainSMART ™ Tools to retain strategies. (4) Track your progress.
© 2000 BrainSMART, Inc.

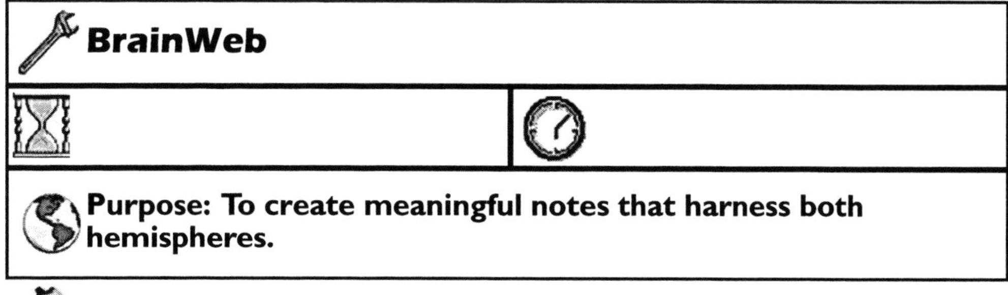

- **Step 1:** Draw an outline of a brain, like the one shown in BrainWeb Happiness.
- **Step 2:** On the left side draw pictures or symbols that are meaningful to you. (This is designed to stimulate the right hemisphere.)
- **Step 3:** Use arrows to show the flow of ideas.
- **Step 4:** On the right hand side, write key information that is meaningful to you. (This is designed to stimulate the left hemisphere.)
- **Step 5:** Practice BrainWebbing television shows, movies, and books.

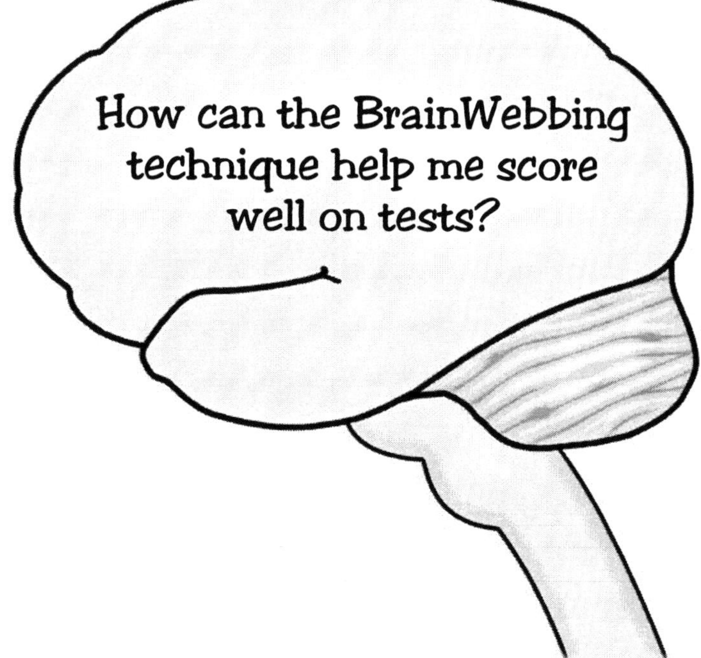

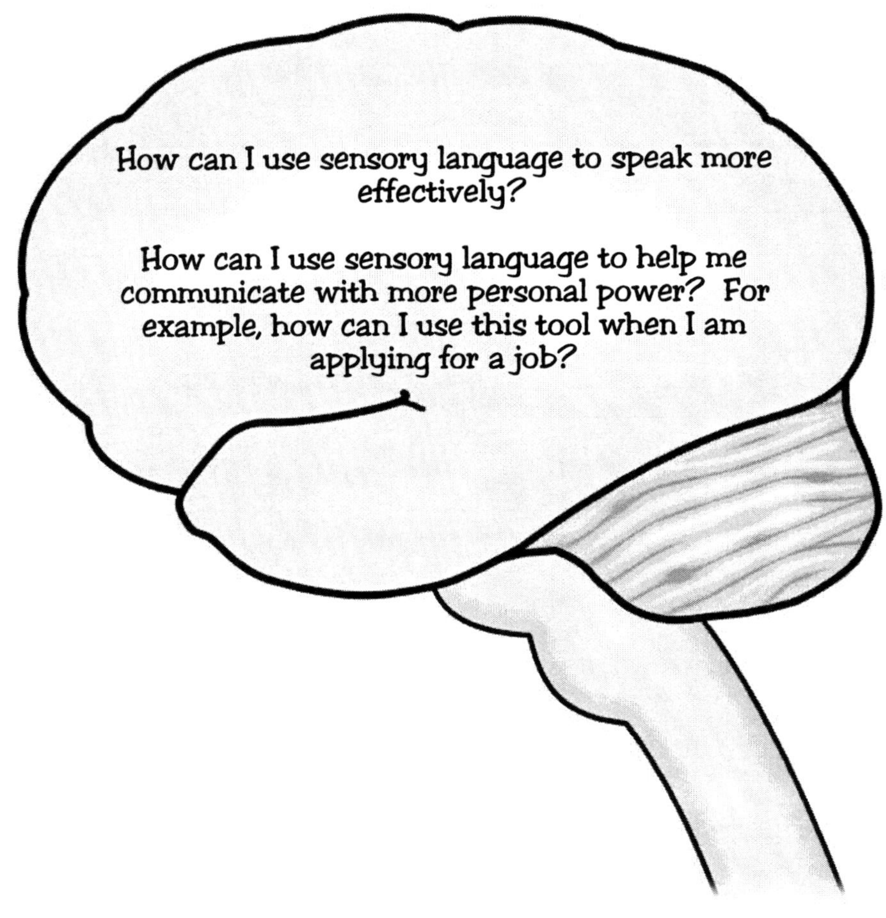

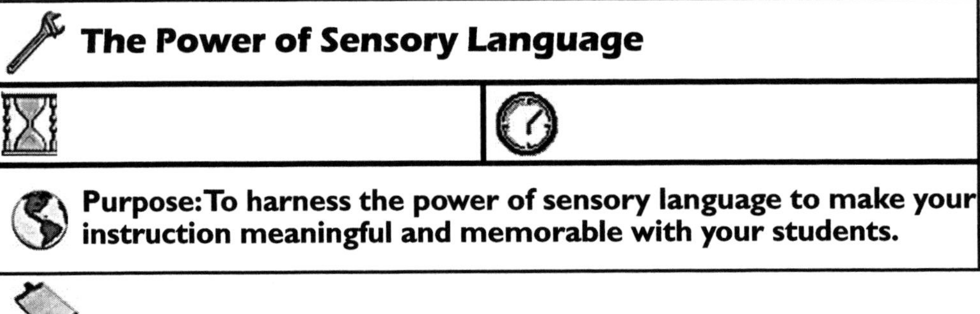

The Power of Sensory Language

Purpose: To harness the power of sensory language to make your instruction meaningful and memorable with your students.

- **Step 1:** Practice reading Script 1 to yourself, and then aloud with gusto.
- **Step 2:** When you feel confident that you can give it everything you've got, read Script 2 to your students. Script 1 uses non-sensory specific language. Script 2 takes full advantage of the power of specific sensory language.

Script 1: The man fell in the water and became very afraid as the shark began to circle him. He did not know if he was going to survive. He thought it could be a long time before the rescue boats found him.

Script 2: You feel your heart pounding from the cold, hard grip of fear in your gut as the shark's jet black dorsal fin cuts through the water. As you look into its dark, dead eye, a shiver runs down your spine as you realize you have only one chance to survive. You feel the rough wood of the mast underneath you and you pull back the cold, hard bolt on the rifle that shakes in your trembling hands. As you look down the sight the sweat and the salt stings your eyes and then you see it moving towards you faster and faster, its great sharp teeth opening up in a menacing smile. You see the bright yellow oxygen tank caught in the side of its great mouth and you hear the click of the bolt as it slams shut. You taste the salt in your mouth as the stench of diesel fills your nostrils. Your cold, numb fingers squeeze the trigger. The rifle leaps in your hand with a deafening sound, and suddenly the shark explodes, shattered into a thousand pieces. Waves of relief flood over you and you laugh out loud. You have survived.

- **Step 3:** Ask students to explain to their partner what they remember from the story.
- **Step 4:** Then ask students to identify what senses you used in the story, for example, sight, sound, touch, taste, and smell.
- **Step 5:** With the whole class develop the theme of another story and ask students in small groups to focus on one particular sentence.
- **Step 6:** Get the class to tell the new story remembering to engage as many senses as possible.

NOTE: By adding sensory-rich language to your own teaching you will both increase attention and retention of information. By encouraging students to do the same you will be equipping them with fabulous language skill.

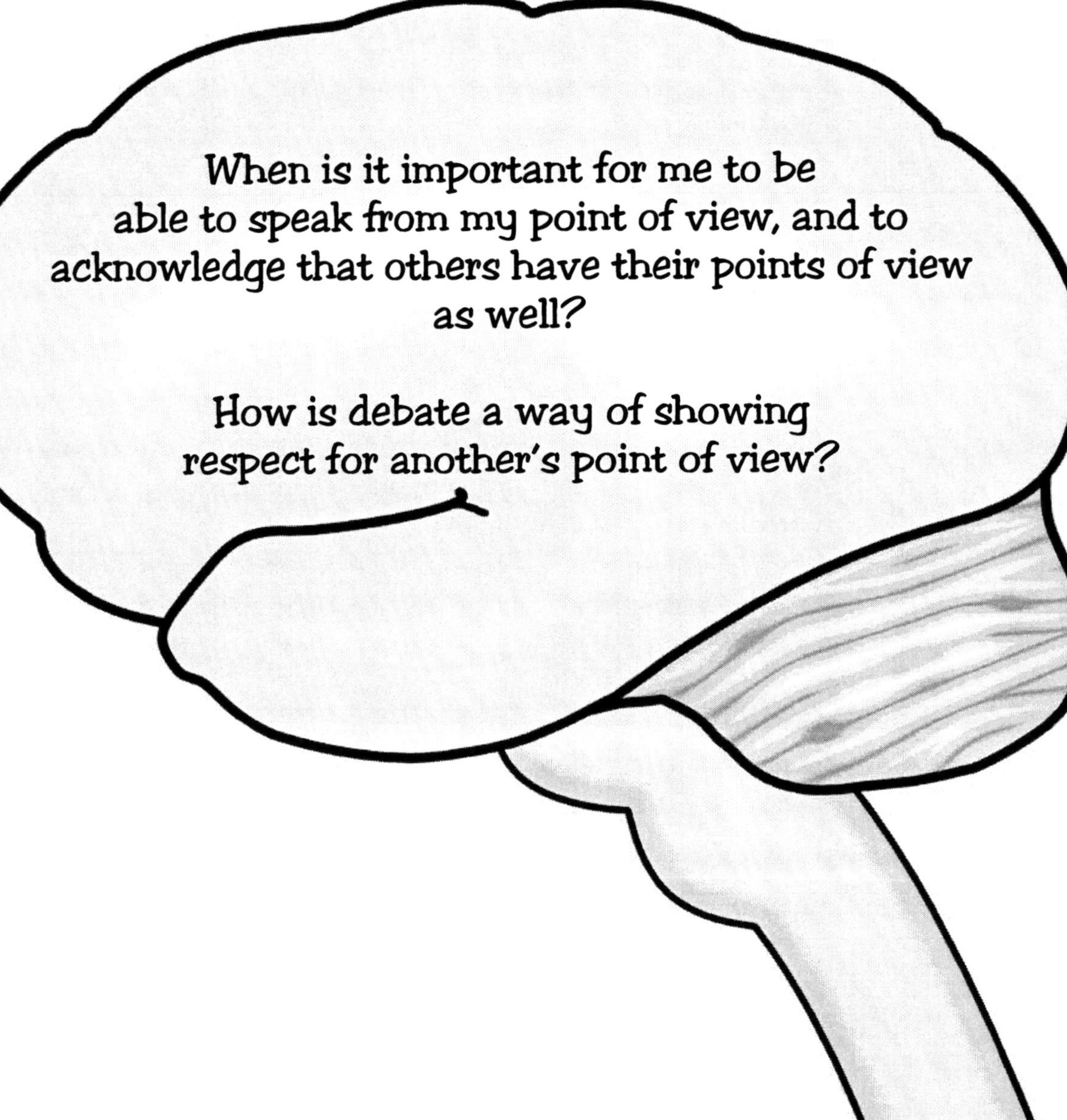
When is it important for me to be
able to speak from my point of view, and to
acknowledge that others have their points of view
as well?
How is debate a way of showing
respect for another's point of view?

The Power of Debating

Purpose: For students to learn skills in appreciating others' points of view and how to build and defend their own case.

- **Step 1:** Select an appropriate topic for debate. **Note:** The more meaningful it is for students, the better.
- **Step 2:** Work with students to identify at least two different points of view about this particular subject.
- **Step 3:** With the class, identify as many arguments as possible for or against the motion.
- **Step 4:** Have students work in groups to draw a mind map of elements that support one side of the argument or other.
- **Step 5:** Have pairs of students debate with each other.
- **Step 6:** Students then swap mind maps and present from the other point of view.
- **Step 7:** Refer to this experience often when presenting new material. It is important that students learn how to see many different points of view

NOTE: The simple act of debating will encourage students to really internalize information and to learn how to transfer information into persuasive communication. It is likely your students will remember this exercise forever.

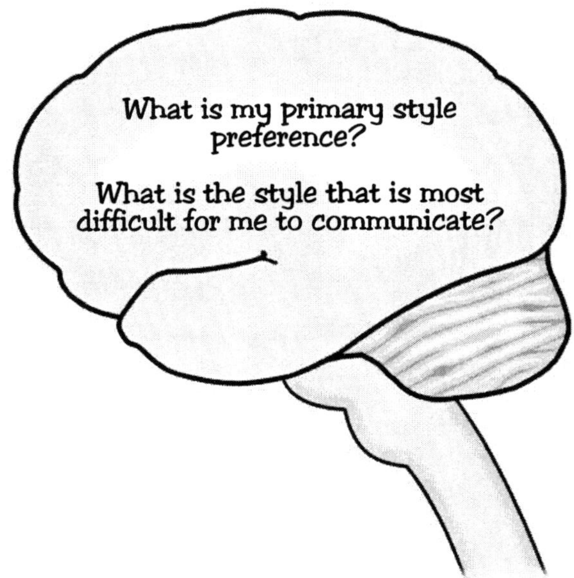

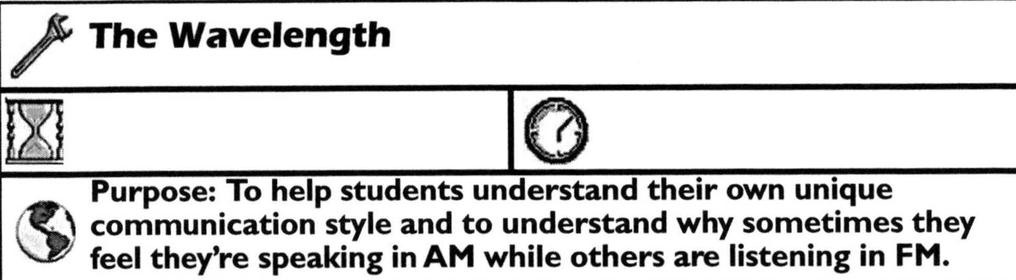

The Wavelength

Purpose: To help students understand their own unique communication style and to understand why sometimes they feel they're speaking in AM while others are listening in FM.

- **Step 1:** Practice presenting the three following scripts in a way that's appropriate for the wavelength you've chosen.
- **Step 2:** After you feel comfortable with each of the scripts, present them to your students.
- **Step 3:** Notice which students respond best to each of the different wavelengths: Visual, Auditory, and Kinesthetic.

Script 1 *Visual* (Please use large gestures and literally paint pictures with your hands as you illustrate what you might have experienced at a fair) Oh, I just love the sights at a fair. There was a bright blue sky with a few white clouds up above. It was wonderful to see the clowns coming down the midway carrying flags of green and red and blue and all kinds of balloons and toys. And then when I got to the top of the roller coaster ride, I had a wonderful view down below. I could see the children's faces and how they were smiling excitedly.

Script 2 *Auditory* (Restrict your body language now and focus just on the power of your voice. Speak in more of a monotone) I was just telling myself how much I enjoyed being at the fair. There were so many sounds to hear. A band was playing music. You could hear the drums, the flutes and many of my favorite songs. Most of all I like to hear the shrieks of the children on the rides. At the end of the day it was great to tell everybody exactly what happened at the fair.

Script 3 *Kinesthetic* (This time use body language which is essentially acting out the activities you are telling your students about) Oh, it felt so good at the fair. You get on this really neat ride, you feel this safety belt clamp across your chest and your heart begins to pound as you begin to go up higher and higher. You can taste the fear in your mouth as you move closer and closer to the top of the ride and then suddenly your stomach feels like it's in your throat as you swing to the left and to the right. You feel the car shudder just before you splash into the water that feels icy cold against your face. Then you get off the ride and your knees feel like jelly. It was great at the fair.

- **Step 4:** Ask students which sense you were using in each of the three scripts.
- **Step 5:** Ask students to pick one sense and work in groups to map out what they can see, hear, or feel at the fair.
- **Step 6:** Review with students all of the different experiences one might have at the fair.
- **Step 7:** Ask students to present a story about the fair using just one sense and get them to rotate through each sense.
- **Step 8:** Explain to students that the reason you did this exercise today was to help them to understand that there are different ways for us to communicate: visually, through words, or using feelings.

NOTE: This exercise is a great deal of fun to do and students will almost immediately begin to understand the power of using language in the different wavelengths.

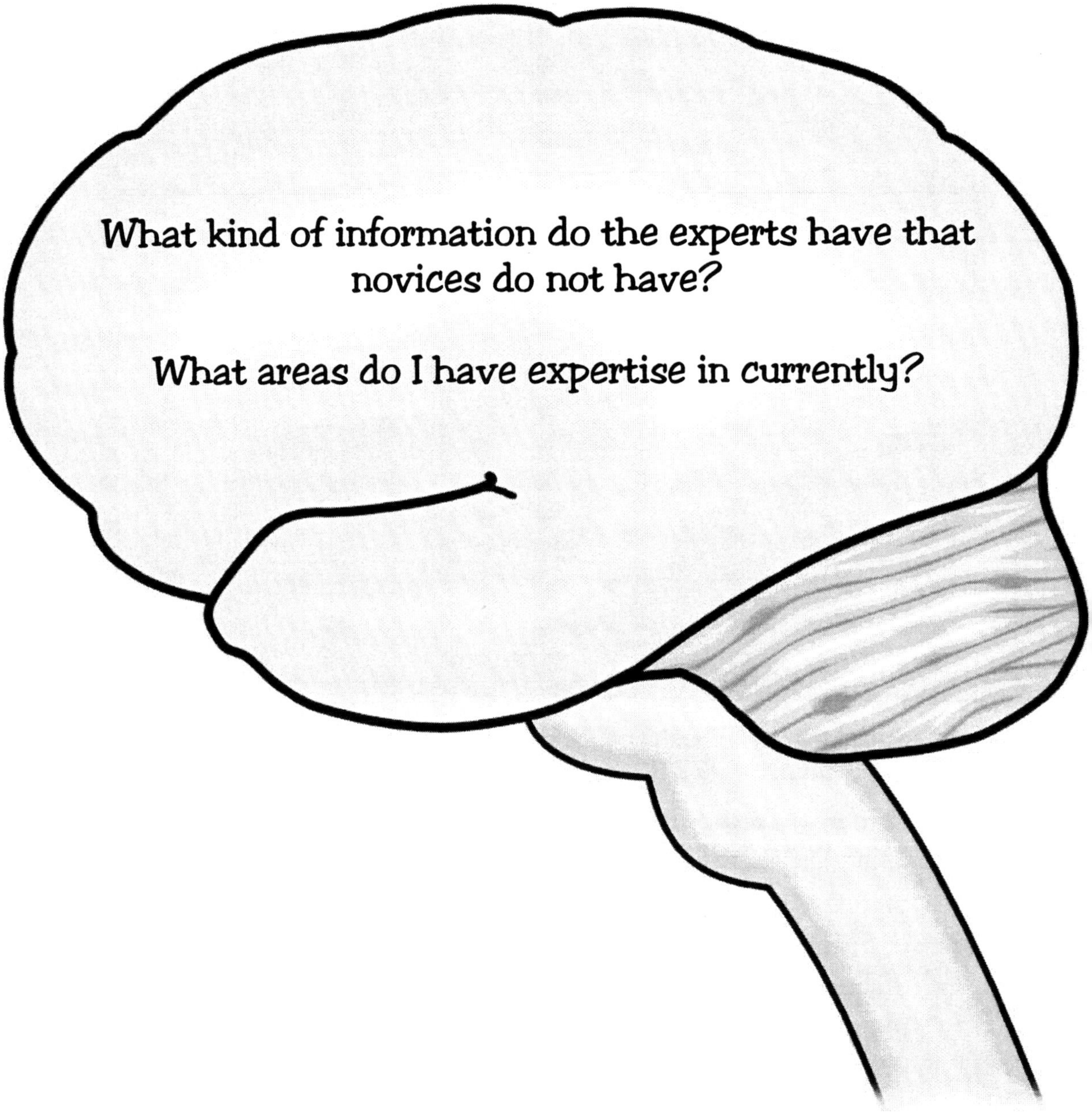

What kind of information do the experts have that novices do not have?

What areas do I have expertise in currently?

Power Interviewing

Purpose: To help students focus attention on important information.

- **Step 1:** Review in literature a list of some experts in the content area that you are teaching.

- **Step 2:** Help individual students identify the resources they need to become expert on the expert. Dialog with them, and help them read and retain the important information.

- **Step 3:** Let them do a mind map of this expert's knowledge on the topic.

- **Step 4:** Either get the group or the class to interview a student who presents himself as the expert in the field.

- **Step 5:** Keep the expert interviewing process going until students have acquired enough information from the student to create their own mind map on the topic.

NOTE: This technique can be used with a wide range of material and particularly works well in terms of social studies where you could interview different generals in the Civil War for example.

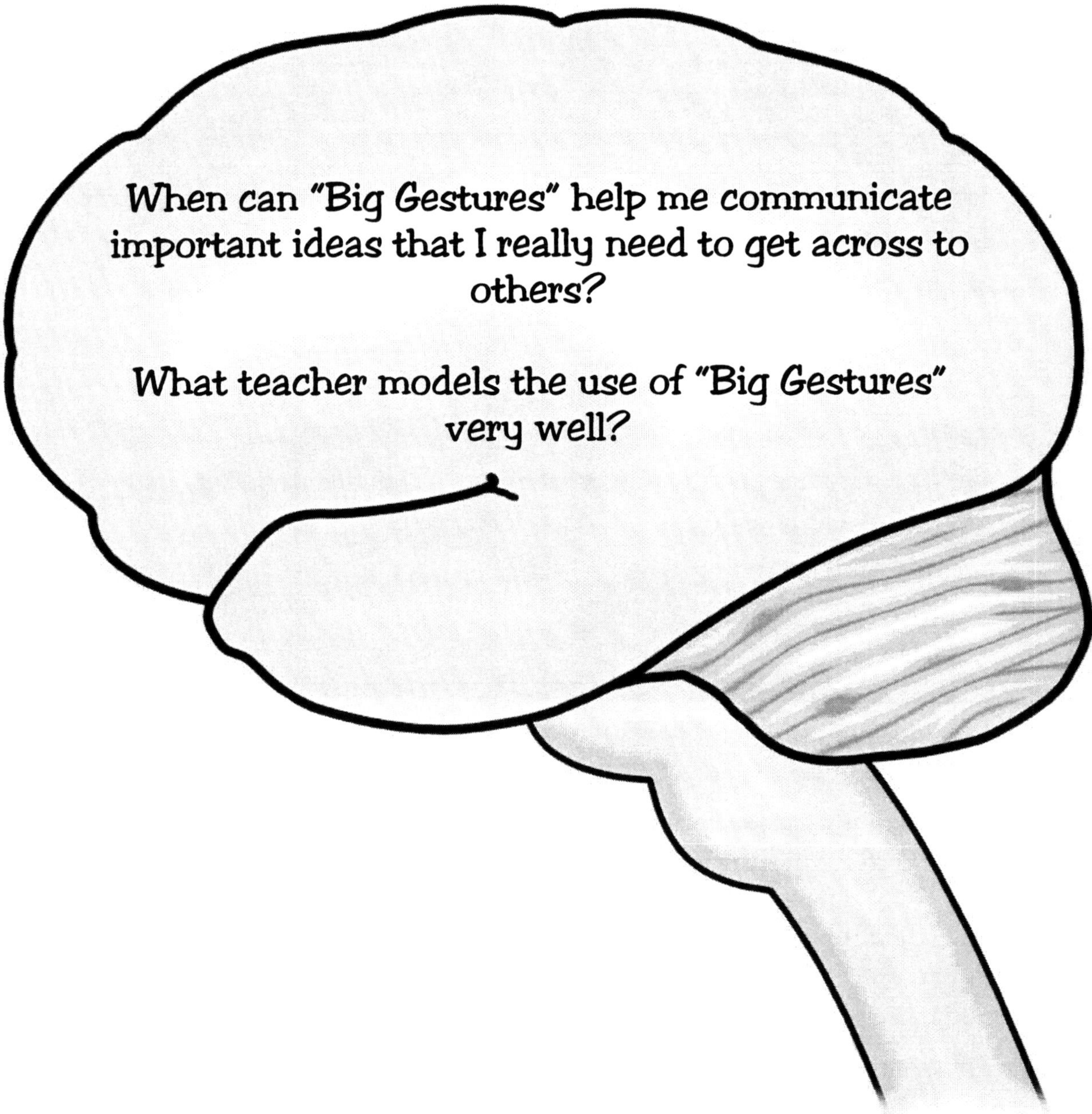

When can "Big Gestures" help me communicate important ideas that I really need to get across to others?

What teacher models the use of "Big Gestures" very well?

Big Gestures

Purpose: To help students learn the power of body language in effective communication.

- **Step 1:** Tell your students a story from your own life that you think they will find engaging and interesting.
- **Step 2:** Now tell the story using big gestures and notice the big difference in the impact it has on your students.
- **Step 3:** Get students to work in small groups to put together their own stories.
- **Step 4:** When students have put together a story, get them to practice acting it out with small gestures and then with big gestures.
- **Step 5:** Get students to tell their stories to their group and to get feedback from other students.
- **Step 6:** Review with students the impact of using big gestures in communication.

NOTE: We know that more than 80% of classroom communication is nonverbal. By helping students develop this skill, you'll be equipping them with a highly effective tool they can use for the rest of their lives.

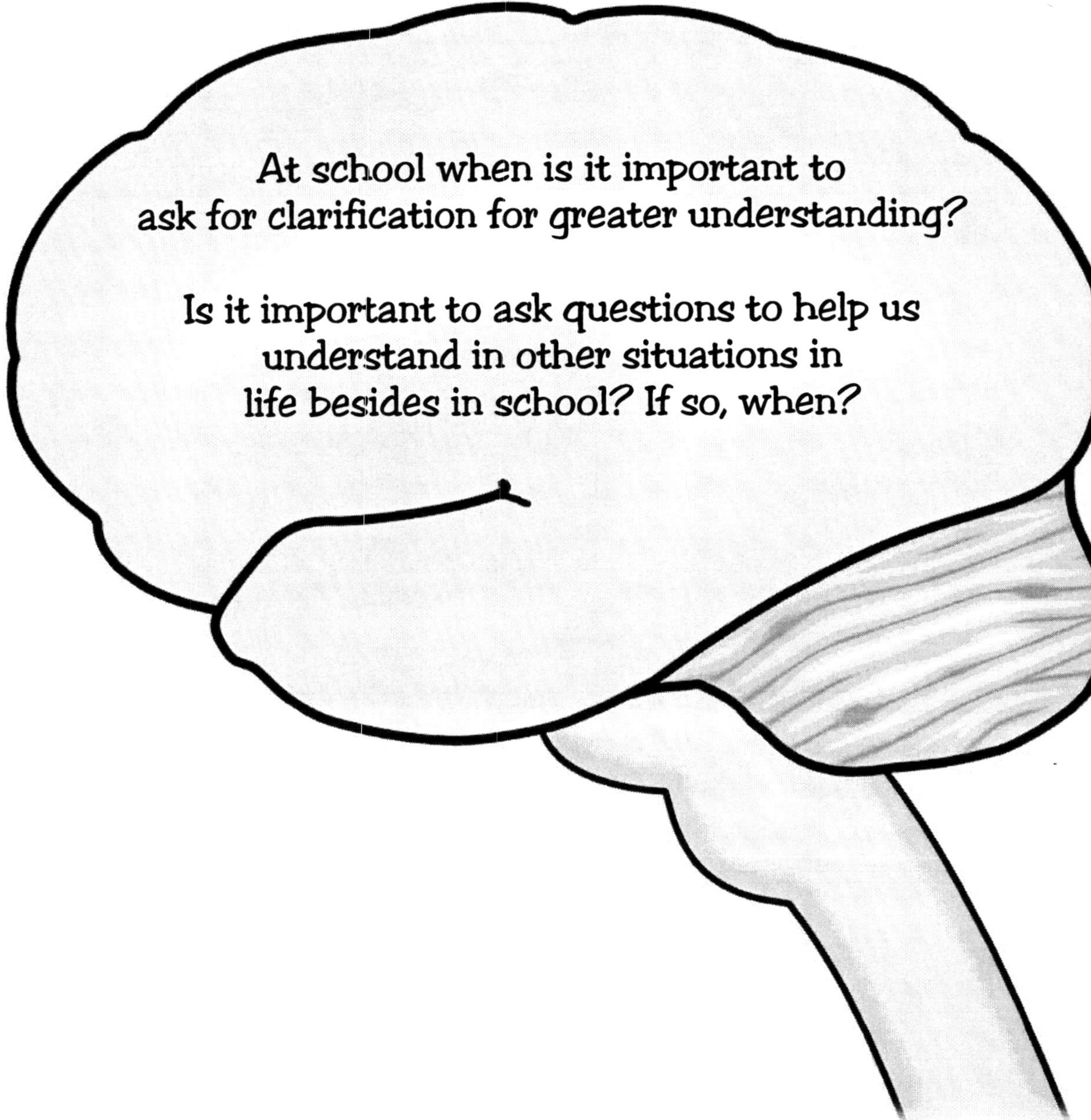
At school when is it important to
ask for clarification for greater understanding?

Is it important to ask questions to help us
understand in other situations in
life besides in school? If so, when?

The Meaning of Words

Purpose: To get students to appreciate the importance of asking what words mean if they do not understand. (Note: This would be a great lesson for adults to learn as well.)

- **Step 1:** Explain to the students that around the world there are thousands of different languages.

- **Step 2:** Further explain that even in the English/American language each culture can have its own special way of speaking.

- **Step 3:** Read the following list and ask students to explain what they think it means:
    - Apples and pears means:
    - Jam jar means:
    - Gregory Peck means:
    - Strawberry tart means:

- **Step 5:** Notice that students will have no idea what you're talking about. Then explain that this is called Cockney rhyming slang. (Cockney is somebody who was born within the sound of Bow Bells in England.)

- **Step 6:** Ask students to identify how this language is created.

- **Step 7:** Review student answers and explain that each of these expressions rhymes to create the meaning of another word. For example: Apples and pears means stairs. Jam jar means car. Gregory Peck means neck. Strawberry tart means heart.

- **Step 8:** Get students to create their own rhyming language.

NOTE: Helping students to appreciate that if they don't understand something it may be because we as teachers have not used language correctly can build their own self-confidence. It can also be a wonderful way to keep us on track.

10 BrainSMART Tools For Attention

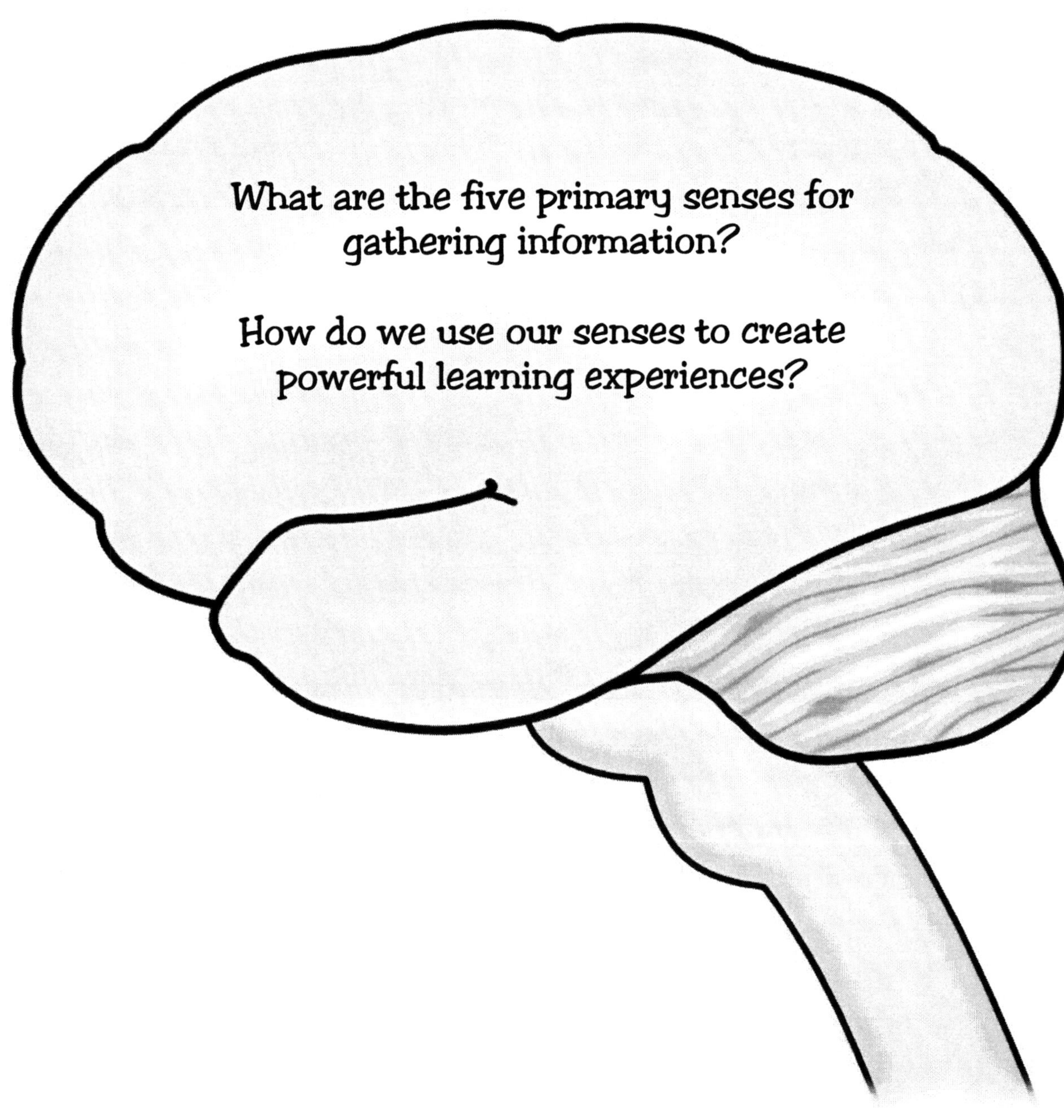
What are the five primary senses for gathering information?
How do we use our senses to create powerful learning experiences?

Mystery Object

Purpose: To get students into a curious, excited state and to boost retention and recall.

- **Step 1:** Map out the number of days you will have with each group of students.
- **Step 2:** Make a list of unique sensory experiences for each day. For example: Smell of a lemon, taste of candy, sound of a song, sticking fingers in jello, stroking a pet.
- **Step 3:** Each day do one small sensory surprise.
- **Step 4:** At the end of each day draw a picture of that sensory surprise and create a mind map of key information that was learned during that day.
- **Step 5:** When you review ask students, for example, "What did we learn on lemon day, or Mozart day?"
- **Step 6:** Consistently build something unique and interesting into each day of teaching.

NOTE: This simple approach to building curiosity can pay big dividends. The brain is wired to remember what is unique and different. It also sends a clear message to your students that you care enough about them to be creative and inventive.

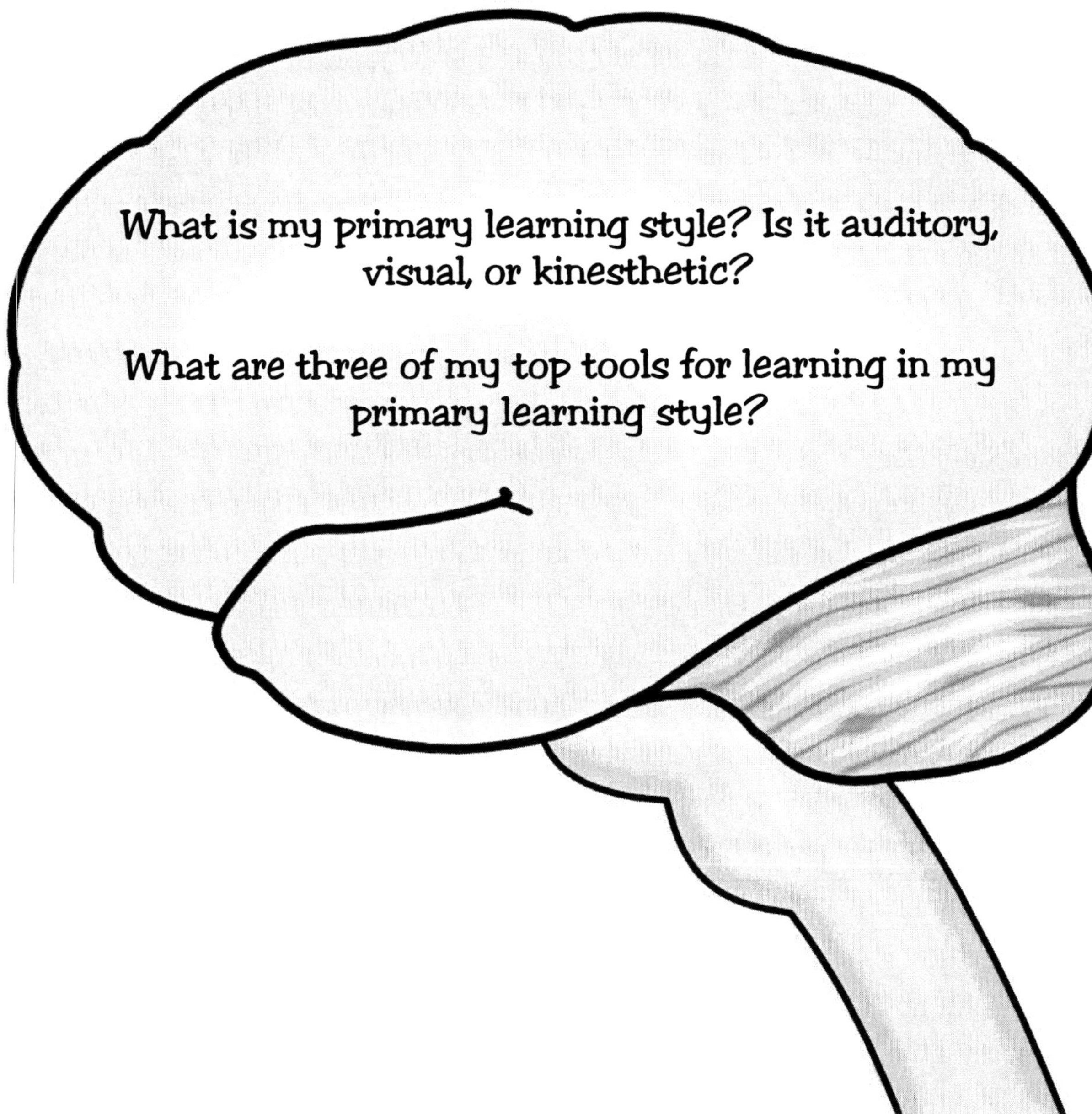
What is my primary learning style? Is it auditory, visual, or kinesthetic?
What are three of my top tools for learning in my primary learning style?

Location Graph

Purpose: To help students understand diversity and to get this concept and content of the location graph into their bodies. It is a great process tool that gives students a chance to move.

- **Step 1:** Identify any important content that can be illustrated through a distribution. For example, you might pose questions around students preferred modality style for learning as a way to help them be more metacognitive about their learning. Questions might be:

  How do you like to learn best?

  Listening, seeing, or experiencing?

  Which would you prefer as recreational activity?

  Listening to music, watching TV, or playing a sport?

  On an output task what would you prefer?

  To draw, speak, or perform an answer?

- **Step 2:** Pick a space in the room that is large enough to get students to sort according to Auditory - Visual - Kinesthetic and have them distribute in the style of a bar graph made of the students in the class.

- **Step 3:** Have the students go to the place on the line that illustrates their strength. As they stand on the graph let the students process the meaning of the differences in style.

NOTE: This is a great activity for honoring individual differences, preferences, and ideas. It also gives kinesthetic students another tool for expression as they engage in movement. It is also another way to use the powerful location memory.

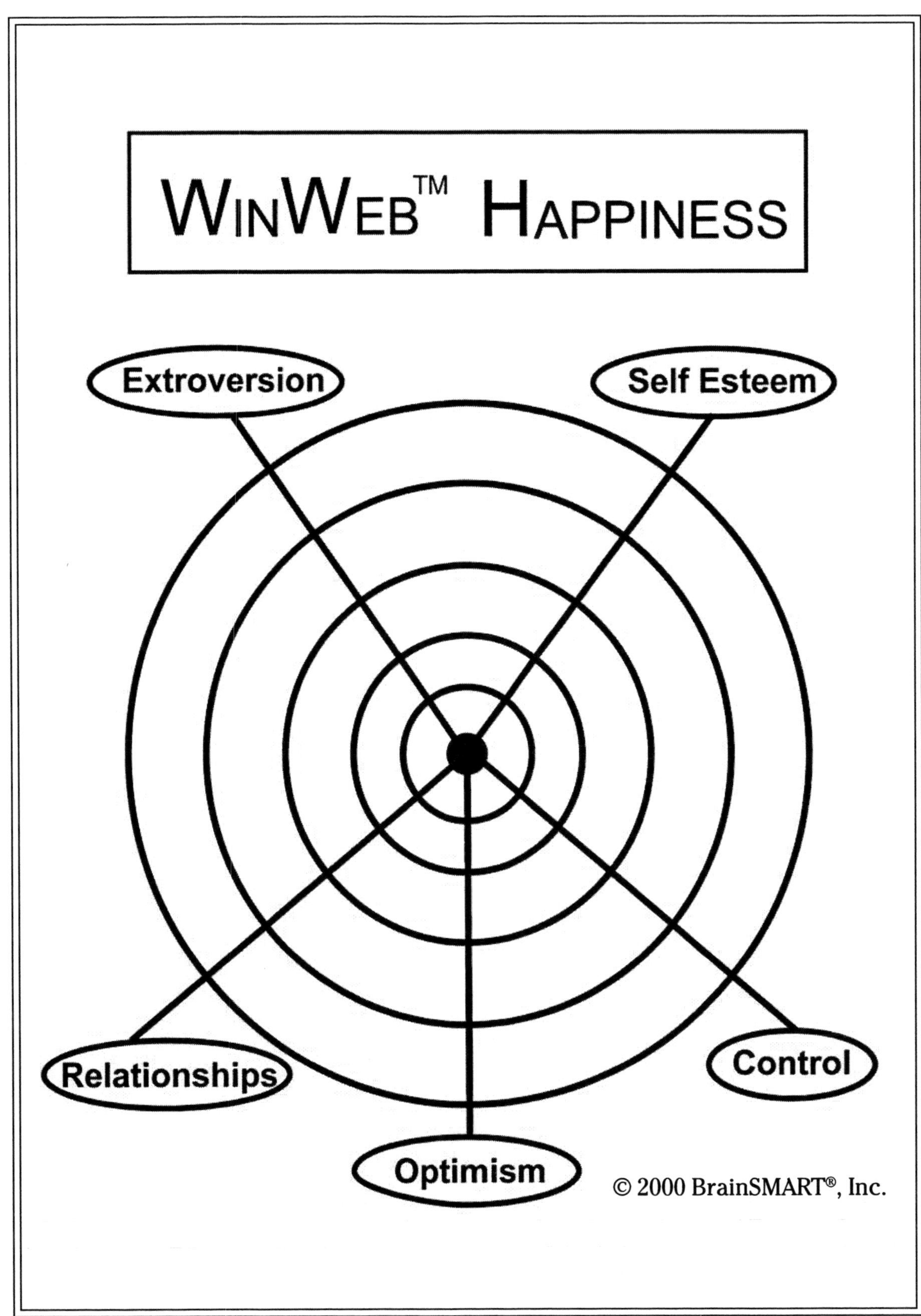
WinWeb™ Happiness
Extroversion
Self Esteem
Relationships
Control
Optimism
© 2000 BrainSMART®, Inc.

WinWeb

Purpose: To focus attention on what's important now (WIN). To give feedback on progress on important tasks. To boost motivation.

- **Step 1:** Many of us have difficulty completing tasks that are important.
- **Step 2:** The WinWeb acts like a target tracking system.
- **Step 3:** The attached shows an example of five keys to boosting happiness.
- **Step 4:** For each key area rate yourself. A bulls-eye in the middle is for perfect, while a rating along the outer edge needs a lot of work.
- **Step 5:** For areas that need improvement, plan to take positive action every day.
- **Step 6:** See the BrainWeb on Happiness tool (pg. 116) for more information.
- **Step 7:** Track your progress over time. All five areas are improvable.

NOTE: This can be used for students tracking their own behavior, homework assignments, achieving mastery in a subject, vocabulary learned, or other areas.

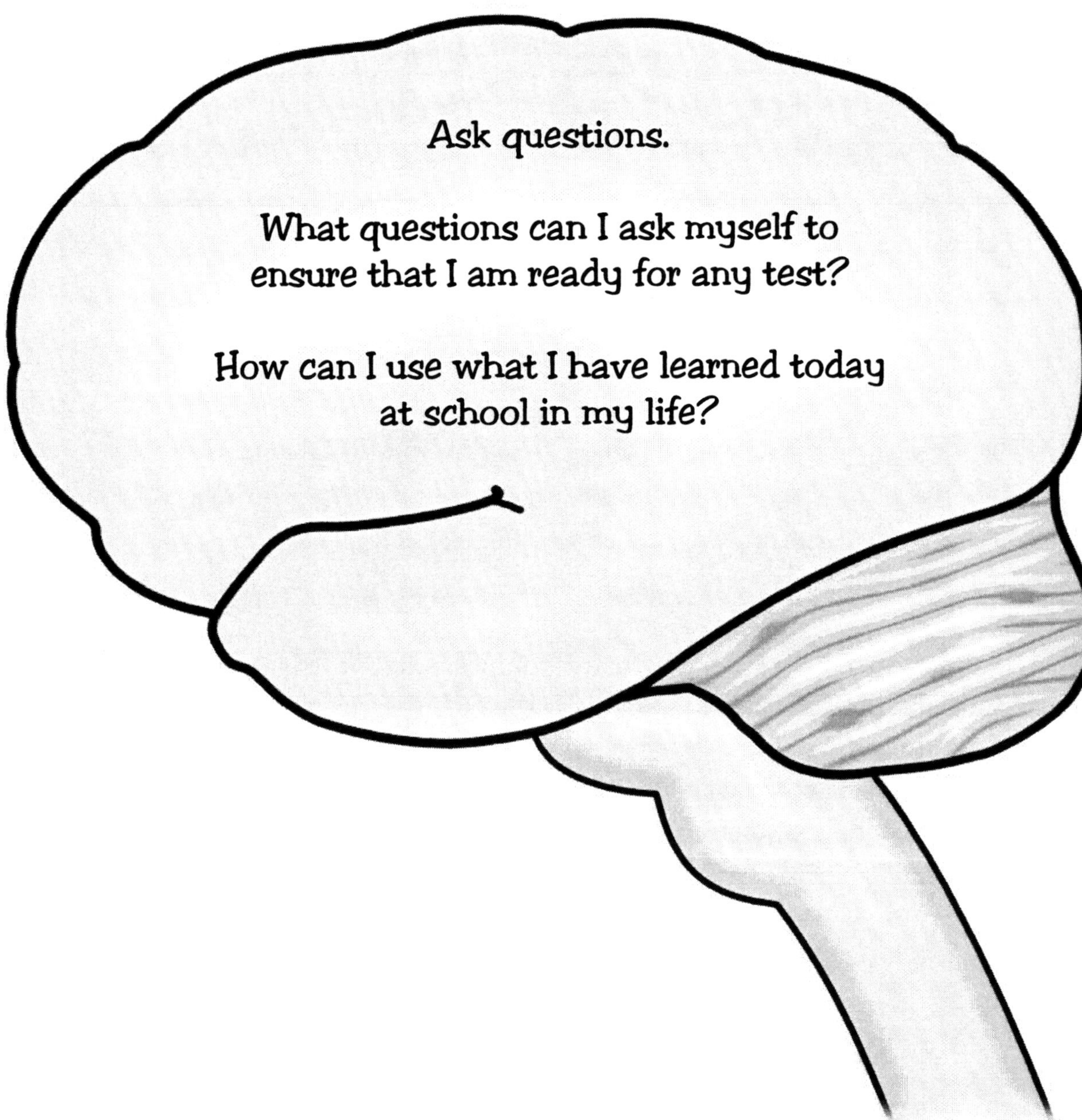
Ask questions.
What questions can I ask myself to ensure that I am ready for any test?
How can I use what I have learned today at school in my life?

C.R.A.V.E. Formula

Purpose: This tool is a general framework for teaching for attention. The C.R.A.V.E. Formula may also be used to guide mentors to work with students. The steps in this formula do not have to be used in the order presented.

Step 1: Build curiosity for learning.

Step 2: Use relevance to increase the level of attention.

Step 3: Ask questions.

Step 4: Remember that variety is the spice of attention.

Step 5: Emotion drives attention.

NOTE: A good idea is to assess how television commercials and news programs use the C.R.A.V.E. model to grab viewers' attention.

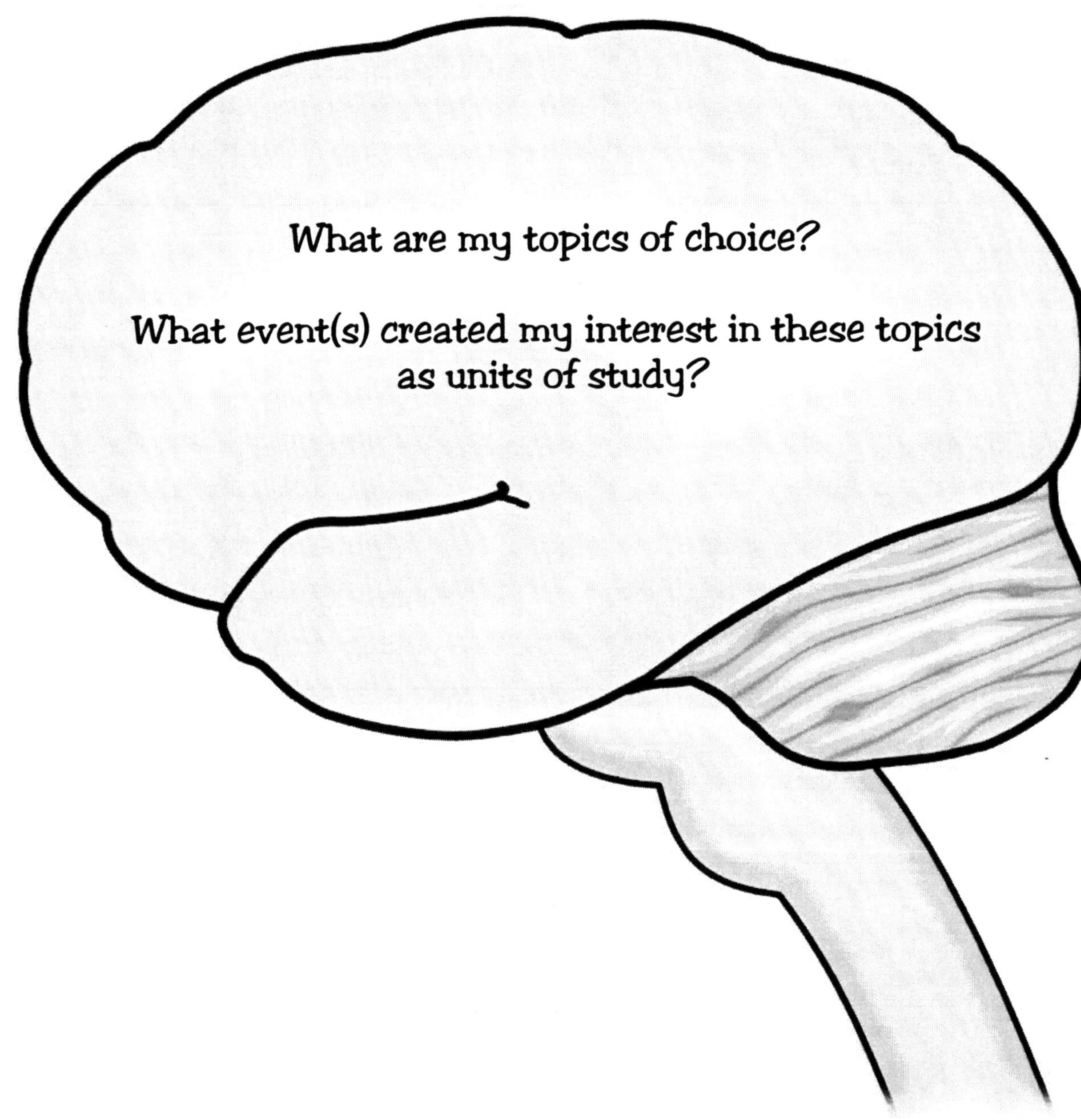
What are my topics of choice?
What event(s) created my interest in these topics as units of study?

Choice

Purpose: To dramatically increase levels of attention and to encourage independent learning.

- **Step 1:** For part of your teaching time select a range of topics that are key to covering curriculum.
- **Step 2:** Offer choice to your students about what they study.
- **Step 3:** When students finish a task early suggest that they work on one of these topics.
- **Step 4:** Set a period of time students can work on these topics throughout the year.
- **Step 5:** Use students as topic experts.
- **Step 6:** If you wish to boost reading comprehension, give students a choice of how they let you know the answer to questions. For example, let students choose from drawing, writing, or acting it out.

NOTE: Be creative in ways which you offer choice in terms of what is studied, how, when, and where as you teach important principles and concepts.

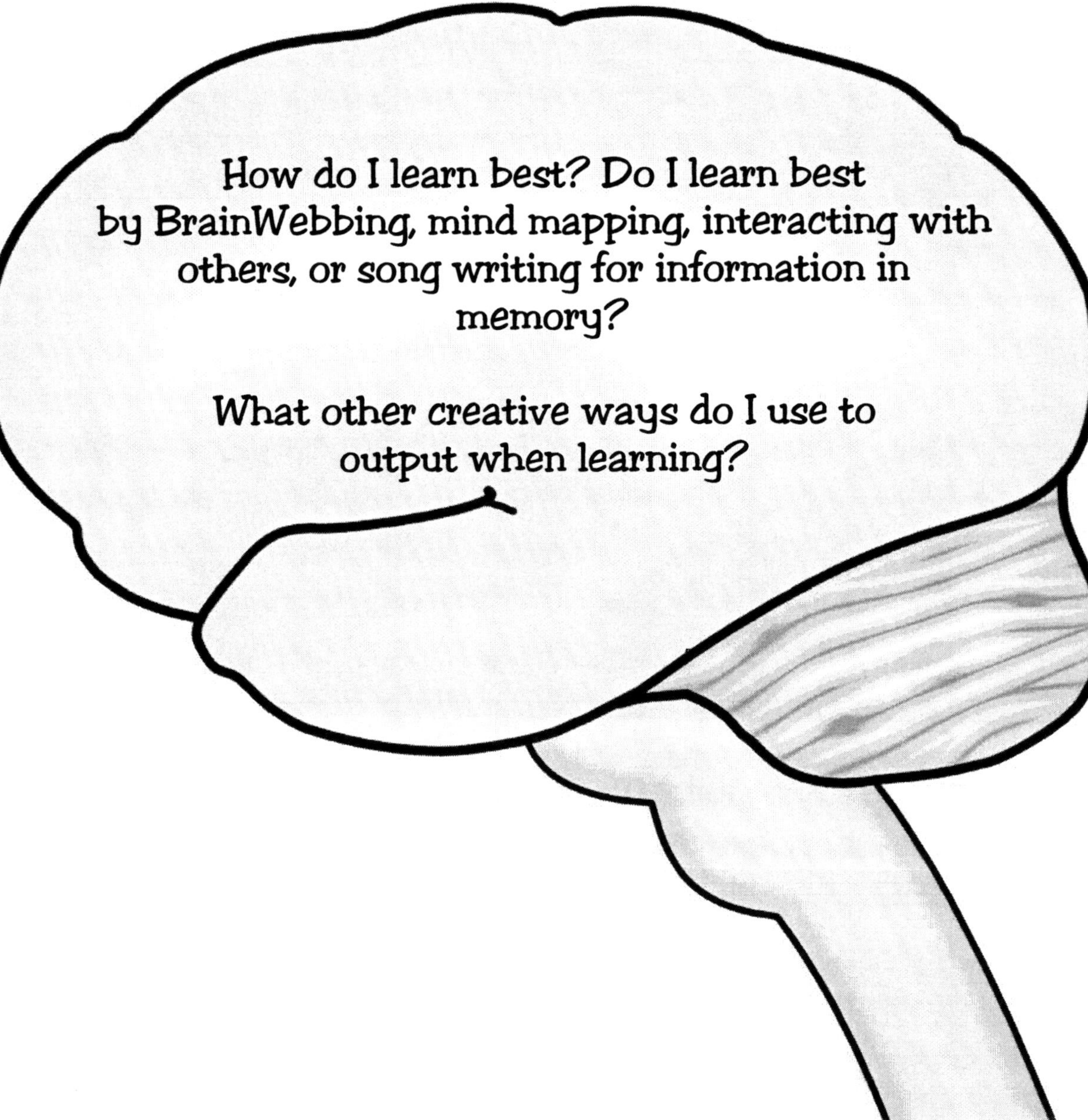
How do I learn best? Do I learn best by BrainWebbing, mind mapping, interacting with others, or song writing for information in memory?
What other creative ways do I use to output when learning?

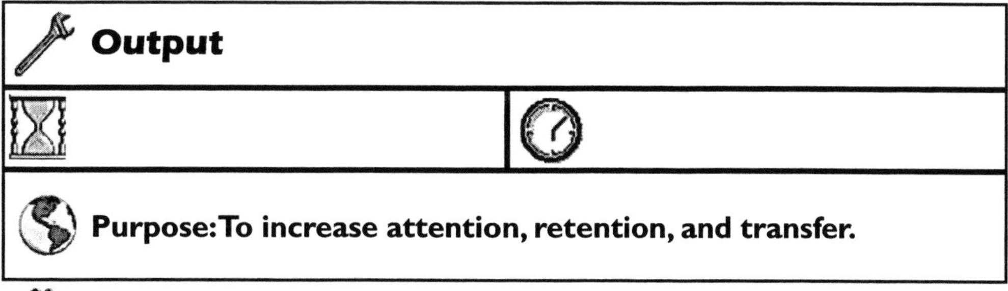

- **Step 1:** Listening to lectures is difficult for many learners.
- **Step 2:** Passive learning will often be deleted.
- **Step 3:** The more students output the higher the attention and retention.
- **Step 4:** Encourage BrainWebbing, model building, story telling, song writing, and other creative ways to output.
- **Step 5:** Observe student output to discover where the learning gaps are.
- **Step 6:** Encourage other students to fill in the gaps.

NOTE: Orchestrating output will free your time to assess where your students are. It will reduce energy drain as it increases student learning.

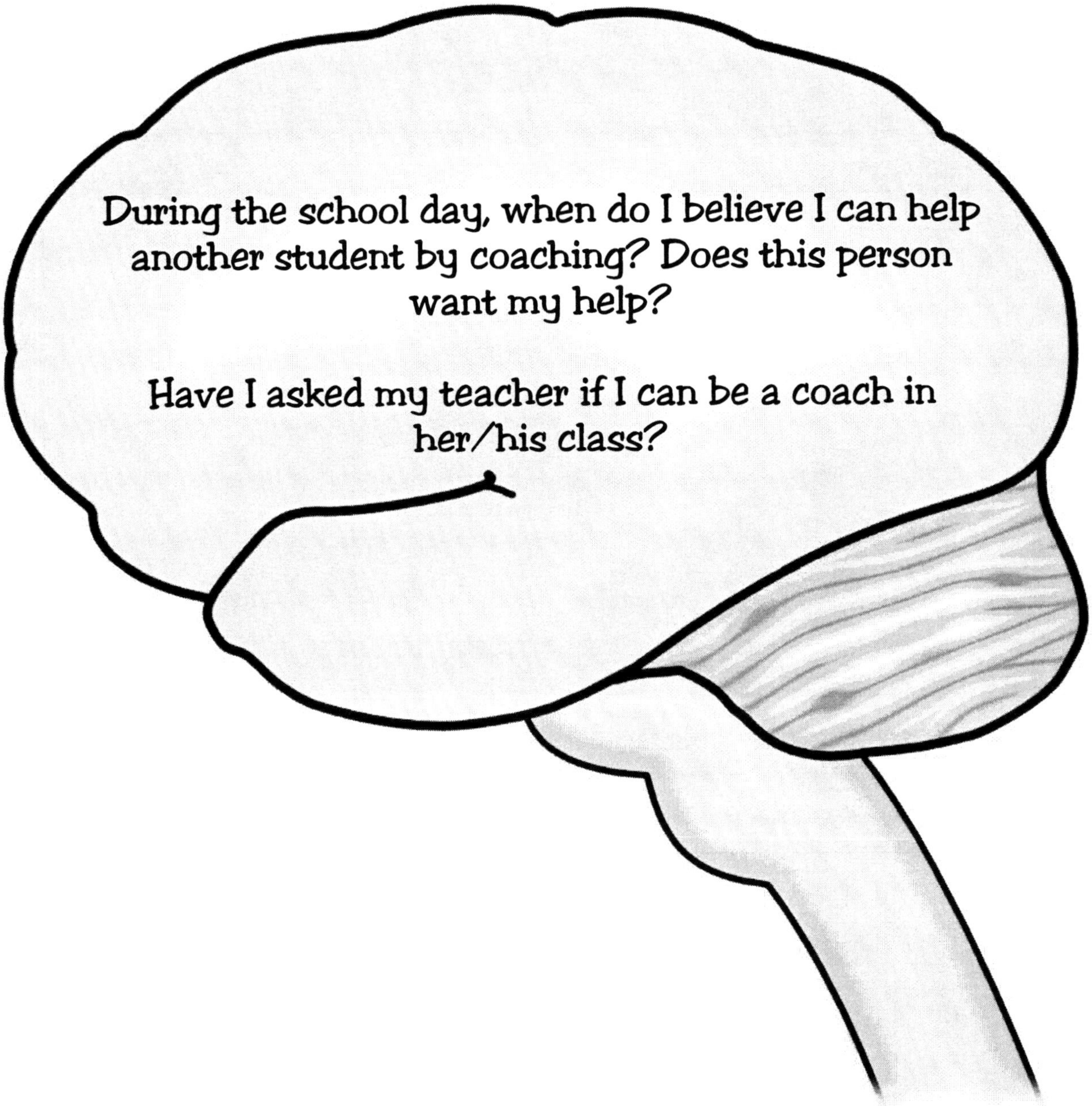

During the school day, when do I believe I can help another student by coaching? Does this person want my help?

Have I asked my teacher if I can be a coach in her/his class?

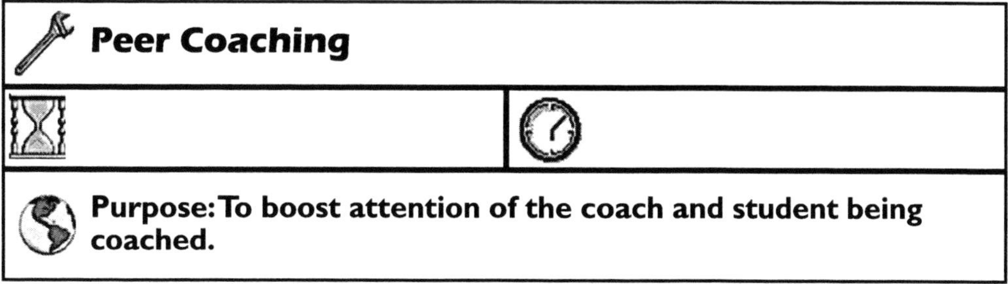

- **Step 1:** Peer coaching was identified by researchers at Stanford University as one of the most effective strategies for facilitating learning.

- **Step 2:** Find students who finish quickly and encourage them to coach another student.

- **Step 3:** Find appropriate rewards for this work. For example, a reward might be to give a student a chance to work on a special project.

- **Step 4:** Listen to what is being taught and how.

- **Step 5:** Correct any inaccuracies through a questioning approach.

NOTE: Peer coaching and teaching is a powerful process to encourage in your classroom. Observe other teachers who do this well.

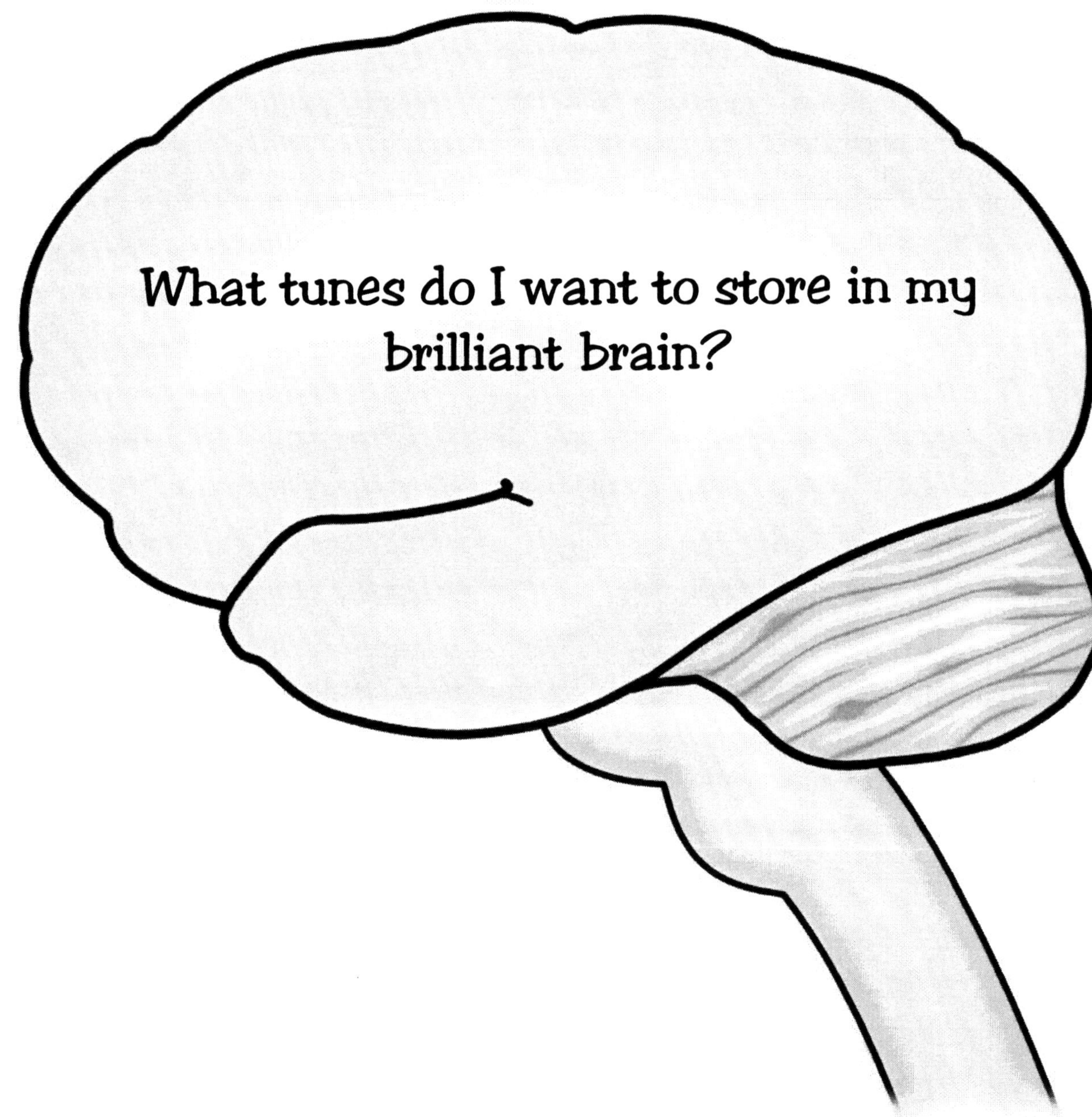
What tunes do I want to store in my brilliant brain?

Name That Tune

Purpose: To help students to appreciate how brilliant their auditory learning capacity is.

- **Step 1:** Put together a tape with just the intros of many tunes that you think your students will know.
- **Step 2:** Play this tape to them in the class, ask them to raise their hands as soon as they remember each tune, and then write down the name.
- **Step 3:** Play the whole tape.
- **Step 4:** Then ask students to review with you the right answers. Ask students how many of them got the answers right.
- **Step 5:** Ask students to dialog with you why this happened.
- **Step 6:** Celebrate with a big "I Feel Good" about the power of the auditory memory.

NOTE: This technique will give students a concrete success experience that you can refer to often throughout the year. Students often have an incredible capacity for remembering tunes, and the same brain that can remember tunes can remember other information when rehearsed and learned in the right way.

H.E.A.R.

When has there been a time at school that it would have been helpful for me to use the H.E.A.R. listening strategy?

How can I use the H.E.A.R. strategy to help me be a better listener?

Is it a surprise to me that I can remember so many tunes? Did I realize that my memory is so good?

Can I use certain music to create memorable learning experiences?

H.E.A.R.

Purpose: To increase students' ability to listen and pay attention with world-class precision.

- **Step 1:** Discuss with students how important listening is for their relationships, for school, and for work.
- **Step 2:** Remind students that listening is often cited as the number one skill for helping people in relationships and in business.
- **Step 3:** Ask students why people don't listen very well and list the reasons the students give you.
- **Step 4:** Ask students to please stand up.
- **Step 5:** Push the flat of your hand straight in front of you and say "Halt." Explain to students that by halting their internal dialog they free their mind to listen on the outside. Now get all students to do the "Halt" exercise.
- **Step 6:** Push your finger out straight in front of you and say, "Engage" making sure that you turn your right ear forward. Explain to students that you are now engaging full-body listening and that by turning your right ear forward the information is going to your left brain where language is best processed.
- **Step 7:** Then stretch out both arms to the side and say, "Anticipate" and get students to do the same. Explain to students that the reason you want them to anticipate is to increase their capacity to listen and remember. Get them to anticipate that they will be learning something absolutely vital.
- **Step 8:** Roll your hands forward in a circular fashion, like the paddle on a river boat and say, "Replay" and ask your students to do the same. Explain that when you replay what you think that you've heard you demonstrate that you've truly listened. This will also boost your memory of what was said.
- **Step 9:** Put the whole sequence together: Halt; Engage; Anticipate; Replay. Then get students to work in groups to discuss how important this technique could be.

NOTE: This technique has been very effective at helping more kinesthetic students to learn truly how to listen. The physical nature of the exercise strongly encodes the information.

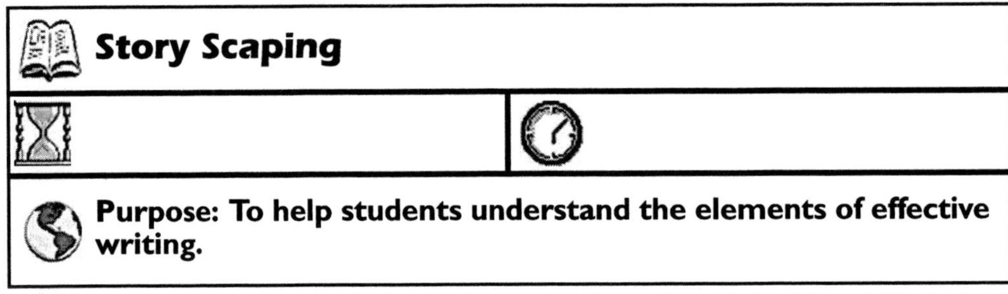

- **Step 1:** Tell your students that today you will all be creating a story.

- **Step 2:** Ask your students to shout out things they would like you to include in that story.

- **Step 3:** Use the following script and let the students fill in the gaps.

NOTE: This exercise works best when you act out the story. Move from your right to your left across the room and back again.

Script: Once upon a time there was a man who was wearing a long brown ____________ and he was out in the woods looking for _________________ when suddenly he heard a loud roar, looked around and saw a huge __________________. So he began to run and the faster he ran the faster the _______ ran. He kept running and running and running until suddenly he came to a very high place. He looked down and he was on the edge of a ________________. " Oh my golly," he said. " What am I going to do?" "I'm being chased by this ________________ standing on the edge of this gap." Suddenly he looked down and saw a long thin ________________ so he jumped off the _______________ and started to hang on to the ________________. He then looked up and saw the _______________ then to his horror he looked down and heard another noise underneath him that was a ______________ He thought to himself, "Well at least I'm safe hanging on to this ______________." Then suddenly another little animal came out and started to chew on the ________________. It was a ____________.

Just as he thought his life was over he looked over and saw a beautiful fruit. It was a ____________. He reached out and grabbed the ______________ and said, "I feel good, yes!" Then he said to the __________ and the ______________, "I'm as strong as a bull. I can hang here all day so you might as well go home." So up above the ________________ went home and down below the ___________ went home and soon he climbed back up the ________________, walked back through the __________ and back through the village.

- **Step 5:** Ask students what they remembered about the story. You'll be amazed at the retention and recall that they had.
- **Step 6:** Get students to act out their own stories, so that they begin to understand the structure of writing a story.
- **Step 7:** Having acted out the stories, allow students to create a mind map of their stories.
- **Step 8:** Have students write their stories in whatever way is most comfortable for them.

NOTE: This simple way of teaching students how to write can remove much of the fear that students associate with the writing process. It also helps them internalize permanently the structure of stories.

20 BrainSMART Tools For Retention

How can I use "The Power of Seven"
to help me study for tests?

How can I use this strategy when I do homework?

The Power of Seven

Purpose: To facilitate effective retention and recall of the major elements of your lesson.

- **Step 1:** Break the content of the lesson into seven major components.
- **Step 2:** Convert these seven components into seven key headlines, each with a key word.
- **Step 3:** Use these headlines as seven branches on your BrainSMART lesson map.
- **Step 4:** Start the class by giving an overview of the key areas that will be covered.
- **Step 5:** Stand in a different part of the room each time you begin one of the seven key areas.
- **Step 6:** At the end of the class review by standing in each of the seven positions and asking the students what they remember. Then add any information the class did not recall.
- **Step 7:** Finally get the class to do their own mind map of the seven key areas that you covered.
- **Step 8:** The next time you meet with the class, review by standing in each of the seven positions and asking what they remember and redoing a group mind map.

NOTE: This is a powerful routine that will develop long term retention of core information and help students discover the power of seven for themselves.

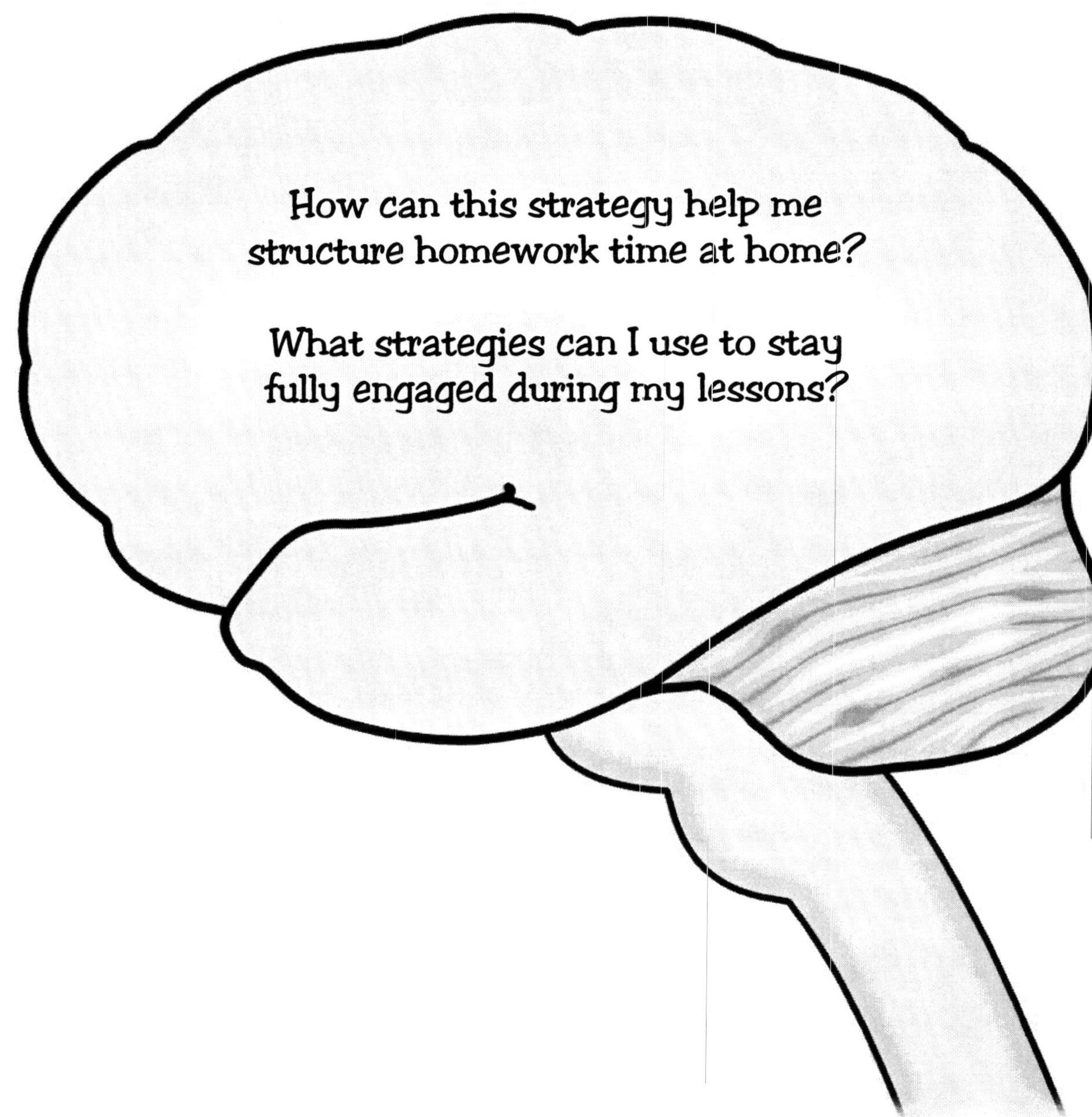
How can this strategy help me
structure homework time at home?
What strategies can I use to stay
fully engaged during my lessons?

The Power of 20 Minutes

Purpose: To maximize attention, retention, and recall by aligning instruction with the brain's natural attention cycles.

- **Step 1:** Break the learning time you have with students down to chunks of a maximum of 20 minutes. (Seven to fifteen minute chunks are often optimum for younger students.)

- **Step 2:** Always begin your lesson with the most important information. The brain is most likely to remember the beginning and end of any lesson.

- **Step 3:** At the beginning of your lesson, also give an overview of what is to be covered and create maximum curiosity.

- **Step 4:** Add as much variety as you can in terms of where you stand in the room, how you use your voice tone, and your use of music and graphics to sustain attention and interest.

- **Step 5:** Towards the end of the 20 minute session, highlight the most important information. Remember the brain retains the first and last things it is exposed to.

- **Step 6:** At the end of 20 minutes, insure a complete state change by using "BrainObics," "think pair share," or giving students a mini break.

NOTE: By respecting the way the brain naturally absorbs information, in 20 minute chunks and capitalizing on the laws of primacy and recency, we can help students learn in a far more joyful and effective way. It is also useful to suggest to students that anytime they do homework they also use The Power of 20 Minutes to maximize the impact of their study time.

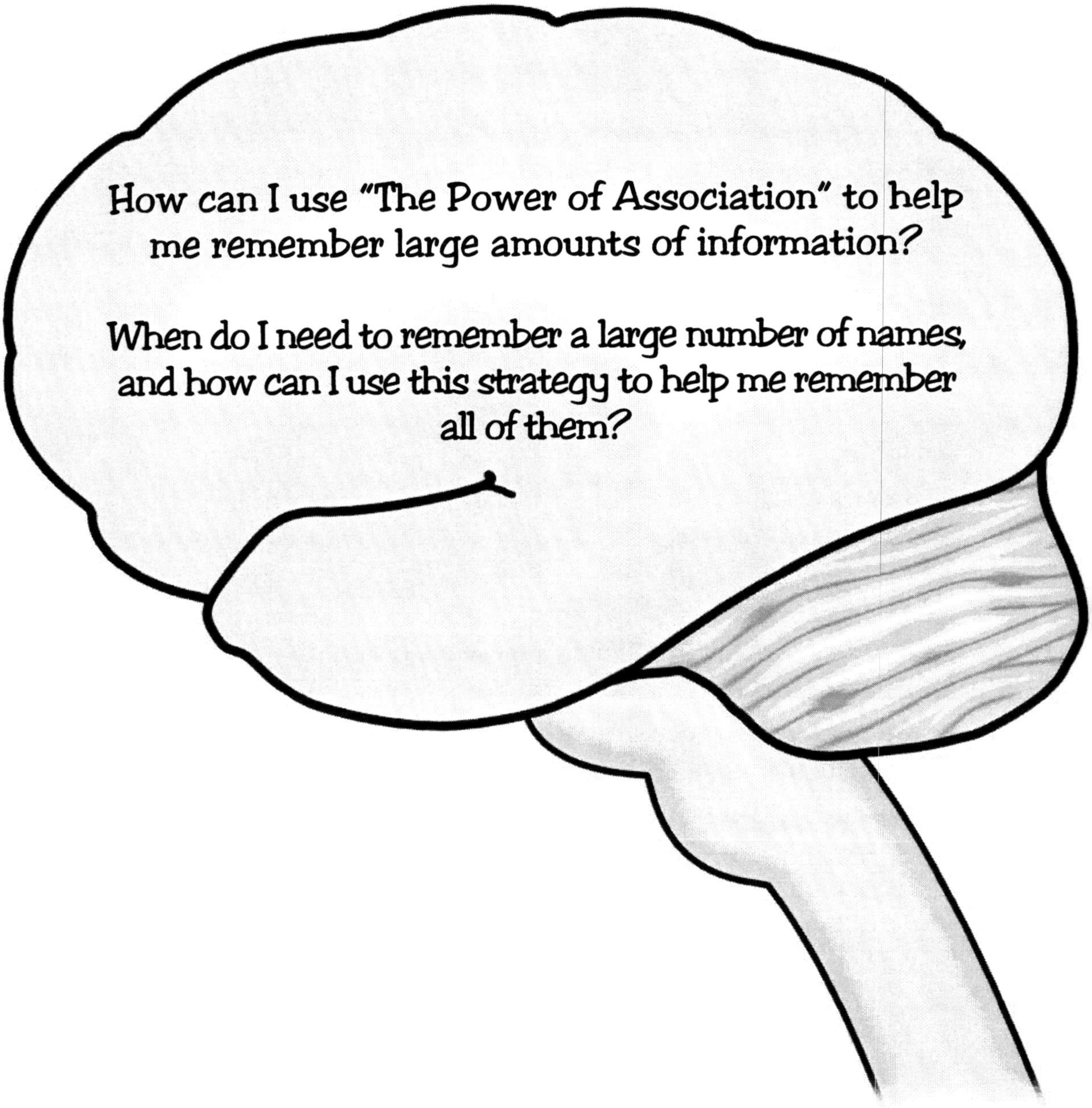

How can I use "The Power of Association" to help me remember large amounts of information?

When do I need to remember a large number of names, and how can I use this strategy to help me remember all of them?

The Power of Association

Purpose: To capitalize on the brain's enormous capacity to store new information when it is associated with information that already exists inside the brain.

- **Step 1:** Get students excited about how their brain can easily remember information that is associated with a picture. We do this by asking them, "Is it easier to remember a face or a name?"
- **Step 2:** Most students will reply, "It's easier to remember a face." We then ask them, "Why?"
- **Step 3:** Having acknowledged and respected the answers, we may suggest that we find it easy to remember pictures and that a picture is worth a thousand words.
- **Step 4:** We then explain to students that when somebody hears the sound of their name it is indeed the sweetest sound they could ever hear.
- **Step 5:** We then show them pictures from a magazine, a picture, or a book and make up names for them. Ask the students to remember the names.
- **Step 6:** Having noted their effectiveness at remembering names, we then show them another way and give them simple examples. Example 1: to remember the name Frank, see a picture of Frank in your mind's eye. Now imagine a frankfurter going through their neck like Frankenstein. Example 2: to remember the name Bill, imagine the picture of Bill in your mind's eye and stick a dollar bill on his forehead. Example 3: to remember the name Ann, make a picture of Ann in your mind's eye and imagine an ant nibbling away at Ann's forehead.
- **Step 7:** Having had fun with this exercise, get students to create their own associations for people whose names they would like to remember. (A good way to do this is for them to remember names of characters when they're watching television.)
- **Step 8:** Review with your students the Power of Association. Get them to reflect on the fact that a picture is worth a thousand words.

NOTE: Giving students the ability to remember names will give them a huge advantage in life. They will also begin to appreciate the Power of Association and begin to tap into the brain's incredible capacity to use this natural ability to remember any key information.

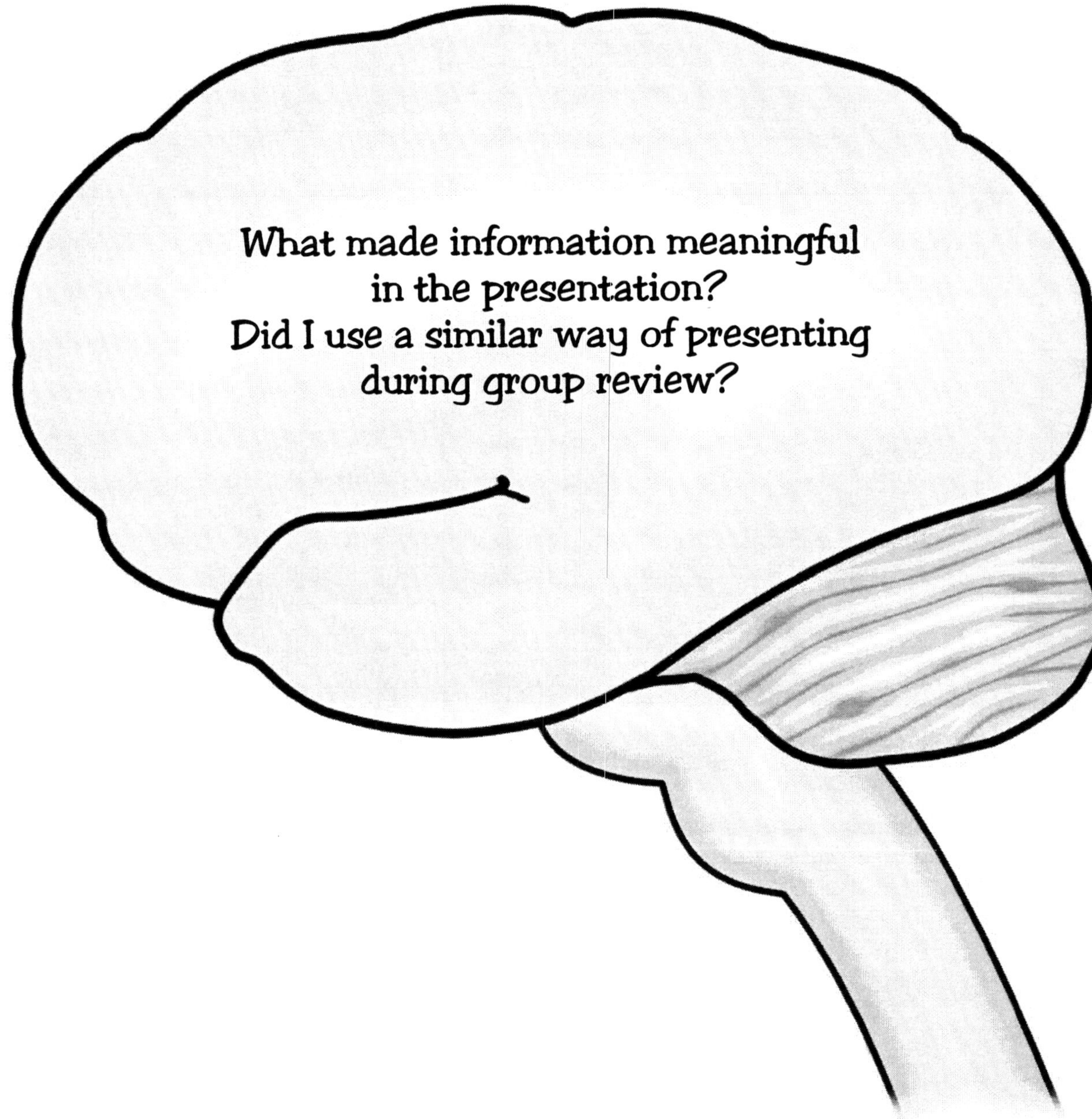
What made information meaningful
in the presentation?
Did I use a similar way of presenting
during group review?

The Power of Rehearsal

Purpose: To equip students with a very simple system for facilitating retention, recall, and transfer of information.

- **Step 1:** Present important information to students in a dynamic and enthusiastic manner.
- **Step 2:** Ask students to review with each other the key information which you just presented.
- **Step 3:** Ask students to present to the whole class what they remember.
- **Step 4:** Correct any information presented that was not accurate (and do this in a positive way) then fill in any gaps.
- **Step 5:** Continue to present information in 7 to 20 minute chunks and repeat the process.
- **Step 6:** Get students into small groups to review the information presented.
- **Step 7:** Ask students to then prepare a brief presentation lasting 60 seconds that summarizes two key points that they would like to remember.
- **Step 8:** Get students to present their summaries in small groups.

NOTE: By getting students into the routine of rehearsing and replaying information that they have been exposed to and doing small group presentations, we can build their capacity to pay full attention, retain, and articulate what they have learned.

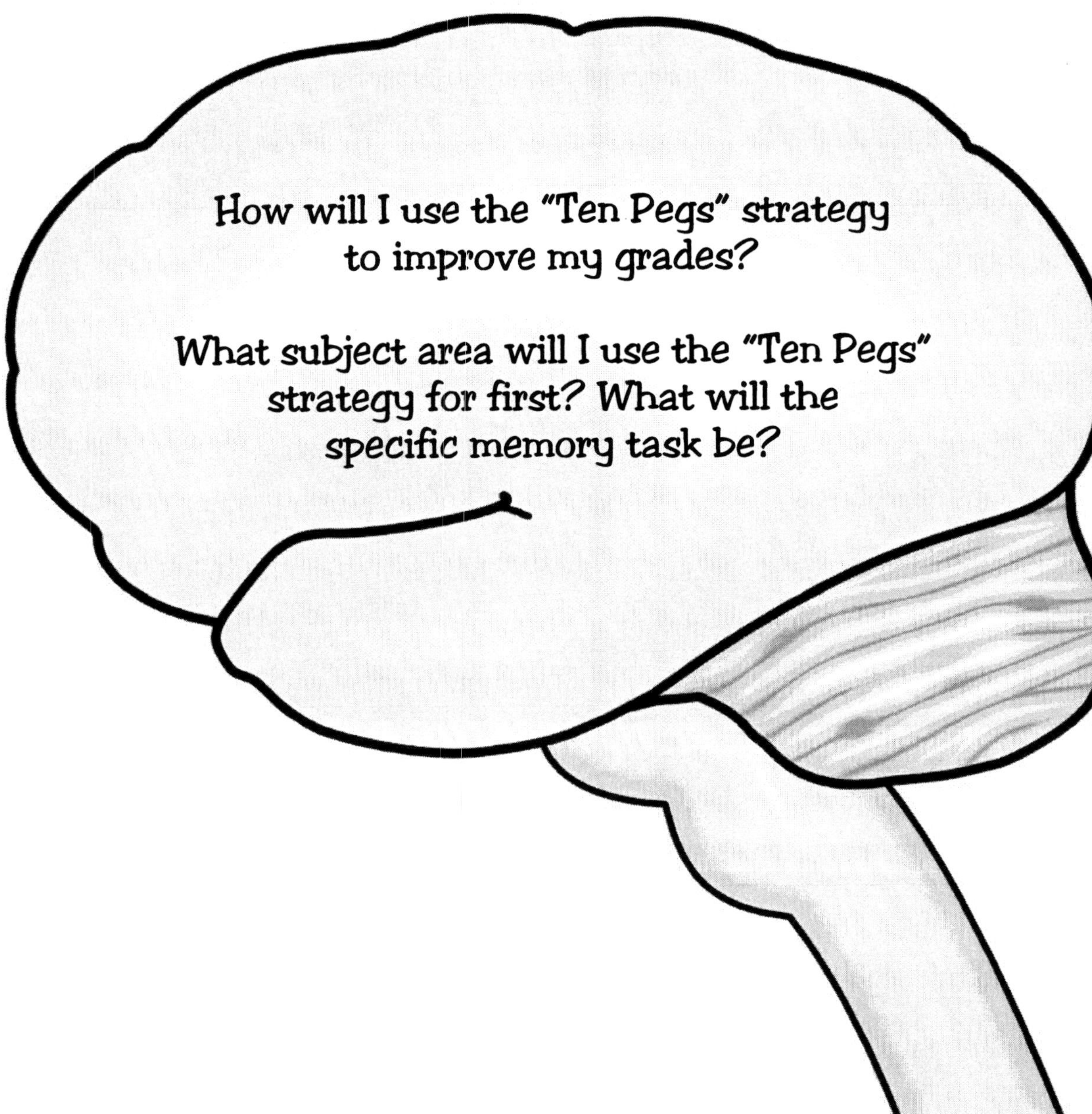
How will I use the "Ten Pegs" strategy
to improve my grades?
What subject area will I use the "Ten Pegs"
strategy for first? What will the
specific memory task be?

 **Ten Pegs**

 **Purpose: To give all students, particularly those who are more kinesthetic, a practical, portable system for retaining and recalling information.**

- **Step 1:** Ask students to please stand up.
- **Step 2:** Ask students, without the use of pen or paper, to listen to a list of 10 words and to try to remember them all.
- **Step 3:** Give them a list of words something like: Tomatoes, Molasses, Steak, Orange, Bananas, Ice Cream, Mustard, String, Band-Aid, and Eggs.
- **Step 4:** Then ask the students to turn to the person next to them and give them the list in order.
- **Step 5:** Ask who remembers all 10 in order, 9 in order, 8 in order, 7 in order, and so on, and make a note of how many people remember how many in order.
- **Step 6:** Ask students if they would like to learn a way in which they could easily remember all 10.
- **Step 7:** Get students to mirror you as you move down the body pegs: 1. head 2. shoulders 3. chest 4. belly 5. hips 6. backside 7. thighs 8. knees 9. shins 10. toes.
- **Step 8:** Ask students to visualize, in a vivid way, each of the 10 items beginning with tomato and ending with eggs.
- **Step 9:** Ask the students to now remember each of the 10 items. Ask if anyone remembered more this time than the previous time and celebrate.

NOTE: The power of the Ten Peg system is that virtually all students can succeed with it, particularly those who are more kinesthetic. You can use this system to remember any amount of information from language arts to science to any content area. This is a highly motivating exercise that can literally change the way students think about themselves.

How can I use this strategy to
improve my test performance?

Eyes Up

Purpose: To equip students with a simple, practical method for boosting recall of information.

- **Step 1:** Ask students how many windows they have in their home.
- **Step 2:** Observe where the students' eyes move in response to your question. Then ask students to freeze.
- **Step 3:** Ask students to notice where their eyes are looking in response to your question. Note that most students are looking up.
- **Step 4:** Ask students if they've ever sat down to take a test and forgotten everything. Notice how many say yes. Then ask them where their eyes were looking when they forgot everything. Notice many of them will say that their eyes were looking down.
- **Step 5:** Explain to students that for most people, looking up switches on their brain's ability to remember things that they have seen.
- **Step 6:** Show the students a mind map of something you would like them to learn.
- **Step 7:** Suggest that they look at the mind map for one minute or so.
- **Step 8:** Take down the mind map and ask students what they remember. Prompt them by suggesting that they look up.
- **Step 9:** Practice this sequence a number of times until the act of looking up to help them remember becomes automatic.

NOTE: Many students will greatly improve their ability to recall information using this technique. Research also indicates that important information can be best stored in students' minds when you are presenting from the students' left side of the room.

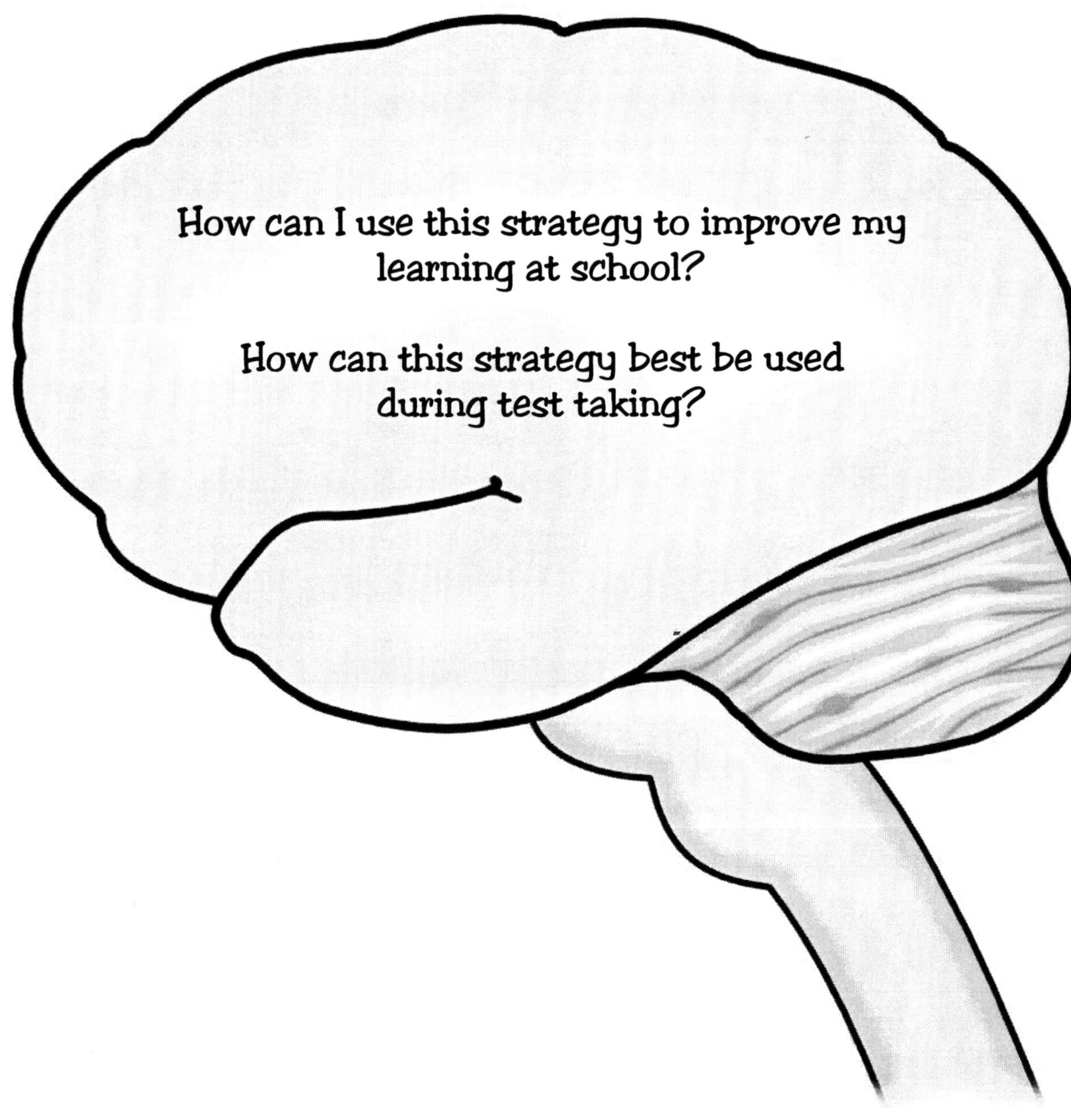
How can I use this strategy to improve my learning at school?
How can this strategy best be used during test taking?

Eyes to the Side

Purpose: To help students increase their ability to remember spoken or other auditory information.

- **Step 1:** Ask students to remember the sound of a dog barking.
- **Step 2:** Notice the direction the students' eyes move to as they recall this information. Notice that for many students it will be to the side. Around 90% of right-hand students will look to their left.
- **Step 3:** Ask students to freeze and discover for themselves where they were looking.
- **Step 4:** Explain to them that looking across to the left switches on their sound memory.
- **Step 5:** Create a positive sound effect like a bell or a chime, repeat a couple of times.
- **Step 6:** Now ask students to remember the sound of the bell or the chime and encourage them to move their eyes to the left or the right, whichever is more comfortable for them.
- **Step 7:** Encourage students to move their eyes to the sound memory position frequently when you would like to help them to remember auditory information.

NOTE: Consistent practice at moving the eyes to the sound memory position may considerably help some students. Also remember that a student's eye movements often are indicating a specific form of mental processing that they need to undertake in order to remember something. Asking for direct eye contact from the student can often shut down effective thinking and memory.

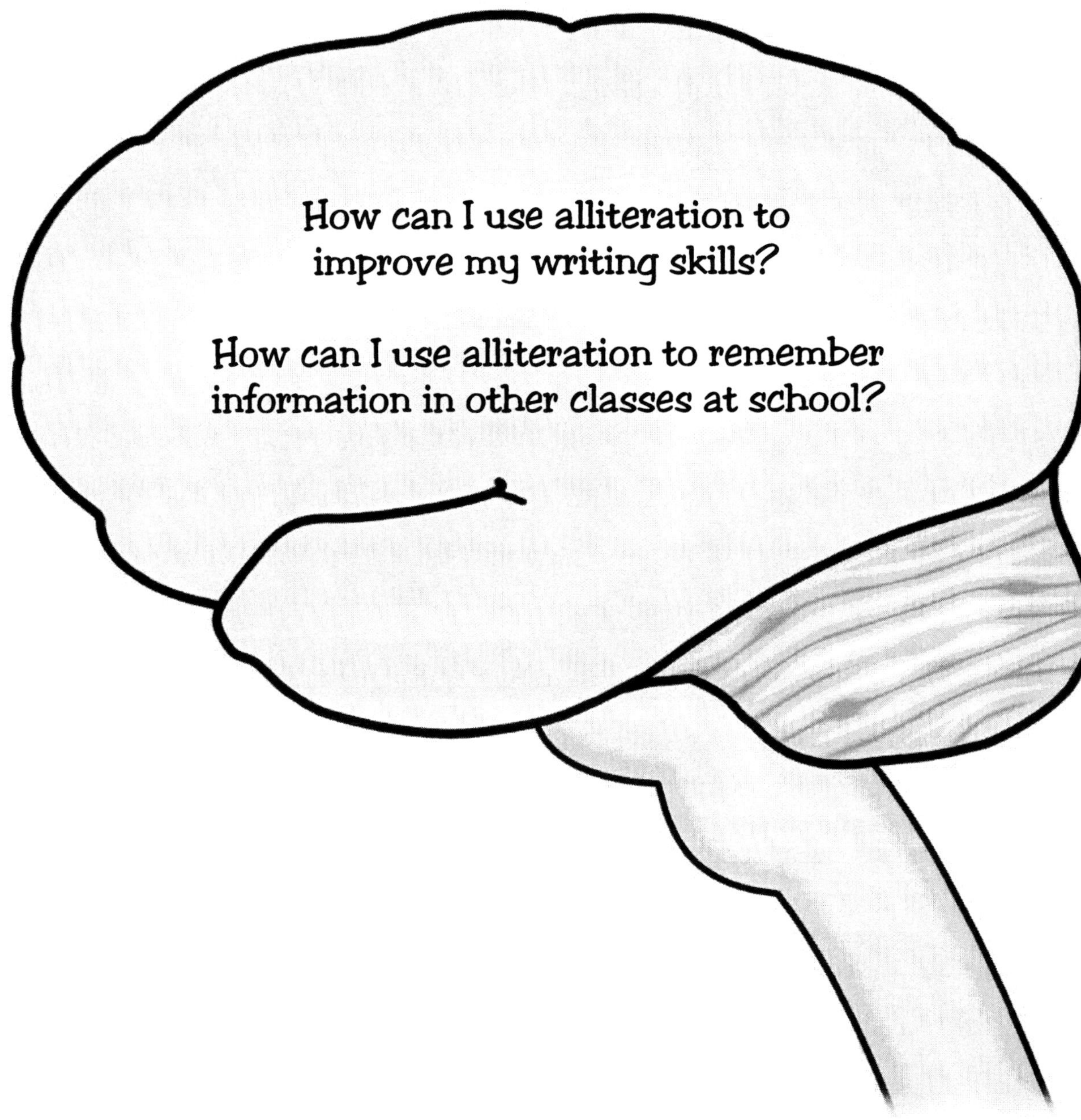
How can I use alliteration to
improve my writing skills?
How can I use alliteration to remember
information in other classes at school?

Power of Alliteration

Purpose: To equip students with a simple tool for remembering more auditory information.

- **Step 1:** Explain to your students that the brain loves patterns and rhymes.
- **Step 2:** Explain that alliteration, where a sentence has words that begin with the same sounding letter can be a powerful way to remember information.
- **Step 3:** Create a list with the students of good examples. For example: Magic moments; Love of learning; Reading, writing, 'rithmetic.
- **Step 4:** In some content area that you are working on, brainstorm with your students ways you could use alliteration to make some things more memorable.
- **Step 5:** Get students into groups to explore some alliterations of their own.
- **Step 6:** Get someone from each of the groups to present their alliterations.
- **Step 7:** Remind students to use the power of alliteration when there is information they want to remember throughout the year.

NOTE: A great follow-up exercise is to review newspaper articles and television news items that use alliteration to attract attention and boost memory. Commercials are also good at doing this as are cartoons such as Merry Melodies.

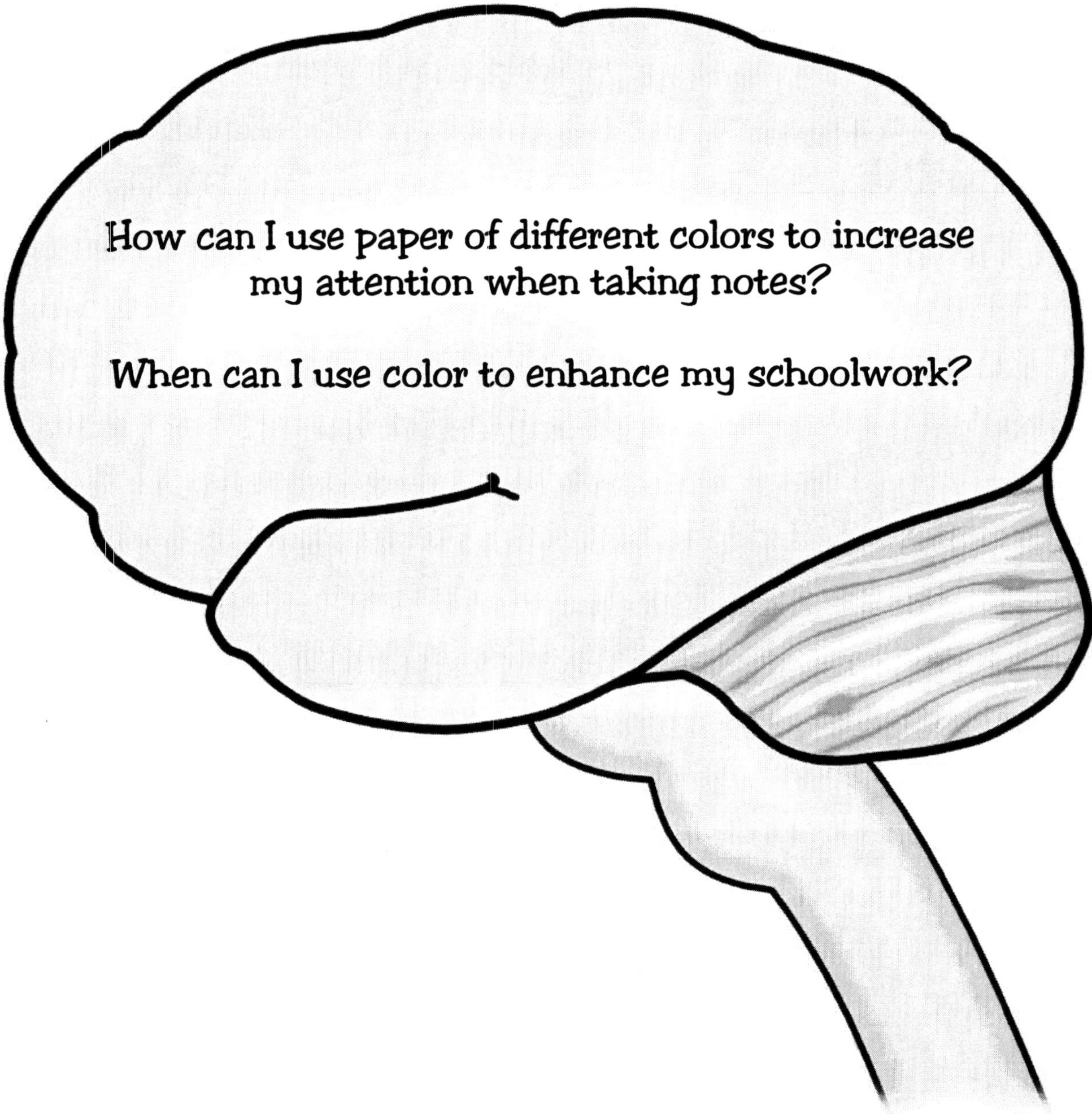

How can I use paper of different colors to increase my attention when taking notes?

When can I use color to enhance my schoolwork?

The Power of Color

Purpose: To help students understand that by using color they can greatly increase attention, retention, and recall of information.

- **Step 1:** Ask students whether most television commercials are black and white or are in color and get responses.
- **Step 2:** Students brainstorm in group, on why commercials are made in color. Also ask if they think they are more expensive to make in color.
- **Step 3:** Debrief information from the groups.
- **Step 4:** Show students a couple of sample magazines and notice how many of the ads are in color and as a group discuss why the ads are in color.
- **Step 5:** Brainstorm with students all the ways in which color could be used to help learning happen. Explain that the human brain tends to think in color and that the human eye is drawn to color.
- **Step 6:** Encourage students to use color in their note taking and in their day-to-day work with you.
- **Step 7:** On an ongoing basis when you use mind maps or other artifacts that use color, reinforce this message.

NOTE: Using color appropriately can have a significant effect on boosting State, Meaning, Attention, Retention, and Transfer. Every year the advertising industry spends billions of dollars because it works. The brain often codes black and white or blue on white as boring. In fact, to the brain, a single color is a monochrome, which is as boring as a monotone in the human voice.

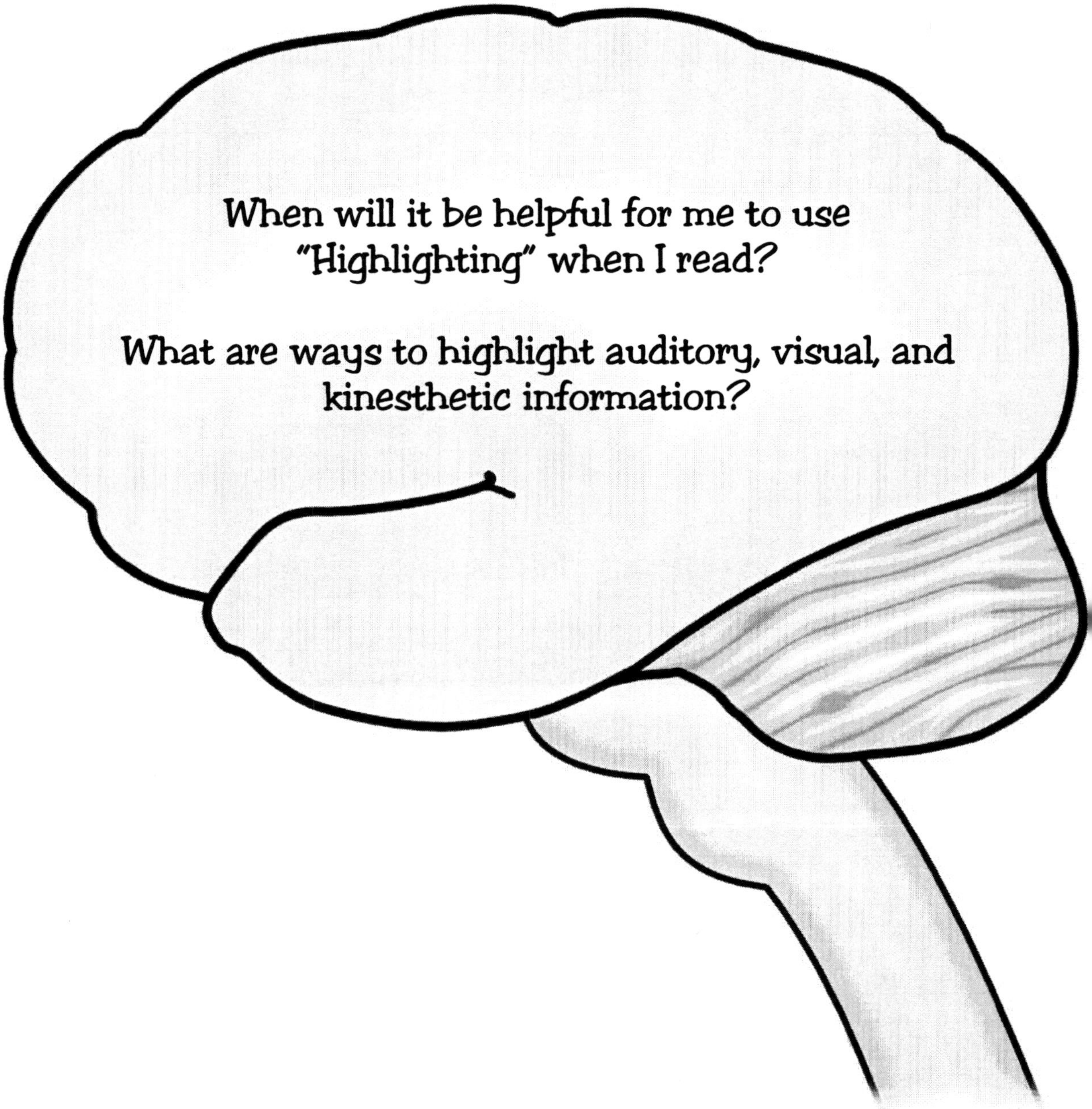

When will it be helpful for me to use "Highlighting" when I read?

What are ways to highlight auditory, visual, and kinesthetic information?

Highlighting

Purpose: To assist students in understanding more of the 80/20 principal. In other words, in most circumstances, 20% of the work produces 80% of the results.

- **Step 1:** In preparing your lesson, identify 10 facts from the content area that you would like to discuss.
- **Step 2:** Pick two facts that are absolutely critical to be remembered and understood.
- **Step 3:** As you present material, when you come to one of the two points, do whatever steps necessary to highlight that this is one of the two most important facts to remember.

NOTE: You may change your voice tone, highlight the fact verbally with the sentence, "Now this is critical to remember," stand in a different part of the room, or use a graphic, for example.

- **Step 4:** Continue with your lesson.
- **Step 5:** A little later in your lesson, stop and ask your students to remember what was the important fact that you highlighted.
- **Step 6:** Continue with the lesson until you come to the next key fact that you wish to highlight. Repeat the procedure.
- **Step 7:** Later in the lesson, once again stop and ask the students, "What are the two key facts that we highlighted today?" and get their feedback.
- **Step 8:** During future lessons, ask students to remember the two key highlights from today.

NOTE: By consistently highlighting content that is most important, you can considerably boost the probability of students remembering that key information. Remember, more is less. The more information that is presented, the less will be remembered. Furthermore, the act of stopping and asking students what was highlighted will heighten their overall level of attention.

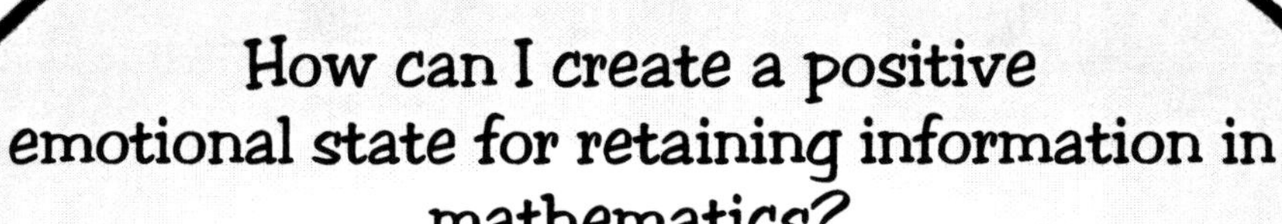
How can I create a positive emotional state for retaining information in mathematics?
What are the three most powerful BrainSMART tools for creating a positive emotional state for test taking?

The Power of Emotion

Purpose: To boost student retention of important information while creating a greater understanding of the roll of emotion in attention and memory.

- **Step 1:** Explain to students that today you will be exploring the power of emotion to help them remember important information.
- **Step 2:** Ask students to think about what they remember about last year.
- **Step 3:** Ask students to discuss with the person next to them what they remember.
- **Step 4:** Write on the board or flip chart some of the key things that people remember from the last year.
- **Step 5:** Ask the students what they notice is similar about all these things.
- **Step 6:** After exploring this, explain the value of emotion in making things memorable. A useful metaphor is that emotions are like files. You may wish to write on files names of some positive emotions like fun, joy, and then another file for sadness.
- **Step 7:** Ask students which emotions they would like to store their memories in.
- **Step 8:** Encourage students to use skills we used in State management to help them build good files of positive emotions and useful learning.

NOTE: Help students understand the power of emotions and boosting attention and memory. Students can become more adept at channeling this powerful resource in a positive way. In your own teaching remember to insure you create emotional "hot-spots" around the key information you would like your students to learn.

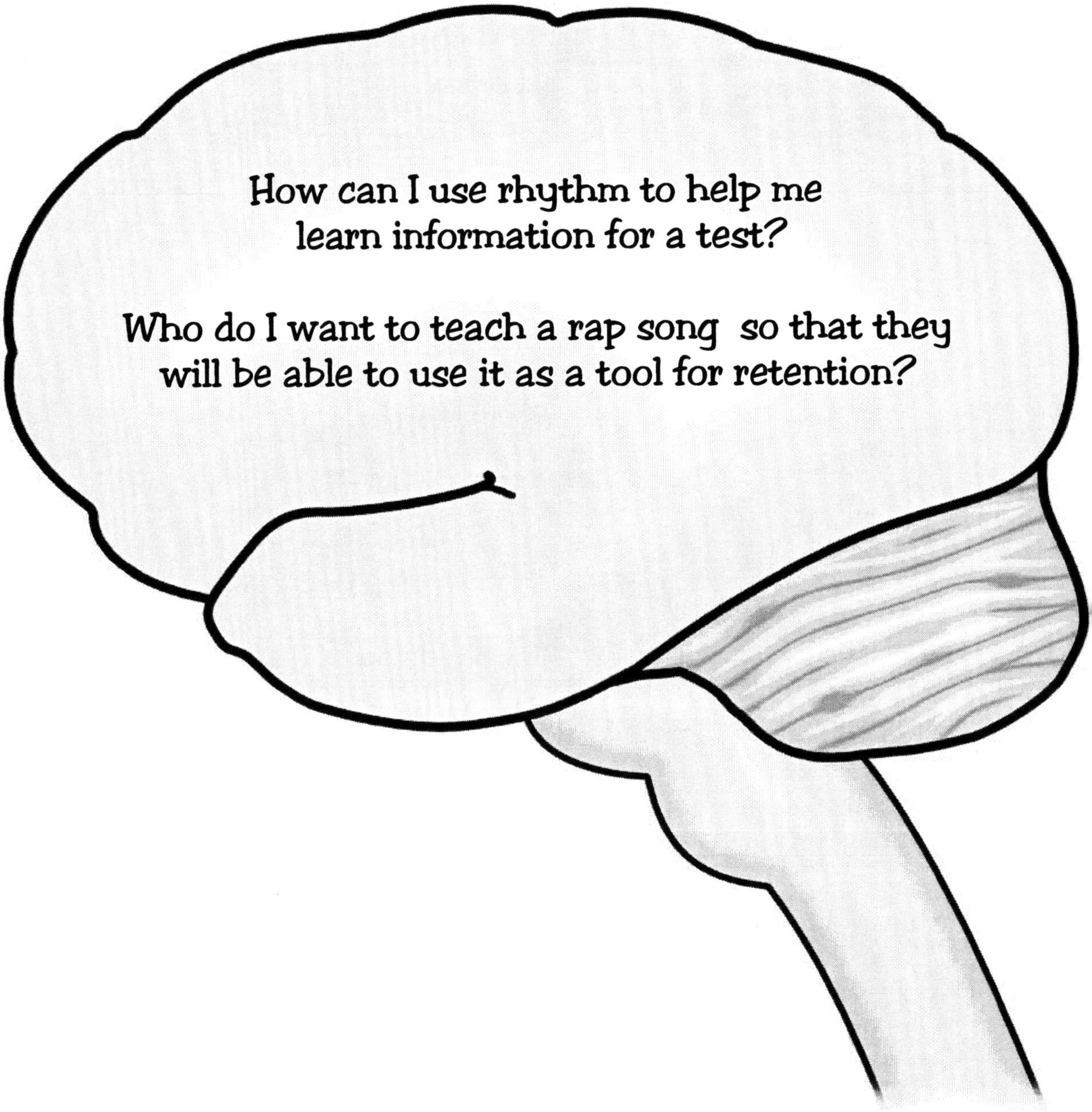

How can I use rhythm to help me
learn information for a test?

Who do I want to teach a rap song so that they
will be able to use it as a tool for retention?

The Power of Rap

Purpose: To help students understand the power of rhythm, rhyme, and rap for boosting attention and recall. It is also designed to help those students with a strong auditory-kinesthetic sense to increase their success in the classroom.

- **Step 1:** Play some rap music for your students (screen for content carefully).
- **Step 2:** Ask students why so many people like rap music.
- **Step 3:** Ask students how rap could be used to help remember information and debrief.
- **Step 4:** Get students into groups to put together their own rap around a content area that is of interest.
- **Step 5:** Present the rap to the rest of the group.
- **Step 6:** Encourage students to develop rap for the key information they want to remember.

NOTE: By using this technique you may be able to reach far more students in the class who do not respond to other forms of teaching. Once again, the act of using this technique will help students develop their overall capacity for retaining and recalling information in the future. If it feels uncomfortable for you, that's good, because it may indicate that you are flexing to reach the students who do not respond to other forms of teaching.

Why do stories help us hit the save key so that we remember?

What is one of my favorite stories that has been handed down through my family?

The Power of Stories

Purpose: To show students how using stories can significantly boost State, Meaning, Attention, Retention, and Transfer of information. Remember the phrase, "Stories stick, facts fade."

- **Step 1:** Read a story to your students or get one of the students to read the story out loud.

- **Step 2:** Ask students to discuss with each other what they remember about that story.

- **Step 3:** Debrief what has been remembered about that story.

- **Step 4:** Ask students why they believe they remember so much information in a story.

- **Step 5:** Explain some of the reasons why stories are so effective in helping us remember information. You may wish to use the metaphor of the "save" key. When we hear a story we can see it, we can animate it with movement and action, and we can vividly experience it with all our senses.

- **Step 6:** Encourage students to use stories in their own communication and for you as a teacher, model great storytelling whenever you have the opportunity.

NOTE: Research in *Scientific American* magazine showed that when high school students were exposed to information written in the *Time* format, retention increased by around 300%. The power of stories to boost learning and a love of learning is immeasurable.

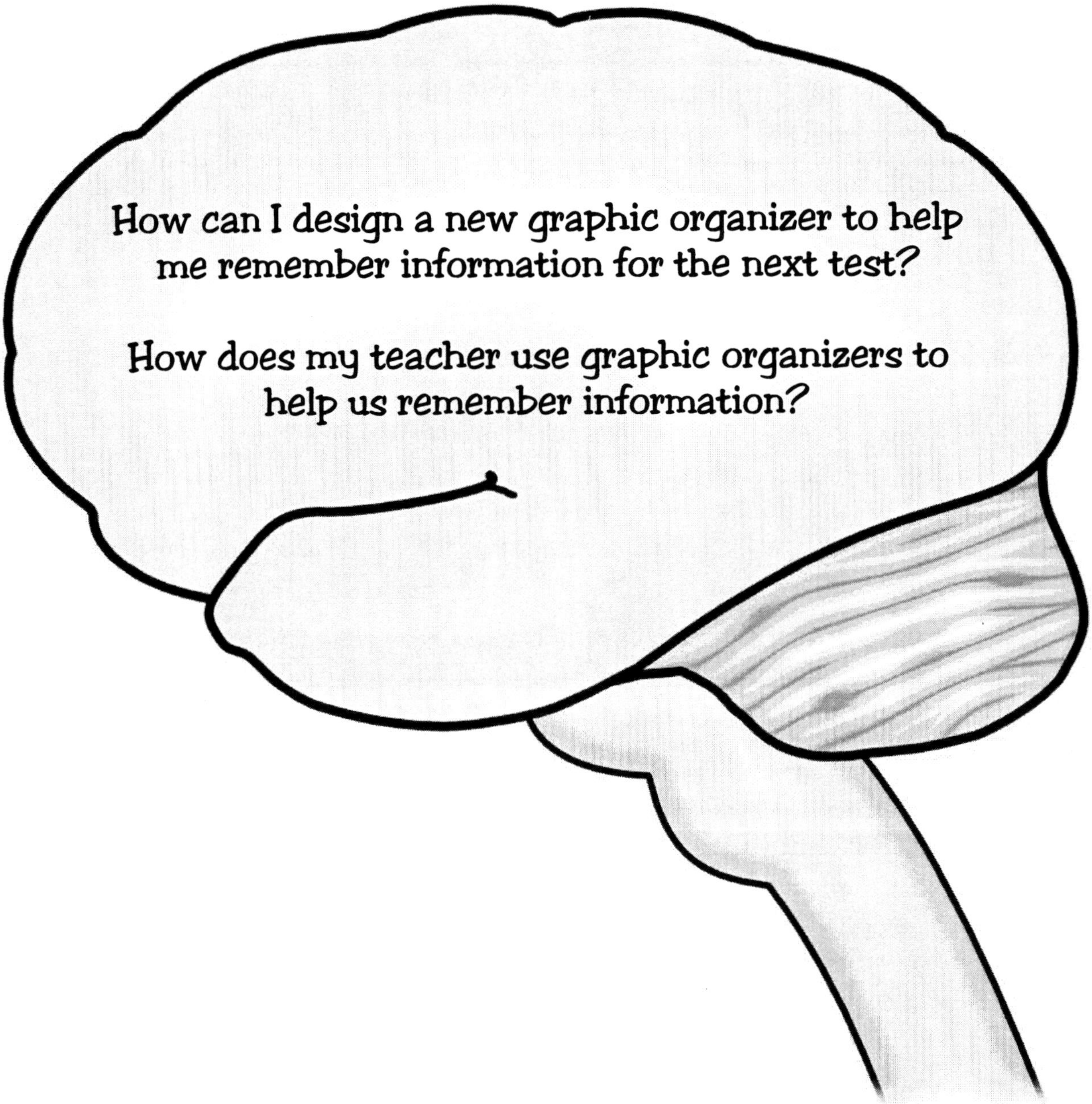

How can I design a new graphic organizer to help me remember information for the next test?

How does my teacher use graphic organizers to help us remember information?

The Power of Graphics

Purpose: To encourage students to use graphics in order to boost their State, Meaning, Attention, Retention, and Transfer of important information.

- **Step 1:** Hold out the front cover of the BrainSMART book or training manual.
- **Step 2:** Ask the students to describe what the front cover looks like.
- **Step 3:** Ask the students how long it took to describe the graphic in words compared with how quickly the eye takes in the information and instantly understands it.
- **Step 4:** Ask students why a graphic is so powerful in helping us understand and remember information and debrief their thoughts.
- **Step 5:** Use the graphics from a *USA Today* newspaper or other good magazine to illustrate the power of graphics in helping them understand.
- **Step 6:** Ask students to use Mind Maps (next Tool) as a way to use graphics to help them remember key information.

NOTE: Computer companies have spent millions of dollars using icons and graphics as a way to facilitate thinking and learning. By building more graphics into your teaching, you can greatly enhance the probability of students learning the material and enjoying it.

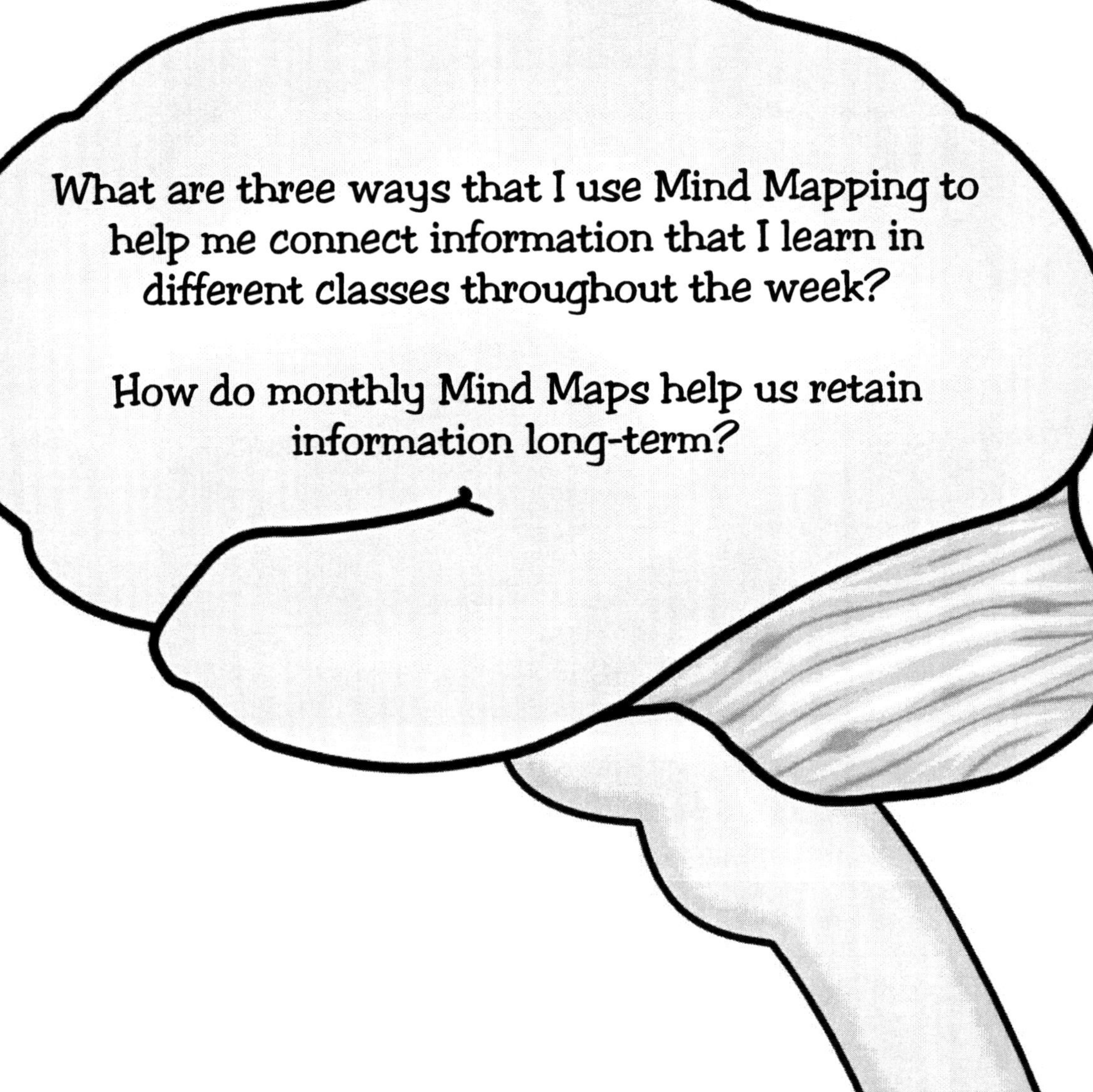
What are three ways that I use Mind Mapping to help me connect information that I learn in different classes throughout the week?
How do monthly Mind Maps help us retain information long-term?

The Power of Organizers (Mind Mapping)

Purpose: To help students tap into the potent power of mind mapping as a way to boost long-term retention and recall as well as a deeper understanding of information.

- **Step 1:** Create a mind map.
- **Step 2:** Lead the class through your mind map noticing how quickly they can grasp the information and how much they enjoy the process.
- **Step 3:** Put the mind map away and ask them what they remember about what was on the mind map.
- **Step 4:** Ask them why they remembered so much information and discuss this with the class.
- **Step 5:** Get the students into groups and get them to put together their own mind maps about the movies.
- **Step 6:** Move from group to group giving them open encouragement and helping them enjoy the process.
- **Step 7:** When the mind maps are completed, get them to present their mind maps to each other.
- **Step 8:** Ask the students if they thought this process was useful and enjoyable and ask them why.
- **Step 9:** Include mind mapping as part of your long-term teaching strategy: Ideally, mind map key information learned each day followed by a weekly mind map and a monthly mind map for use as regular review.

NOTE: See Marcus Conyers' Power Mapping Program for full details of how to create effective mind maps. Also read Tony Buzan's *The Mind Map Book*. Please note: Mind mapping is one of the most powerful processes available in the world for helping all students succeed. As of now there are more than 100 million mind mappers and many students are transforming their success in school as a result of this process.

How can I use "First Letter Cueing"
in a language class to help me remember
important facts?

What is my favorite "First Letter Cueing" device
that helps me to remember key information?

First Letter Cueing

Purpose: To equip students with a simple technique for helping them retain and recall important information.

- **Step 1:** Explain to students that the brain works in a way similar to a computer. One small piece of information can bring the whole file back.
- **Step 2:** Show students examples of how first letter cueing, which in essence cues the whole memory, have been successfully used. For example, to remember the order of musical notes use Every Good Boy Deserves Food, or for remembering how to learn SMART, use State, Meaning, Attention, Retention, Transfer.
- **Step 3:** Get students to think about any sets of first letter cueing that they know and review these in the class.
- **Step 4:** Present to your students an example of first letter cueing that you've used from your own content area. (This could be a lot of fun to do and will build a great deal of credibility with your students.)
- **Step 5:** Get students to review the content area that you are presently studying and allow them to work in groups to come up with their own first letter cueing.
- **Step 6:** Get students to present their first letter cueing to the rest of the class.
- **Step 7:** Suggest to the students on an ongoing basis to use first letter cues to aid retention and recall.

NOTE: This incredibly simple technique can help you and your students remember huge chunks of information. The real payoff comes when it is time to review what you've learned throughout the year before test taking. Have fun with this process.

Home Pegs

You can use familiar surroundings of your own home to remember even more pegs! Here are examples of objects you can use.

Kitchen
Refrigerator
Microwave
Sink
Dishwasher
Oven

Living Room
Bookshelf
Couch
Lamp
TV
Table

Bathroom
Bathtub
Toilet
Mirror
Sink
Towel Rack

Bedroom
Laundry Basket
Curtain
Picture
Bed
Wardrobe

Front Door
Rocket, to connect home list to rocket list

Exercise

1. Practice moving quickly forwards and backwards through your own personal home peg list.
2. Practice connecting your body list to your home list to your rocket list to your alphabet list.

The Power of the Open House Technique

Purpose: To give students a reliable, fun system for boosting retention and recall or getting them to understand the importance of location in learning.

- **Step 1:** Ask students what they had for lunch on Saturday.
- **Step 2:** Ask them if they first had to remember where they were in order to remember what they ate.
- **Step 3:** Highlight to students the importance of location. Explain that the way the brain remembers things is by filing them in geographical locations. So, for example, information on what they had for lunch on Saturday is stored in their memory bank in the location of wherever they were.
- **Step 4:** Explain to your students that they can remember a great deal of information by attaching that information to a familiar location.
- **Step 5:** Use the example of their home or the classroom. (If you use the example of home see the attached open house lesson.)
- **Step 6:** Ask the students to pick five areas in their home or classroom and to think about them and to imagine moving around their home or classroom to each of those locations. For example if they move to the kitchen they move from the refrigerator, to the microwave, to the sink, to the dishwasher, to the oven.
- **Step 7:** Now get them to visualize a list of items. For example on the refrigerator put an orange, on the microwave put a monkey, on the sink put the Titanic, on the dishwasher put a book, on the oven put a one dollar bill.
- **Step 8:** Help the students to imagine clearly, in great detail, those different items in those different locations.
- **Step 9:** Ask the students to play back to you what they remember.
- **Step 10:** You may wish to break down your key content into 20 component areas. Create a mental picture that represents each component and help students memorize the location and information.

NOTE: Once again, this technique can really transform students' self-perception in terms of intelligence. The system uses the brain's natural ability to remember information in an easy and effortless way. The time it takes to store this information will pay great dividends when it comes time for testing for that information.

Visual Pegs
Your Rocket List

Number	Peg	Association
1	Rocket	1 looks like a rocket ready for launch
2	Duck	2 looks like a duck
3	Triangle	A triangle has three sides
4	Horse	A horse has four legs
5	Hand	A hand has five fingers
6	Phone	6 looks like a phone
7	Boomerang	7 looks like a boomerang
8	Hourglass	8 looks like an hourglass
9	Cloud	Cloud 9
10	Knife & Plate	10 looks like a knife and plate
11	Chopsticks	11 looks like chopsticks
12	Roses	A dozen roses
13	Black Cat	Bad luck
14	Valentines	February 14 is Valentine's Day
15	Tax Return	Yours is due on the 15th
16	Sugar	Sweet sixteen
17	Magazine	Seventeen is a magazine
18	Voting Booth	When you're 18, you're old enough to vote
19	Teenager Waving	A 19-year old waves goodbye to the teen years
20	Spectacles	Spectacles give you 20/20 vision

Exercise

In your mind's eye run forwards and backwards through your rocket list.

The Power of the Rocket List

Purpose: To equip students with a simple tool for remembering 20 critical pieces of information. Secondary benefit is to sustain focused attention.

- **Step 1:** Give your students a list of 20 things to remember. (See the attached.)
- **Step 2:** Ask students to write that list of 20 things in order.
- **Step 3:** Ask students how they did.
- **Step 4:** Help students use their imagination to remember the rocket list attached.
- **Step 5:** After they've memorized the rocket list, help them use their imagination to link the list to the new information they want to remember. For example, if the first item you'd like them remember is cheese, get them to imagine the rocket flying to the moon and landing on a huge cheese that is the moon.
- **Step 6:** Once again give the students the list of objects to remember and ask them to use the rocket list to retain that information.
- **Step 7:** Review how many items they remembered.

NOTE: After the rocket list is committed to memory, it can significantly boost the students' self-confidence. Once again, it would make sense to break your material down into around 20 critical components that you would like the students to remember.

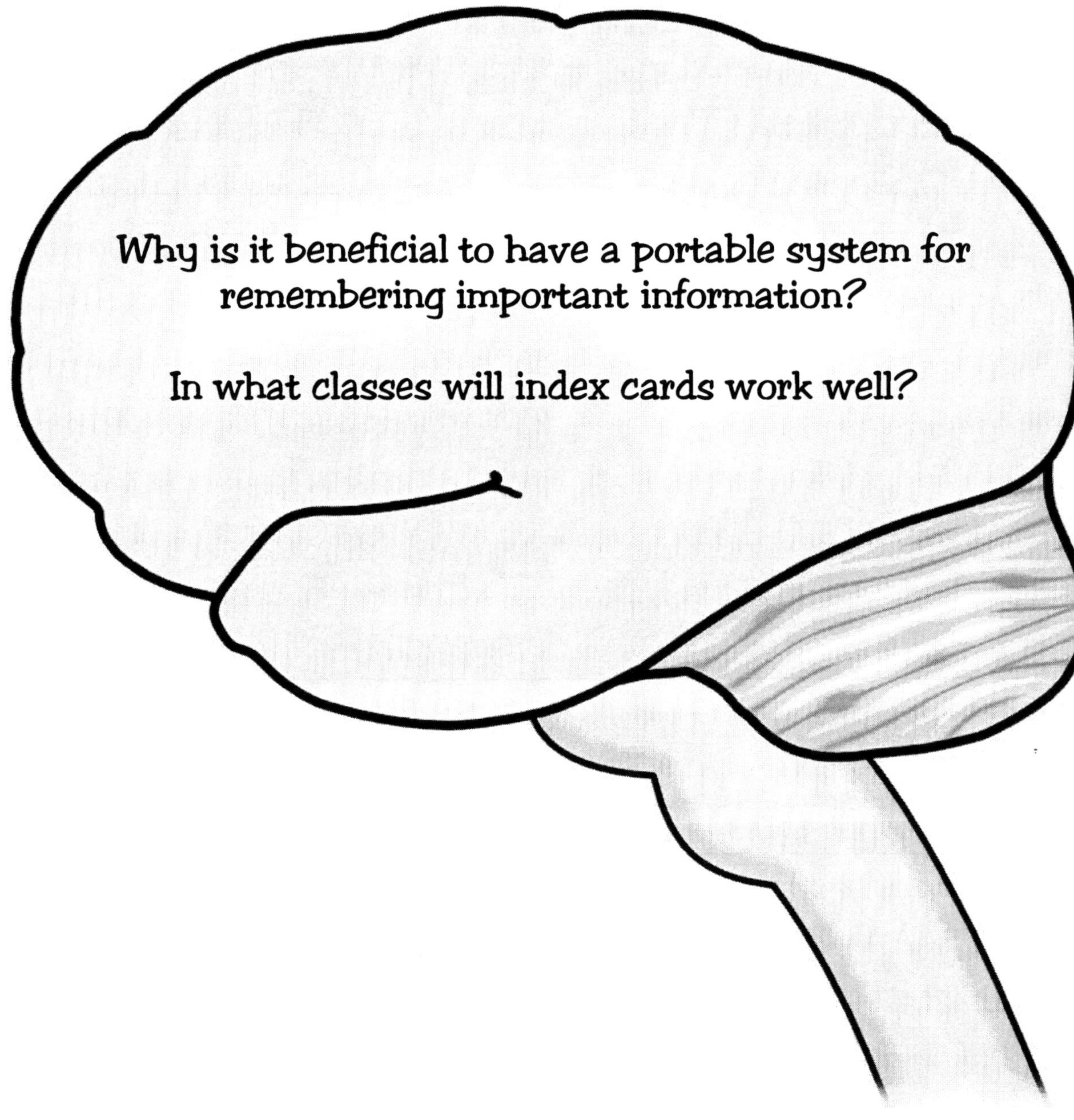
Why is it beneficial to have a portable system for remembering important information?
In what classes will index cards work well?

The Power of Index Cards

Purpose: To equip students with a portable system for reviewing, retaining, and recalling important information.

- **Step 1:** Insure you have a good quantity of index cards.

- **Step 2:** Write on one side of the index cards a piece of information you'd like the students to remember and on the other side write a question that relates to it. For example, on one side of the card you might write, "The American Civil War started in 1861." On the other side of the card you might write, "In what year did the American Civil War start?"

- **Step 3:** Get students to begin to create their own index cards of information you would like them to learn.

- **Step 4:** Explain to students that they can carry the index cards with them and whenever they have the opportunity on the bus or some other time of the day they can just go through their index cards.

- **Step 5:** Help students understand the benefit of this system. As soon as they know information they delete that index card from their deck. For example, once they know the American Civil War started in 1861, they no longer keep it in their deck.

- **Step 6:** On an ongoing basis help students create learning decks for all the key information you would like them to learn.

NOTE: This simple and powerful learning system puts students in the driving seat in terms of how quickly they learn information. The act of writing the cards does a great deal to load them into their memory bank.

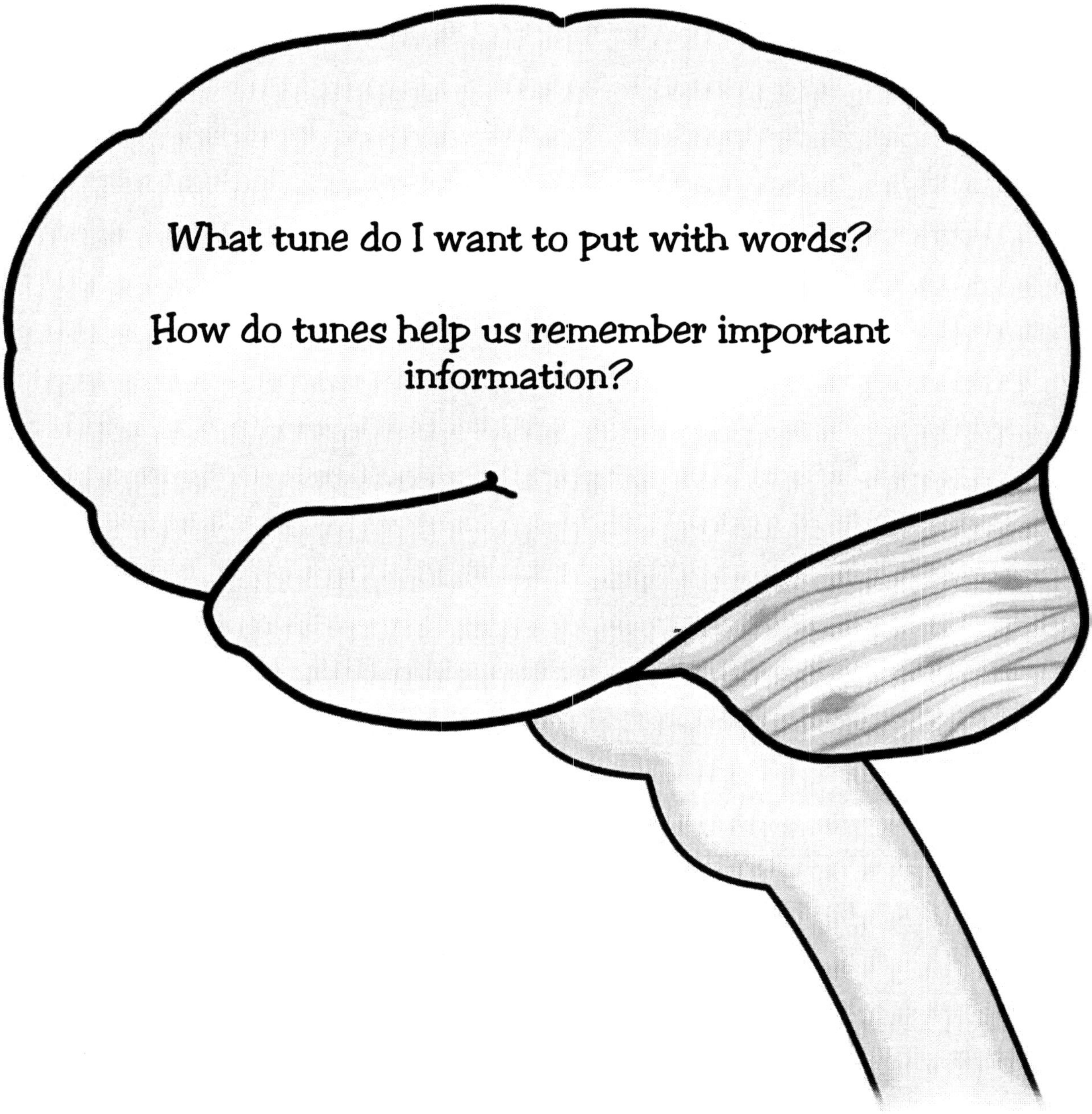

What tune do I want to put with words?

How do tunes help us remember important information?

The Power of Tunes

Purpose: To help students understand how music and tunes can help them remember important information.

- **Step 1:** Play the "Twinkle, Twinkle, Little Star" music.
- **Step 2:** Start to sing the alphabet song.
- **Step 3:** Notice how many of your students continue this after you stop.
- **Step 4:** Ask students why they think information is so well remembered by tunes and debrief.
- **Step 5:** Sing to students the BrainSMART song, (to the tune of "If I Only Had A Brain," which is this: "Brain stem and cerebellum are really quite reptilian in your brain and hypothalamus, and thalamus are in your limbic brain. Neocortex and cerebrum are good for higher thinking in your higher brain. This idea was put together by a very clever fella Dr. Paul McClain."
- **Step 6:** Work with your students to put together a song about some critical information that you would like them to remember.
- **Step 7:** On an ongoing basis return to memory songs you've created.

NOTE: Enjoy using the power of music and tunes to help students learn. It not only boosts retention, but boosts state in a positive way.

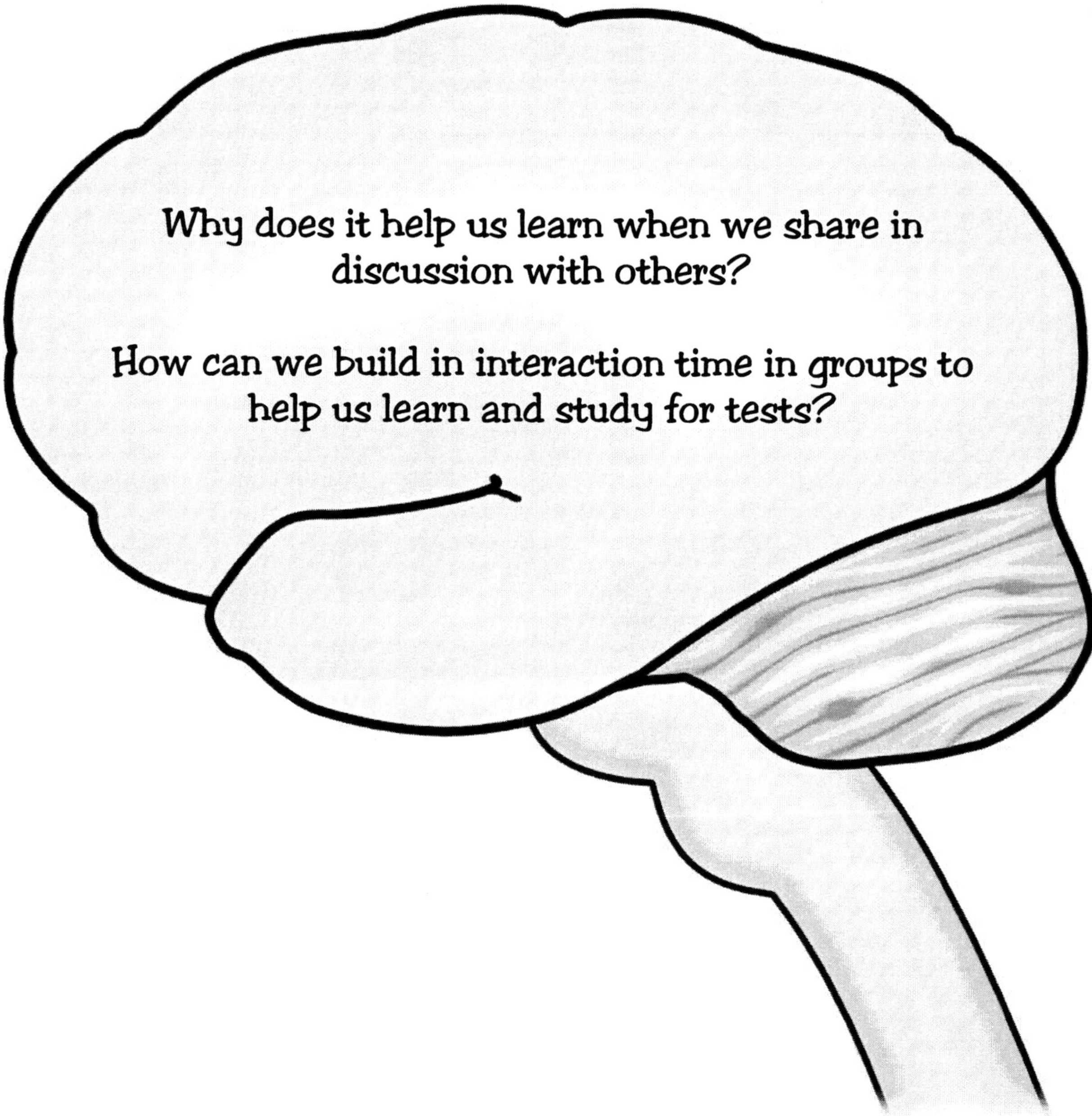

Why does it help us learn when we share in discussion with others?

How can we build in interaction time in groups to help us learn and study for tests?

Partner Share/Reflect Pair Share

Purpose: To have a very quick (if needed) and easy way to build in interaction time, much needed for learning.

- **Step 1:** Pairs may either be chosen by the teacher or students may pair off at their tables

- **Step 2:** In their pairs, students share information relative to the topic. If reflection time is needed, ask students to reflect for a set amount of time and jot down important points from this time

- **Step 3:** This is effective as an exercise timed for approximately 2-15 minutes.

NOTE: We generally use the Partner Share for short exchanges (2-5 minutes in length). There are two key factors that ensure effective Partner Shares:

1. Make sure the students understand and practice sharing when both partners have opportunity to speak.
2. Build in accountability in the Partner Share by asking students to use information gained in the Partner Share.

This is also a great tool to turn into a Nature Walk in partnership when the weather is beautiful outside. It allows the pairs to have the partnership activity in the beauty of nature while walking. Allow a little bit more time (15 minutes or so) for this one, or have students do a Nature Walk at lunch when appropriate.

10 BrainSMART Tools For Transfer

How can the "Success Seat" help me
score better on the next test?
Are there other times I need to use
"Success Seat"?

Success Seat

Purpose: To help students delete negative failure files and build positive success files and improve test-taking performance.

- **Step 1:** Ask students if they've ever sat down to take a test and forgot everything.
- **Step 2:** Listen to their replies and notice how often 80% to 90% of students have experienced this.
- **Step 3:** Reassure students that there are some simple things that they can do to improve their memory during test taking.
- **Step 4:** Get students to physically take all of the old torture test seats where they failed before out of the classroom.
- **Step 5:** When they're out of the classroom get them to dust down those failure seats and bring back success seats.
- **Step 6:** After students bring back the success seats use a combination of the tools from the retention toolbox to insure they all succeed.
- **Step 7:** Get them to anchor this success with the "I feel good!" "Yes!" system.

NOTE: The more we can do to get students to delete their failure files and fill their success files the higher level of achievement they will achieve.

How can we use "Quick Maps" to help us perform well on tests?

Quick Mapping

Purpose: To use as a technique for students to break through the fear barrier when they take tests

- **Step 1:** Arrange a mock test for your students.
- **Step 2:** Demonstrate to students how they could do a quick map of everything they remember on the topic before starting the test.
- **Step 3:** Explain that a quick map is simply a process where you dump the key information on the topic onto a mind map before you start answering any questions.
- **Step 4:** Ask students how it might be useful to do a quick map before they started a test.
- **Step 5:** Review their answers and give additional feedback that this technique allows them to break through the fear barrier and gets their minds focused on what they do know rather than what they don't know.
- **Step 6:** Now give the students a test and observe how they do their own quick maps.
- **Step 7:** On an ongoing basis get students to do quick maps during mock tests.

NOTE: By getting students familiar with this process they may be able to greatly reduce test anxiety; furthermore, they will be used to accessing those states of moderate stress and will therefore be able to access more information at test taking time

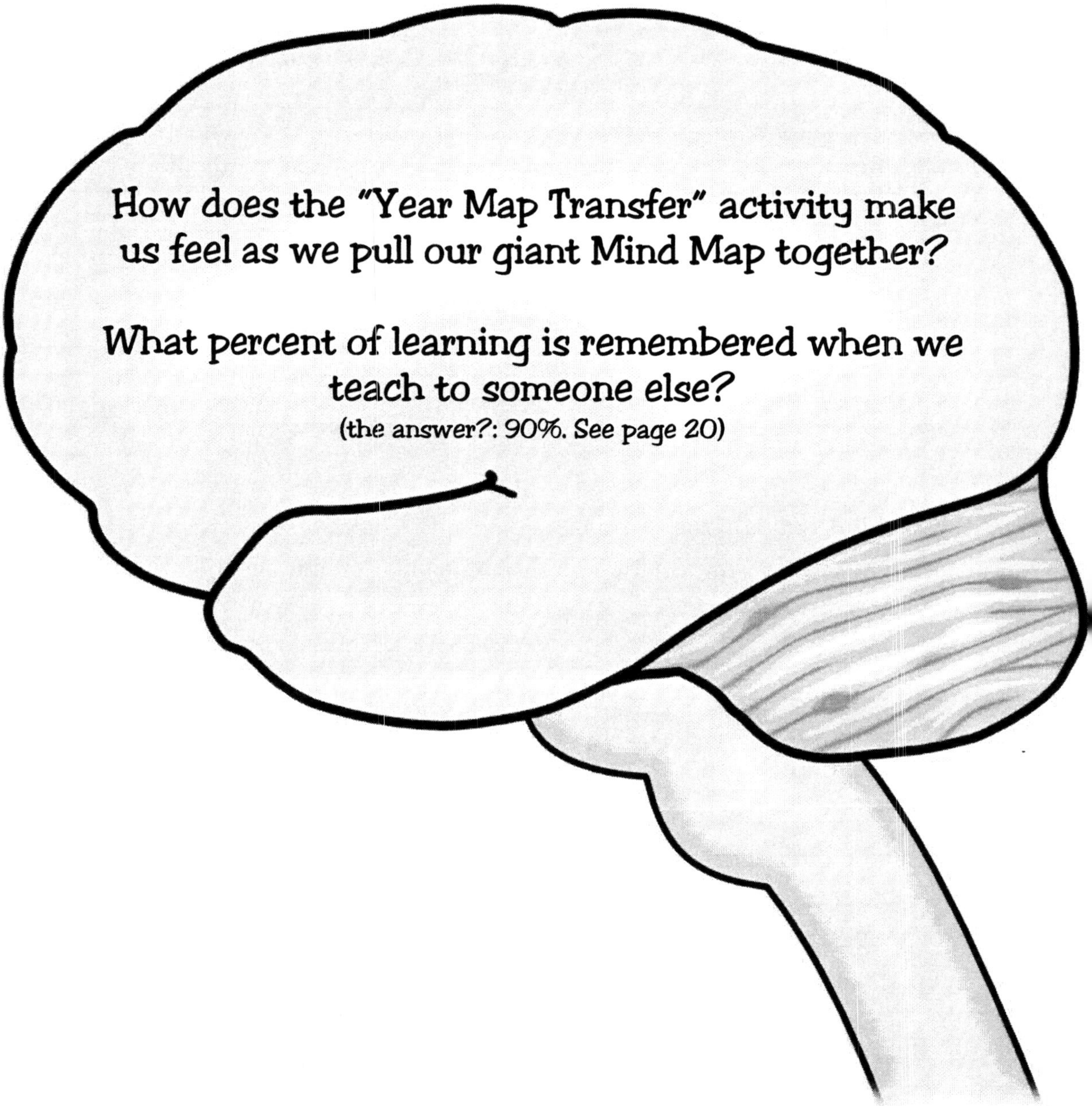

How does the "Year Map Transfer" activity make us feel as we pull our giant Mind Map together?

What percent of learning is remembered when we teach to someone else?
(the answer?: 90%. See page 20)

Year Map Transfer

Purpose: To help students coming into a new year to build confidence that they will succeed

- **Step 1:** As you approach the end of the year with your students announce there is an exciting project for them.
- **Step 2:** Let students know that what you're going to do is to create a giant mind map of everything they've learned about your topic.
- **Step 3:** Get student groups to work on a specific part of the year's curriculum.
- **Step 4:** Then assemble the giant mind map (made up of a collection of the group mind maps) ideally on the left hand wall of a classroom.
- **Step 5:** Now ask each student in turn to present one part of the map.
- **Step 6:** Have a rehearsal.
- **Step 7:** Then invite the new class that you will be teaching to come and be taught by your current class.

NOTE: This simple exercise can do much to help students feel good about what they've already learned; furthermore, incoming students can get to see the big picture and see real evidence that students can learn at this. It will also make you feel very good knowing that the information has really been retained. This is a great exercise to do before test time as a way for really locking in the belief that students can succeed.

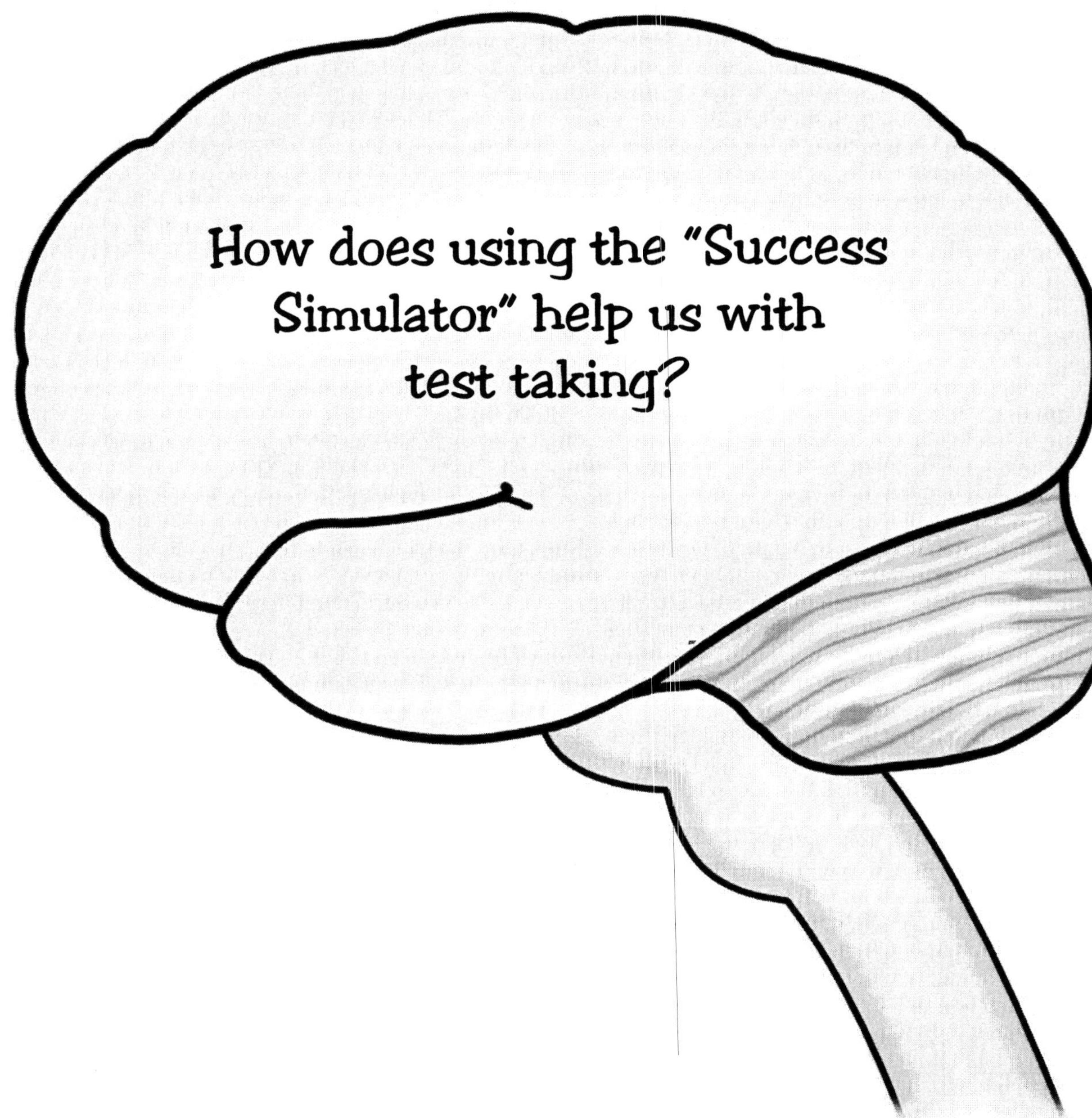
How does using the "Success Simulator" help us with test taking?

Success Simulator

Purpose: To help students practice effective transfer of knowledge in a way that will boost test performance.

- **Step 1:** Ask students if they've ever sat down to take a test and forgotten everything.
- **Step 2:** Identify a time in your life when the same thing happened to you.
- **Step 3:** Ask students if they would like a way to remember information better when they take a test.
- **Step 4:** Explain that airline pilots practice in flight simulators to get really good at flying and that students can use the power of their imagination to create a success simulator when they take tests.
- **Step 5:** Get students to practice the following ritual: (1) Start with the "I feel good! Yes!" exercise, (2) Sit in your seat, (3) Shake the stress from your shoulders, (4) Take a deep breath and relax, (5) See yourself remembering all the information you need to do well on the test.
- **Step 6:** Repeat this exercise frequently with your students.

NOTE: Many students who do not succeed well in test taking are rehearsing failure over and over again until it becomes a self-fulfilling prophecy. By using the success simulator you can greatly improve their chances of succeeding.

What BrainSMART Tools have I
used over the past three days to improve my
retention?

Who do I know that can benefit from knowing
how to use these three tools?
Teach them.

The BrainSMART Carousel

Purpose: To help students appreciate the five key components of effective learning.

- **Step 1:** Put five pieces of flip chart paper around the room. One is marked STATE, one MEANING, one ATTENTION, one RETENTION, and one TRANSFER.

- **Step 2:** Select one or two of your favorite tools from the training manual and write them up on the charts.

- **Step 3:** Explain to students that you want them to explore all the different ways in which they can improve their learning in terms of improving state, making learning meaningful, helping them pay attention, helping them to remember information, and helping them to transfer it during a test.

- **Step 5:** Let the students begin to work in groups. Each group will stand by one of the sheets and begin to write anything that comes to mind on the topic.

- **Step 6:** After the students have written on one sheet, they then move to the next until all the students have attended each of the five SMART stations.

- **Step 7:** Then get students to review all the different tools that they could use to improve learning.

NOTE: This is a great technique to use after a few weeks of teaching the BrainSMART way. It will give you great feedback as to the tools they've seen you using and it will give you a wealth of ideas of how to make your teaching even more effective.

BrainSMART® *Lesson Planner*

State	Meaning	Attention	Retention	Transfer
Getting students into positive low stress \ high challenge states	Making learning meaningful and relevant to learner	Sustaining focused learner attention followed by downtime and feedback	Using multiple strategies for facilitating natural memory	Facilitating transfer of information learned to real life and test taking

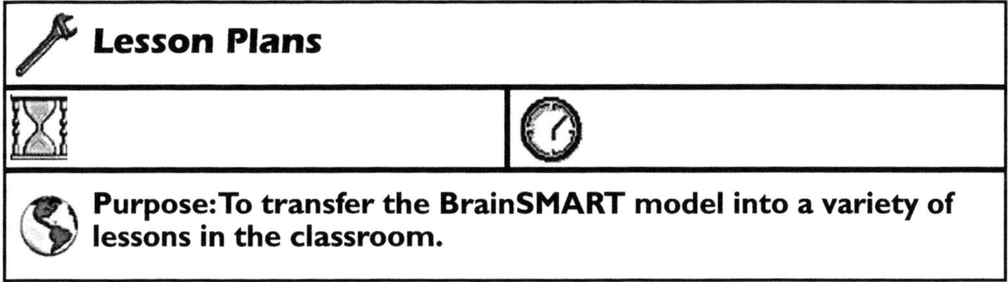

- **Step 1:** Now that you have the road map of the BrainSMART model, and a toolbox of strategies at your disposal, here is a BIG tool for lesson planning. The lesson planning chart is designed to be simple. You begin by merely adding whichever tools you find most useful into your existing routine, so that you become comfortable with them. The more tools you explore, the more students you'll begin to reach in your classroom. Remember, only one student in six, about 15%, learn best through traditional teaching. By planning your lesson around how the brain learns best, you can reach more students more of the time, and reduce burnout and stress at the same time.

- **Step 2:** You may find that you use more tools in one part of the model than in others. For example, creating possibilities for retention can be enhanced by using multiple retention strategies. In areas such as transfer, you may use fewer tools overall, but find that the same tools are consistently effective.

- **Step 3:** Also use the Future Map as a way to incorporate BrainSMART into future plans for the year. The Future Map is a tool that can be used to develop plans in any important area.

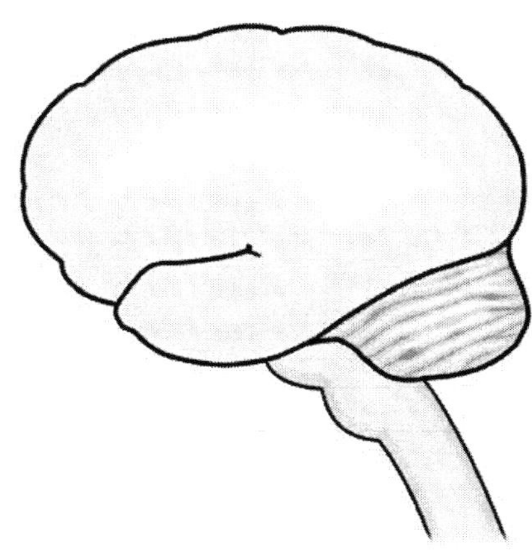

A Question for Students

How can I organize my homework so that I ensure correct completion?

Is my organizational system working so that I am making good grades? If not, how can I modify to ensure maximum benefit?

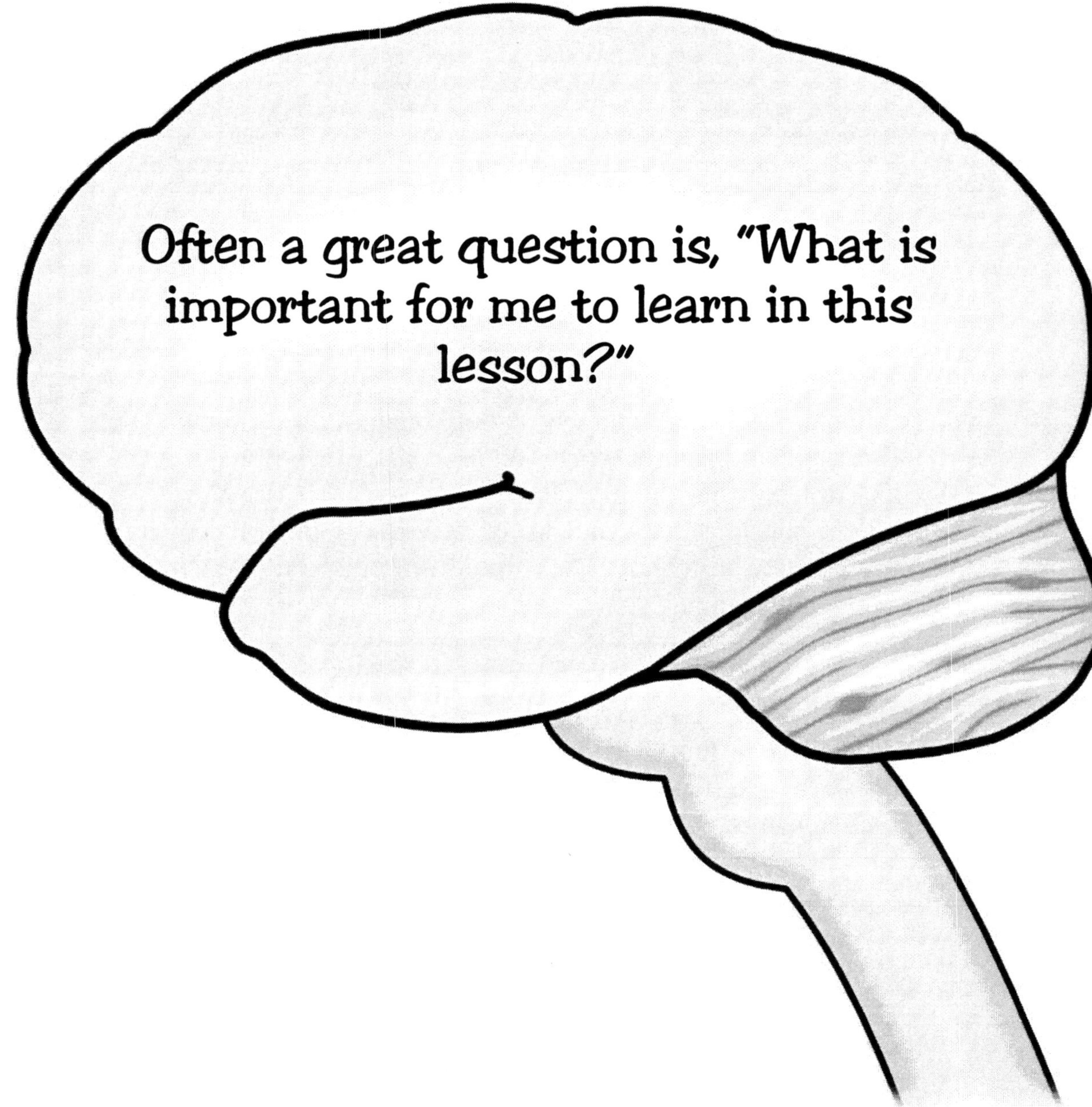
Often a great question is, "What is important for me to learn in this lesson?"

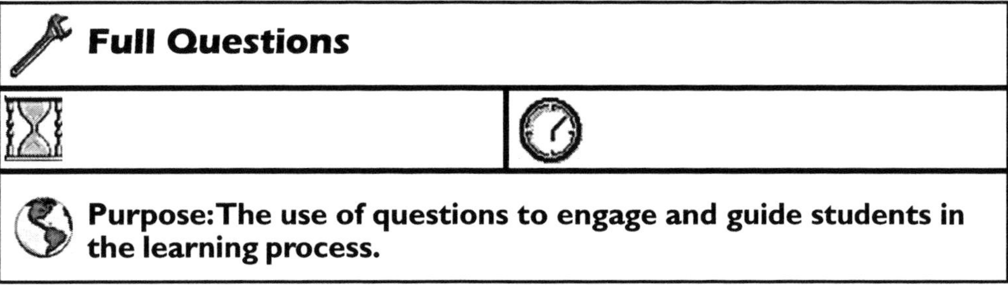

Full Questions

Purpose: The use of questions to engage and guide students in the learning process.

- **Step 1:** This tool is a powerful teacher skill that will help guide your students' learning.

- **Step 2:** To guide students to greater depth of understanding, ask full or broad questions.

- **Step 3:** These "full questions" are often How and Why questions that allow for student elaboration.

- **Step 4:** For maximum transfer allow students time to respond to the full questions with many examples from their lives. We know that the application to many diverse situations is what greatly aids transfer. For example, when studying the 20/80 Principle, (next page), we might ask "How can we use this powerful principle in our lives?"

NOTE: This technique has been used by many teachers through the years. A few among these users are Socrates, Vygotsky, and Feuerstein.

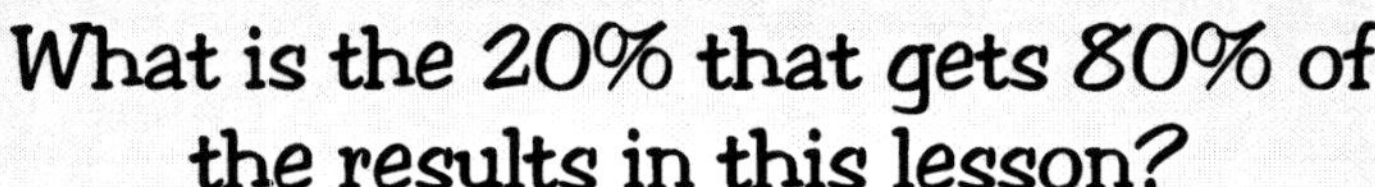
What is the 20% that gets 80% of
the results in this lesson?
For example, as I read this book, what is the 20% that gets 80% of the results? That is, what is the most important part of the book, or the part I want to remember?

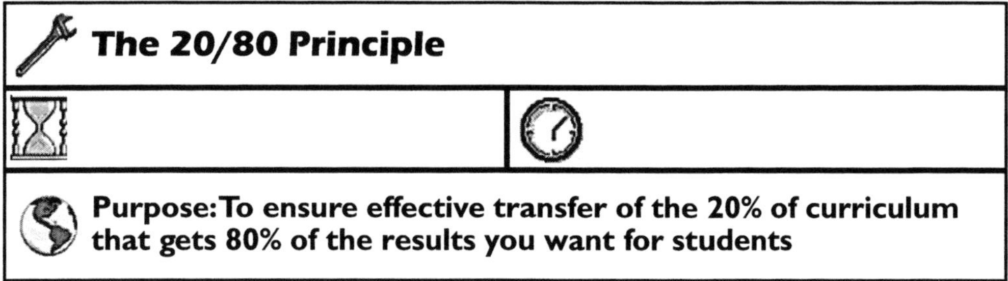

The 20/80 Principle

Purpose: To ensure effective transfer of the 20% of curriculum that gets 80% of the results you want for students

- **Step 1:** For centuries humankind has known that a few inputs produce most outputs and a few causes produce most consequences.
  For example, consider the following:
  20% of a book has 80% of the key ideas,
  20% of criminals account for 80% of the crime,
  20% of a journey to work causes 80% of delays,
  20% of what is remembered for a test is remembered two years later while 80% is forgotten.

- **Step 2:** For effective transfer to take place it is essential to focus on the 20% of curriculum that gets 80% of the results.

- **Step 3:** Dialogue with colleagues around the following question: What is the 20% that gets 80% of the results?

NOTE: By focusing on the 20% that gets you 80% of results you can reduce stress and burnout.

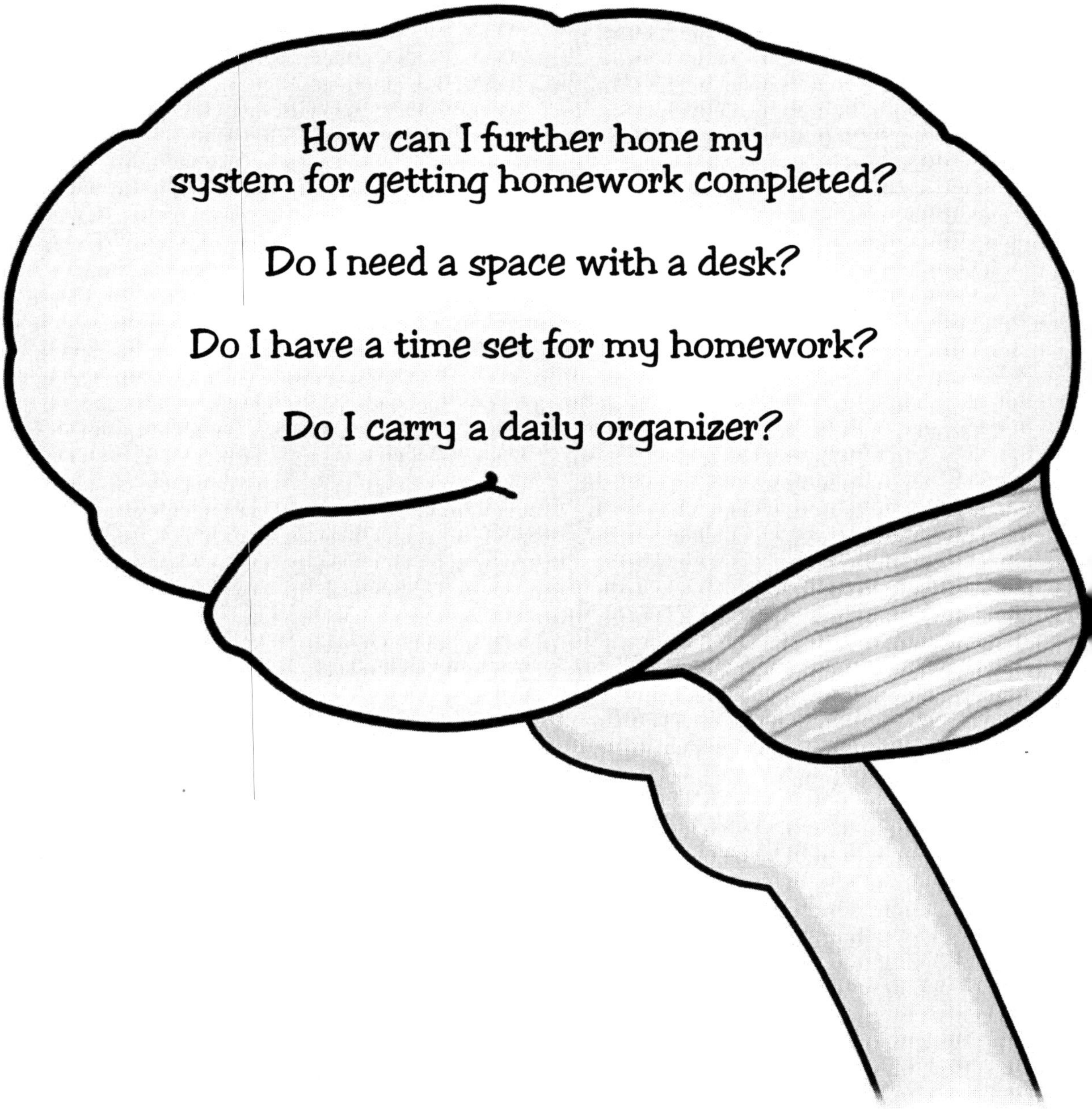

How can I further hone my
system for getting homework completed?

Do I need a space with a desk?

Do I have a time set for my homework?

Do I carry a daily organizer?

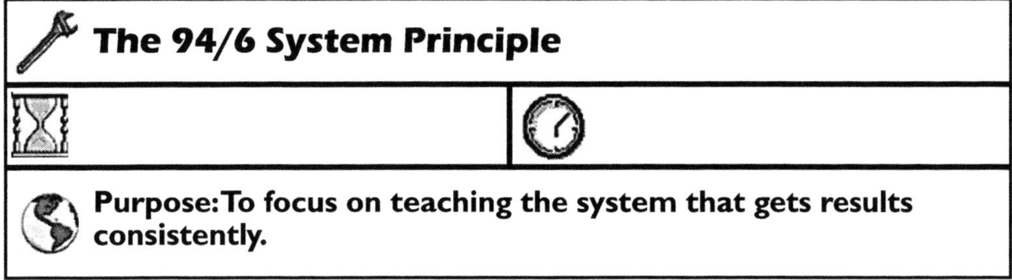

The 94/6 System Principle

Purpose: To focus on teaching the system that gets results consistently.

- **Step 1:** Quality expert W. E. Deming discovered during 60 years of consulting that 6% of problems and opportunities are caused by special events and 94% are caused by the system.

- **Step 2:** Ask this question; What is my system for creating the following in my classroom:
  State,
  Meaning,
  Attention,
  Retention,
  Transfer.

- **Step 3:** Focus your energy on constantly improving the system of instruction you are using.

NOTE: If students don't listen, teach them a system for listening. If they don't remember, teach them a system for remembering.

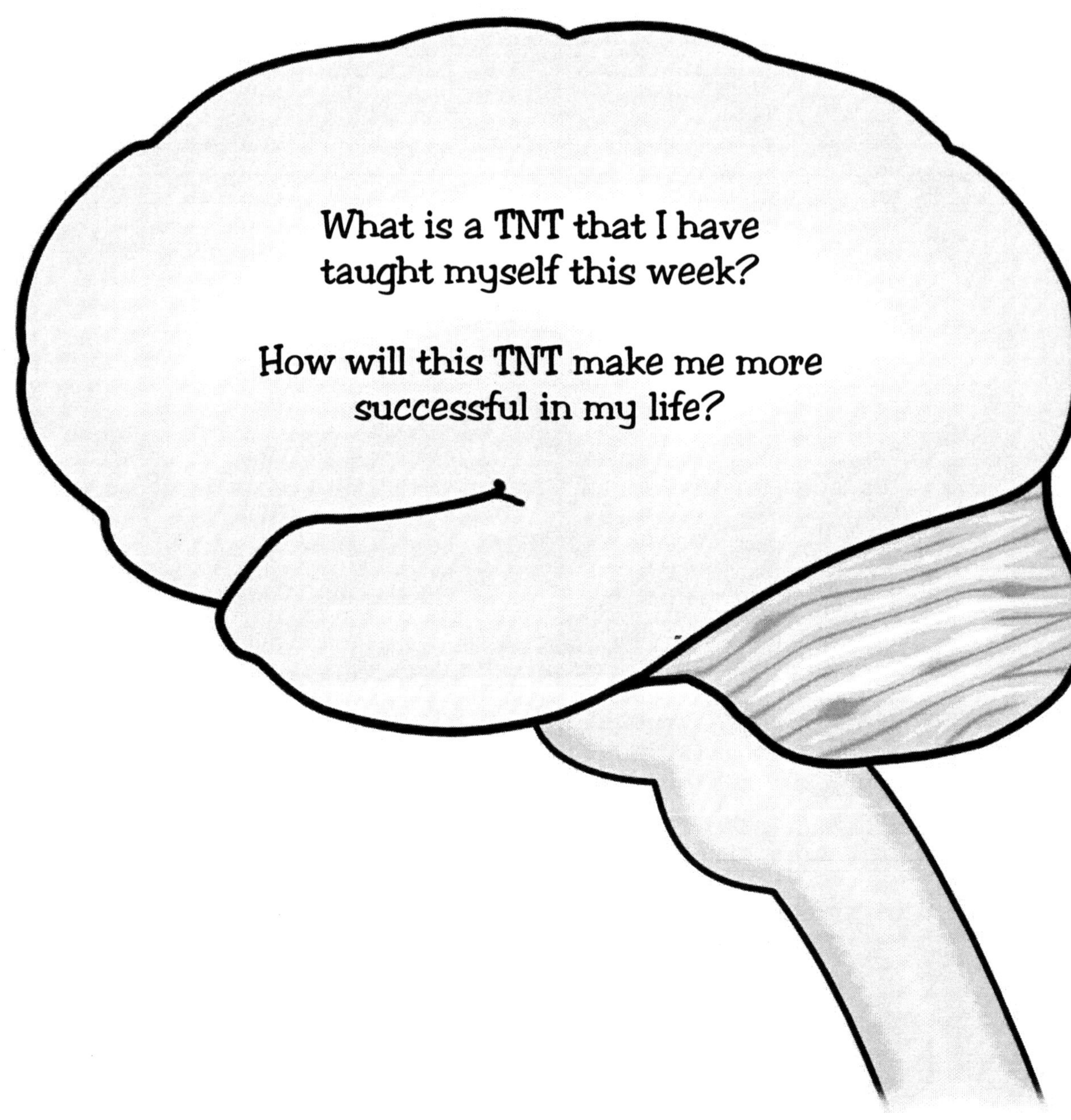
What is a TNT that I have
taught myself this week?
How will this TNT make me more
successful in my life?

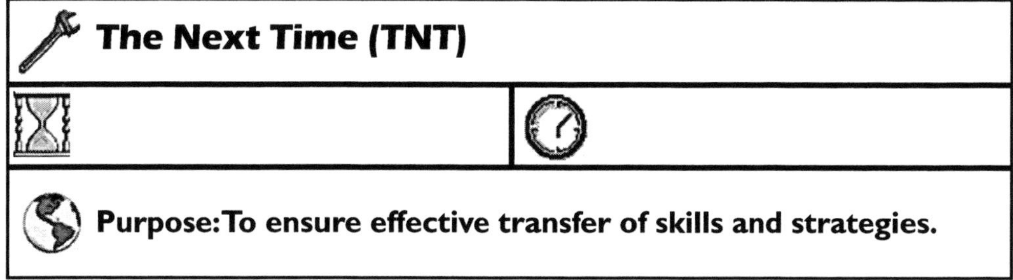

- **Step 1:** The Next Time (TNT) is a dynamic idea for changing behavior.

- **Step 2:** When you find yourself frustrated about making mistakes, stop. Deal with the situation at hand and say, "The next time I will..." See yourself doing something different. Notice how you feel about it. Make it real.

- **Step 3:** Practice this process over and over again until it becomes automatic.

- **Step 4:** Use this system with your students to help them create change.

NOTE: Research suggests that little time is spent specifically working on TNTs. It is a powerful way to make a difference.

References and Resources for Further Learning

Adams, P. (1998). *Gesundheit!* Rochester, VT: Healing Arts Press.

Amen, D. (1998). *Change your brain change your life.* New York: Random House.

Amen, D. (2001). *Healing ADD: The breakthrough program that allows you to see and heal the 6 types of ADD.* New York: Putnam.

Amen, D. & Routh, L. (2003). *Healing anxiety and depression.* New York: Putnam.

Applin, D. (2004). *Medical physiology.* Cambridge, England: Cambridge University Press.

Arnot, R. (2000). *The biology of success.* New York: Little Brown.

Ayres, A. (1972). *Sensory integration and learning disorders.* Los Angeles: Western Psychological Services.

Bandler, R. (1985). *Using your brain for a change.* Moab, UT: Real People Press.

Bellanca, J., & Wilson, D. (1998). *Mediated learning in and out of the classroom.* Arlington Heights, IL: Skylight.

Benson, H. (1997). *Timeless healing.* New York: Simon-Schuster.

Berg, H., & Conyers, M. (1997). *Speed reading the easy way.* New York: Barrons.

Bensen, H., & Proctor, W. (2003). *The break-out principle.* New York: Scribner.

Berliner, D., & Casanova, G. (1996). *Putting research to work in your school.* Arlington Heights, IL: Skylight.

Bernstein, J. (2004). *Before it happens to you: A breakthrough program for reversing or preventing heart disease.* Cambridge, MA.: Perseus Books.

Blades, J. (2000). *Action based learning: Linking movement to learning.* Paper presented at Eric Jensen's Learning Brain Expo 2000, San Diego, CA.

Bloom, F., Beal, M., & Kupfer, D. (Eds.) (2003). *The Dana guide to brain health.* New York: Free Press.

Bragdon, A., & Gamon, D. (1999). *Building left-brain power.* Bass River, MA: Allen Bragdon.

Bragdon, A. & Gamon, D. (2003). *Use it or lose it! How to keep your brain fit as it ages.* New York: Walker & Company.

The brain, the mind, and the classroom. (Cassette recording No. 1 & No. 2). (1996). Alexandria, VA: Association for Supervision and Curriculum Development.

Bransford, J., Brown, A., & Cocking, R. (Eds.). (1999). *How people learn: Brain, mind, experience, and school.* Washington, DC: National Academy Press.

Brewer, C., & Campbell, D. (1991). *Rhythms of learning: Creative tools for developing lifelong skills.* Tucson, AZ: Zephyr Press.

Bruner, J. (1966). *Toward a theory of instruction.* Cambridge, MA: Belknap Press.

Buzan, T. (1983) *Use both sides of your brain.* New York: Dutton.

Caine, G., & Caine, R. (1997). *Education on the edge of possibility.* Alexandria, VA: Association for Supervision and Curriculum Development.

Caine, R., & Caine, G. (1991). *Making connections: Teaching and the human brain.* Alexandria, VA: Association for Supervision and Curriculum Development.

Campbell, D. (1992). *100 ways to improve your teaching using your voice and music.* Tucson, AZ: Zephyr Press.

Carper, J. (2000). *Your miracle brain.* New York: Harper-Collins.

Carter, R. (1998). *Mapping the mind.* Los Angeles: University of California Press.

Casey, A. & Benson, H. (2004). *Harvard medical school mind your heart: A mind/body approach to stress management, exercise, and nutrition for heart health.* New York: Free Press.

Childre, D. (1998). *Freeze frame: A scientifically proven technique for clear decision making and improved health.* Boulder Creek, CO: Planetary Publications.

Childre, D., Martin, H., & Beech, D. (1999). *The heartmath solution.* New York: Harper-Collins.

Conners, C. (1989). *Feeding the brain.* Reading, MA: Perseus Books.

Conyers, M. & Wilson, D. (2001). *Boosting attention – improving metacognition.* (Video recording). Orlando, FL: Video Magic.

Conyers, M. & Wilson, D. (2001). *Gateways to learning: Perception, senses & emotion.* (Video recording). Orlando, FL: Video Magic.

Conyers, M. & Wilson, D. (2001). *Increasing retention and recall.* (Video recording). Orlando, FL: Video Magic.

Conyers, M. & Wilson, D. (2001). *Introduction to the BrainSMART Model™* (CD recording). Orlando, FL: Video Magic.

Conyers, M. & Wilson, D. (2001). *Teaching for meaning.* .(Video recording). Orlando, FL: Video Magic.

Conyers, M. & Wilson, D. (2001). *Teaching to strengths: How to R.E.A.D. and reach your students.* (Video recording). Orlando, FL: Video Magic.

Conyers, M. & Wilson, D. (2001). *The body brain system: Leaner body sharper mind.* . (Video recording). Orlando, FL: Video Magic.

Conyers, M., & Wilson, D. (2001). *Science of learning and the brain.* (CD recording). Orlando, FL: Video Magic.

Conyers, M. & Wilson, D. (2001). *Six master cylinders for high student achievement.* (CD recording). Orlando, FL: Video Magic.

Cooper, P., (1998). *Effective teaching and learning.* Buckingham, England: Open University Press.

Cooper, P., & Bilton, K. (Eds.). (1999). *ADHD: Research, practice, and opinion.* London: Whurr.

Costa, A. (Ed.) (1991). *Developing minds: Programs for teaching thinking* (Vols. 1-2). Alexandria, VA: Association of Supervision and Curriculum Development.

Covey, S. (1989). *The seven habits of highly effective people.* New York: Simon-Schuster.

Crick, F. (1994). *The astonishing hypothesis.* New York: Touchstone Simon-Schuster.

Csikszentmihalyi, M. (1990). *Flow: The psychology of optimal experience.* New York: Harper-Row.

Damasio, A. (1994). *Descartes' error.* New York: Putnam's Sons.

Damasio, A. (1999). *The feeling of what happens.* Orlando, FL: Harcourt.

Deming, W. (1994). *The new economics for industry, government, and education.* Cambridge, MA: MIT Press.

Dewey, J. (1938). *Experience and education.* New York: Collier.

Dennison, P., & Dennison, G. (1994). *Brain gym: Teachers' edition.* Ventura, CA: Edu-Kinesthetics.

Diamond, M. (1988). *Enriching heredity: The impact of the environment on the anatomy of the brain.* New York: Free Press.

Diamond, M., & Hopson, J. (1998). *Magic trees of the mind: How to nurture your child's intelligence, creativity, and healthy emotions from birth through adolescence.* New York: Penguin.

Dryden, G., & Vos, J. (1999). *The learning revolution.* Auckland, New Zealand: The Learning Web.

Edelman, G. (1992). *Bright air, brilliant fire.* New York: Harper-Collins.

Eisner, E. (1994). *Cognition and curriculum reconsidered.* New York: Teachers College Press.

Elias, M. (1999, November 30). Depressing trend: Eroding support for kids. *U.S.A. Today.*

Erickson, H. (1998). *Concept-based curriculum and instruction.* Thousand Oaks, CA: Corwin Press.

Feuerstein, R., Klien, P., & Tannenbaum, A. (1991). *Mediated learning experience (MLE): Theoretical, psychosocial, and learning implications.* London: Freund.

Feuerstein, R. (1980). *Instrumental enrichment.* Baltimore: University Park Press.

Fogarty, R. (1997). *Brain compatible classrooms.* Arlington Heights, IL: Skylight.

Fullen, M. (1995). *Change forces: Probing the depths of educational reform.* New York: Falmer Press.

Gardner, H. (1983). *Frames of mind: The theory of multiple intelligences.* New York: Basic Books.

Gardner, H. (1992). *The unschooled mind.* New York: Basic Books.

Given, B. (2002). *Teaching to the brain's natural learning systems.* Alexandria, VA: ASCD.

Goldman, R., Klantz, R., & Berger, L. (1999). *Brain fitness.* New York: Doubleday.

Goleman, D. (1995). *Emotional intelligence: Why it can matter more than IQ.* New York: Bantam Books.

Gordon, B. (1995). *Memory: Remembering and forgetting in everyday life.* New York: MasterMedia.

Goodlad, J. (1984). *A place called school.* New York: McGraw-Hill.

Greenberg, B. (1999). *Stress management: How to improve performance, motivation, and behavior.* Paper presented at the conference of the Public Information Resources, Inc., Boston, MA.

Greenfield, S. (1997). *The human brain: A guided tour.* New York: Basic Books.

Grinder, M. (1991). *Righting the educational conveyor belt.* Portland, OR: Metamorphous Press.

Haberman, M. (1995). *Star teachers of children in poverty.* Madison, WI: Phi Delta Kappa.

Hart, L. (1983). *Human brain and human learning.* New York: Longman.

Hannaford, C. (1995). *Smart moves.* Arlington, VA: Great Ocean.

Hannaford, C. (1997). *The dominance factor.* Arlington, VA: Great Ocean.

Healy, J. (1990). *Endangered minds: Why our children don't think and what we can do about it.* New York: Simon-Schuster.

Hilliard, A. (1987). The learning potential assessment device and instrumental enrichment as a paradigm shift. *The Negro Educational Review 38*(2), 200–208.

Hooper, J., & Terisi, D. (1986). *The 3-pound universe.* New York: Macmillan.

Howard, P. (1994). *The owner's manual for the brain: Everyday applications from the mind-brain research.* Austin, TX: Bard Productions.

Hunter, M. (1982). *Mastery teaching.* El Segundo, CA: T.I.P.

Hynd, G., & Willis, G. (1988). *Pediatric neuropsychology.* Orlando, FL: Grune-Stratton.

Jensen, E. (1996). *Completing the puzzle: A brainbased approach to learning.* Del Mar, CA: Turning Point.

Jensen, E. (1998). *Teaching with the brain in mind.* Alexandria, VA: Association for Supervision and Curriculum Development.

Joyce, B., & Weil, M. (1996). *Models of teaching* (5th ed.). Boston, MA: Allyn-Bacon.

Klinger, E. (1990). *Daydreaming.* New York: Tarcher.

Koch, R. (1998). *The 80/20 principle: The secret of achieving more with less.* New York: Doubleday.

Kolb, B. (1995). *Brain plasticity and behavior.* Mahwah, NJ: Erlbaum.

Kolb, D. (1984). *Experiential learning: Experience as the source of learning and development.* Englewood, NJ: Prentice-Hall.

Kotulak, R. (1996). *Inside the brain: Revolutionary discoveries of how the mind works.* Kansas City, MO: Universal Press.

Kozulin, A., & Rand, Y. (2000). *The experience of mediated learning: An impact of Feuerstein's theory in education and psychology.* Oxford, England: Elsevier Science.

LeDoux, J. (1996). *The emotional brain: The mysterious underpinnings of emotional life.* New York: Simon-Schuster.

Longo, P. (1999). *Distributed knowledge in the brain: Using visual thinking to improve student learning.* Paper presented at the conference of the Public Information Resources, Inc., Boston, MA.

Maguire, J. (1990). *Care and feeding of the brain.* New York: Doubleday.

Mazano, R. (2003). *What works in schools: Translating research into action.* Alexandria, VA: ASCD.

Meier, D. (2000). *The accelerated learning handbook.* New York: McGraw-Hill.

Nolte, J., & Angevine, J. (1995). *The human brain in photographs and diagrams.* St. Louis, MO: Mosby-Year Book.

Peoples, D. (1992). *Presentations plus.* New York: Wiley.

Perkins, D. (1992). *Smart schools: Better thinking and learning for every child.* New York: Free Press.

Perkins, D. (1995). *Outsmarting IQ: The emerging science of learnable intelligence.* New York: Free Press.

Pert, C. (1999). *Molecules of emotion* (2nd ed.). New York: Touchstone.

Peskin, B., & Conyers, M. (2000). *Peak performance and radiant health.* Houston, TX: Noble.

Piaget, J. (1954). *The construction of reality in the child.* New York: Basic Books.

Piaget, J. (1977). *The development of thought: Equilibration of cognitive structures.* New York: Viking Press.

Presseisen, B. (1988). *At risk students and thinking perspectives from research.* Washington, DC: National Education Association.

Ornstein, R., & Thompson, R. (1984). *The amazing brain.* Boston, MA: Houghton-Mifflin.

Rapp, D. (1991). *Is this your child?* New York: Morrow.

Ratey, J. (1999). *The care and feeding of the brain.* Paper presented at the conference of the Public Information Resources, Inc., Boston, MA.

Rath, T. & Clifton, D. (2004). *How full is your bucket? Positive strategies for work and life.* New York: Gallop Press.

Restak, R. (1994). *The modular brain.* New York: Scrober.

Robbins, J. (1996*). Reclaiming our health.* Tiburon, CA: Kramer.

Roizen, M. (1999). *Real age: Are you as young as you can be?* New York: Harper-Collins.

Sanders, W., & Rivers, J. (1996). *Cumulative and residual effects of teachers on future student academic achievement.* (Research Progress Report). Knoxville, TN: University of TN. Value-Added Research and Assessment Center.

Sapolsky, R. (1998). *Why zebras don't get ulcers.* New York: Freeman.

Sarason, S. (1971). *The culture of the school and the problem of change.* Boston, MA: Allyn-Bacon.

Schacter, D. (1996). *Searching for memory: The brain, the mind, and the past.* New York: Basic Books.

Schmidt, M. (1997). *Smart fats.* Berkley, CA: North Atlantic Books.

Seligman, M. (2002*). Authentic happiness: Using the new positive psychology to realize your potential for lasting fulfillment.* New York: Free Press.

Seligman, M. (1998). *Learned optimism: How to change your mind and your life.* New York: Simon-Schuster.

Sharron, H. (1987). *Changing children's minds: Feuerstein's revolution in the teaching of intelligence.* London: Souvenir Press.

Siegel, D. (1999). *The developing mind: Toward a neurobiology of interpersonal experience.* New York: Guilford.

Somer, E. (1995). *Food and mood: How the nutrients in food improve memory, energy levels, sleep patterns, weight management, and attitude.* New York: Holt.

Sousa, D. (1995). *How the brain learns.* Reston, VA: National Association of Secondary School Principals.

Springer, S., & Deutsch, G. (1998). *Left brain right brain.* New York: Freeman.

Sternberg, R. (1983). *How we can teach intelligence.* Philadelphia: Research for Better Schools.

Sternberg, R. (1997). *Successful intelligence.* New York: Simon-Schuster.

Stronge, J. (2002). *Qualities of effective teachers.* Alexandria, VA: ASCD.

Sullivan, G., & Harper, M. (1998). *Hope is not a method: What business leaders can learn from America's army.* New York: Doubleday.

Sylwester, R. (1995). *A celebration of neurons: An educator's guide to the brain.* Alexandria, VA: Association of Supervision and Curriculum Development.

Sylwester, R. (1998). *Student brains, school issues.* Arlington Heights, IL: Skylight.

Sylwester, R. (2000). *A biological brain in a cultural classroom: Applying biological research to classroom management.* Thousand Oaks, CA: Corwin Press.

Teddlie, C., & Reynolds, D. (2000). *The international handbook of school effectiveness research.* New York: Falmer Press.

Vygotsky, L. (1978). *Mind in society.* Cambridge, MA: Harvard University Press.

Wadsworth, B. (1978). *Piaget for the classroom teacher.* New York: Longman.

Walker, D., & Soltis J. (1997). *Curriculum and aims.* New York: Teachers College Press.

Wang, M., Haertel, G., & Wahlberg, H. (1993). Toward a knowledge base for school learning. *Review of Educational Research 63*, 249–294.

Washington, V., & Andrews, J. (Eds.). (1998). *Children of 2010.* Washington, DC: National Association for the Education of Young Children.

Weinstein, E., & Rosen, E. (1999). *Teaching children about health: A multidisciplinary approach.* Englewood, CA: Morton.

Wheatley, M. (1992). *Leadership and the new science.* San Francisco: Berrett- Koehler.

Willett, W. (2001). *The Harvard medical school guide: Eat, drink, and be healthy.* New York: Simon & Schuster.

Wilson, D., & Church, S. (1993). *Norman public schools' three year study of at-risk students: Teaching thinking and problem solving.* (12) pp. 9-11. Philadelphia: Research for Better Schools.

Wilson, D., & Conyers, M. (2003). *Thinking for results.* Orlando, FL: BrainSMART Publishing.

Wilson, D., & Conyers, M. (2000) *Courageous learners: Unleashing the brain power of students at risk.* Orlando, FL: BrainSMART Publishing.

Wilson, D., & Greenberg, K. (2000). Learning to learn. In A. Costa (Ed.). *Teaching for Intelligence 1999.* Arlington Heights, IL: Skylight.

Wolfe, P. (1994). *A staff developer's guide to the brain* (Cassette recordings). Front Royal, VA: National Cassette Services.

Wolffe, R., & Robinson, H. (2000). *Connect learning through movement.* Paper presented at Eric Jensen's Learning Brain Expo 2000, San Diego, CA.

Wong, H., & Wong, R. (1998). *The first days of school: How to be an effective teacher.* Mountain View, CA: Harry T. Wong Publications.

Wurtman, J. (1986). *Managing your mind and mood through food.* New York: Harper and Row.

Appendix

About the Authors

International author, speaker, and consultant, Marcus Conyers, conducts dynamic keynotes and workshops for superintendents, principals, teachers, and other educators on increasing student learning through brain-based leading and teaching. He is author of 10 books including *BrainSMART® Strategies for Boosting Test Scores*. Marcus and his partner, Dr. Donna Wilson, have co-developed the on-line Ed.S. degree specializing in *BrainSMART® Instructional Leadership* with Nova Southeastern University as well as the Master's with a specialization in *BrainSMART® Teaching and Learning*. Now principals and teachers in over 30 U.S. states, Canada, and Japan are applying strategies learned in these innovative programs.

Marcus devoted 25 years in 35 countries to developing the BrainSMART approach to effective leading and teaching. Florida Department of Education chose the approach for a successful 3-year statewide implementation. The model was then awarded a prestigious Annenberg Challenge Grant for implementation through work with Florida Atlantic University.

Marcus has shared the BrainSMART approach with leaders from the Army Rangers and Navy Seals through his work with Joint Special Operations University. He and Donna have personally worked with 75,000 administrators and educators. Marcus' dynamic presentation style has been influenced by his work with fellow Englishman John Cleese of Monty Python fame. Marcus has worked with a wide range of clients from the fields of law enforcement, counter-terrorism, and from Fortune 500 companies including Ford, Bell, AT&T, and Sony. He has presented at most major national conferences including a keynote at the *Learning and the Brain Conference* alongside leading MIT and Harvard faculty. Today Marcus focuses on supporting long-term initiatives with districts across the United States. He has inspired millions by his appearances on more than 600 TV and radio shows around the world. The Texas Education Agency selected the *BrainSMART HealthWise* program as a statewide initiative following the program's success with the Winter Park Health Foundation in Florida.

Marcus Conyers, BrainSMART Inc.
127 W. Fairbanks Ave. #235
Winter Park, FL. 32789
Toll Free: 866-SMART61Fax 800 725 5508
E-mail: marcus@brainsmart.com

Donna Wilson, Ph.D.

"All students can be successful when they are taught the thinking and learning tools they need to achieve their highest potential. This is how we bridge the achievement divide in education and keep students safe and drug free."

Dr. Donna Wilson
Author and Professional Developer
Former University Faculty Chair Education

Dr. Donna Wilson delivers dynamic research-based professional development keynotes and workshops for schools and districts throughout the United States. She presents at leading conferences such as Association of Supervision and Curriculum Development, National Title 1 Conference, National Staff Development Conference, Harvard's Learning and the Brain Conference, American Educational Research Association Conference and many more.

Prior to co-developing the BrainSMART process, Donna's quest to develop the most effective tools for increasing student achievement led her to complete post-doctoral studies in Israel. She is a recognized leader in translating implications of brain and cognitive research into tools for increasing student achievement and creating safe and drug free schools. Donna is author of seven books on learning and the brain as well as a number of articles including the books *BrainSMART 60 Strategies for Boosting Test Scores, Courageous Learners: Unleashing the Brain Power of Students From At-Risk Situations, BrainSMART In the House, Thinking for Results: Safer Schools and Higher Student Achievement, BrainSMART HealthWise*, and teachers' guidebooks for the *Drive Your Brain: The Road to Reading Success* and *Thinking for Reading* series.

Donna has worked with the BrainSMART team to co-develop on-line Master's and Ed.S. degrees with partner Nova Southeastern University. She co-led a 3 year Florida Department of Education initiative for raising student achievement with students at-risk of dropout. As president of BrainSMART, Wilson is leading a number of long-term initiatives for raising student achievement across the United States and Canada. She is the co-author of two curricula called *Drive Your Brain: The Road to Reading Success* and *Thinking for Reading.* She is known as one of the most dynamic presenters in education today. Donna's passionate belief that all educators and students can reach their true potential by applying effective strategies shines through in everything she does.

Donna Wilson, Ph.D.
127 West Fairbanks Avenue #235
Winter Park, FL. 32789
Toll Free: 866-SMART61 Fax 800 725 5508
E-mail: donna@brainsmart.com

"BrainSMART presenters Donna Wilson and Marcus Conyers bring fascinating research to life, then model practical strategies with students. This is a great way to enhance professional and personal life."

Beth Brissette, Teacher
Orlando, Florida

Bring the benefits of decades of brain research into your classroom and earn a graduate education degree with a BrainSMART specialization to advance your career in as little as 14 months of study.

Delivered through convenient and user-friendly distance education systems, these degree programs allow you the flexibility to complete your program of study from home while maintaining your full-time job. Unique program features include:

- practical BrainSMART approaches shared with 75,000 educators who reach more than a million students
- powerful learning you can use in your classroom and apply in your professional and personal life

BrainSMART Professional Development is a recognized leader in translating implications of brain and student achievement research into a practical process for effective teaching and learning. This BrainSMART process has been shared with state departments of education and high achieving school districts across the United States and Canada. Major BrainSMART accomplishments include

- the Florida Department of Education chose the BrainSMART model for a successful three-year statewide initiative
- the BrainSMART model has been supported by a prestigious Annenberg Challenge Grant award through Florida Atlantic University for an initiative in two large school districts
- the National Association of Elementary School Principals features the work of the BrainSMART team as part of their on-line leadership academy
- BrainSMART was chosen for a statewide "Train the Trainer" program in Texas
- a federally-funded program is using BrainSMART in Palm Beach County, Florida

Since 1980, Donna Wilson, Ph.D., and Marcus Conyers, founders of BrainSMART, have been translating the implications of brain research into tools for teaching and learning. They developed their approach after working with more than 10,000 K–12 students before sharing their strategies with more 75,000 educators who reach over a million students. They have written 10 books on the brain and student achievement, which include *60 BrainSMART Strategies for Boosting Test Scores*, a top 10 best-seller at the National Association of Elementary School Principals conference. They have given keynote speeches and workshops at many national and international conferences, which include

- the National Association of Elementary School Principals
- the National Association of Secondary School Principals
- the National Board for Professional Teaching Standards
- the National Dropout Prevention Network
- the National Staff Development Council

In March 2000, BrainSMART Professional Development and Nova Southeastern University began working together to make the BrainSMART approach available internationally through innovative on-line graduate programs. To date, educators from three countries and nearly 30 states have entered these highly rated programs that are regarded as the first of their kind in the world.

Nova Southeastern University

Located on a beautiful 300-acre campus in Fort Lauderdale, Florida, NSU has more than 21,000 students and is the largest independent institution of higher education in Florida. Nova Southeastern University is the 10th largest independent university in the United States and the largest in the Southeast. NSU awards associate's, bachelor's, master's, educational specialist, doctoral, and first-professional degrees in a wide range of fields. It has an undergraduate college and graduate schools of medicine, dentistry, pharmacy, allied health and nursing, optometry, law, computer and information sciences, psychology, education, business, oceanography, and humanities and social sciences. The institution also enjoys an excellent reputation for its programs for families offered through the Jim & Jan Moran Family Center Village and University School, including innovative parenting, and preschool, primary, and secondary education programs.

The Fischler Graduate School of Education and Human Services

NSU's Fischler Graduate School of Education and Human Services (FGSEHS) offers dozens of programs of postgraduate study in the fields of education and related human services. With more than 30 years of experience in distance education, FGSEHS offers almost all programs via site-based, cluster-based, and online curriculum delivery in a manner that adapts to students' work schedules and locations.

Master's, educational specialist, and doctoral degrees, and certificates are available in fields ranging from educational and organizational leadership to higher education administration; child, youth, and human services, specializations within teacher education, speech-language pathology, distance education and technology, addiction studies, training and professional development, and many others.

The Fischler Graduate School of Education and Human Services is the largest graduate school of education at an accredited university (Southern Association of Colleges and Schools) in the United States, with more than 12,000 students in some 55 cities and 29 states in the United States, plus nearly a dozen other countries.

Headquartered in North Miami Beach, Florida, on a modern, 18-acre, 250,000-squarefoot campus, FGSEHS has nearly 300 full-time employees, including full-time faculty members and administrative, professional services, and support personnel—all working to serve students' needs in education and human services. FGSEHS also calls on the talents and insights of hundreds of highly-qualified part-time adjunct faculty members, facilitators, and national lecturers who add a depth to our curriculum that no single school of education faculty could offer on its own.

All FGSEHS programs are designed to ensure they support individuals' needs to become more effective in their current positions, to fill emerging roles in education and human services, and to be ready to accept changing responsibilities within their own institutions and organizations.

M.S. in Education with a Specialization in BrainSMART Learning and Teaching (36 Credits)

Overview

This distance education degree program is designed for educators who want to earn their master's degree, gain powerful knowledge, and learn cutting-edge skills without leaving their homes and classrooms. The program focuses on equipping participants with knowledge of how breakthroughs in brain research, student achievement, and cognition can be translated into best practices in their classroom.

The Courses

BrainSMART Science, Structure, and Strategies (6 credit hours)

Learn the principles that drive the BrainSMART process for effective instruction; discover strategies that have been shared with more than 75,000 educators who reach more than a million students; see BrainSMART authors model strategies with students; discover fascinating breakthroughs in brain and student achievement research that explain why some approaches to instruction work so well; learn how nutrition impacts mood and learning, and how learning changes the physical structure of the brain.

Thinking for Results: Applying the Science of Student Achievement (6 credit hours)

Experience the exhilaration of discovering a process for increasing students' ability to think more effectively; learn about the cognitive assets that increase student achievement; discover the Drive Your Brain system for maximum learning from the BrainSMART authors; and equip yourself with a toolbox of strategies for helping students learn more effectively. The question will no longer be, "How smart am I?" but "How smart will I become?"

Differentiated Instruction: Respecting Brain-Based Learner Differences (6 credit hours)

Research suggests that less than 25 percent of students learn best with standard instruction techniques. Learn how male/female brain differences may impact communication and learning; discover a process for reading the barcode of your students' brains; gain strategies for presenting lessons in ways that maximize achievement by energizing and engaging students' brains in meaningful learning; master a toolbox of approaches for facilitating learning; and avoid seven of the most common teaching mistakes.

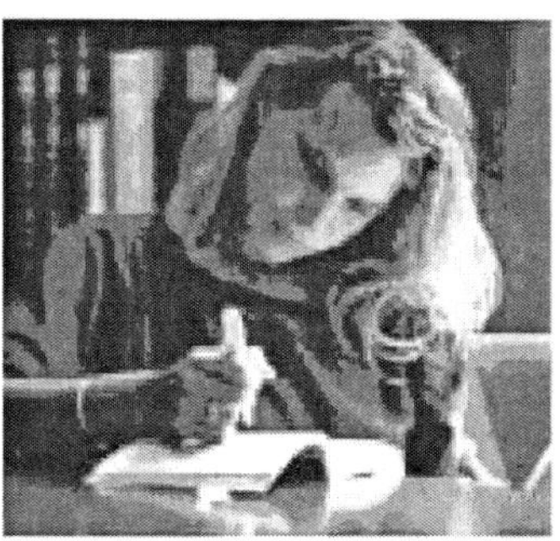

Courageous Learners: Tools for Teaching Students at Risk **(6 credit hours)**

In many classrooms today, teachers are faced with the challenge of supporting the success of students who are at risk of academic failure. Learn the Courageous Learners framework for looking at this challenge; master a new approach for understanding and reaching students with attention deficit disorder (ADD); discover tools for increasing motivation and enhancing academic achievement by all students; and see the BrainSMART authors model strategies that work well with students who learn differently.

Student Achievement and Classroom Management **(6 credit hours)**

Research suggests that the application of cognitive strategies enhances both student achievement and classroom management; discover ways for enhancing academic success that may be applied to all curriculum areas. Research suggests that 80 percent of classroom management problems may be avoided by a brain-friendly approach to instructional design; learn how to harness five forces of classroom management that influence the climate of your classroom.

Teacher Leadership Institute: Action Research Project **(6 credit hours)**

One of the most powerful ways to deepen your understanding of what you are studying is to conduct research in your own classroom. Learn how to design, implement, and evaluate an action research project using a topic that relates to what you have learned in the program and publish your research as a way to contribute to the knowledge base about practical applications of research on the brain and learning.

Admission Requirements

- completed admission application (including $50 nonrefundable application fee payable to Nova Southeastern University)
- earned baccalaureate or graduate degree from a regionally accredited college, university, or administratively approved equivalent
- photocopy of highest-degree earned transcript
- official transcripts from all schools attended (required within 90 days of the starting term)

Tuition and Fees

For information on current tuition rates, fees and materials costs, visit *www.brainsmart.com.*

Ed.S. with a Specialization in BrainSMART Instructional Leadership (36 Credits)

Program Overview

This distance education degree program is designed for teacher leaders, educators in all disciplines, district administrators, professional developers, and school personnel who have already earned their master's degree and want to move their professional skills to the next level without leaving their homes and schools. The program focuses on equipping participants with knowledge of how breakthroughs in brain research, student achievement, instructional leadership, and cognition can be translated into best practices in the classroom and on a schoolwide basis. A series of instructional leadership projects are designed to support skills in taking classroom best practices to a wider audience with a greater scope for enhancing school culture and climate.

The Courses

The Neurobiology of BrainSMART Instructional Leadership (6 credit hours)

Effective leaders facilitate professional development that translates student achievement research into results in the classroom. Research by the National Research Council suggests that learning changes the physical structure of the brain. Some 90 percent of all books on the brain and learning have been published in the last five years and the insights that flow from recent brain research are consistent with the last 50 years of cognitive studies. Discover ways in which these implications are being translated into powerful approaches to learning and teaching in schools that maximize learning.

Best Practices in Thinking for Leading (6 credit hours)

Mental models have a powerful influence on how schools function and connect with key stakeholders. Common language and metaphors can help galvanize support for the implementation of critical initiatives. Equip yourself with a toolbox of powerful strategies for effective thinking with the Thinking for Results framework, which gives students the thinking tools for maximum academic achievement and lifelong learning success. These include strategies for gathering and processing information, techniques for effective expression, effective use of time and space, and practical optimism, along with many other foundational tools.

Differentiated Instructional Leadership (6 credit hours)

The theory of differentiated instruction offers a powerful lens for looking at effective instructional leadership. The course explores several approaches to helping instructional leaders identify learner differences and adapt instruction. These approaches include gender differences, cognitive strengths, learner preferences, and a tool for reading the barcode for the brain. Methods of varying instruction including the keys to effective presenting and facilitating will be explored.

Curriculum Trends and Innovations (3 credit hours)

This course focuses on the analysis of current educational practices, models, and futuristic approaches. Emphasis is placed on the investigation of educational curricular policies and techniques developed for a variety of settings (i.e., community schools, hospital-based instruction, distance education, home schooling). Integration of technology and multimedia is also included.

Research and Design in Education (3 credit hours)

This course provides an in-depth analysis of appropriate educational research methodologies. Attention is placed on the discussion of quantitative (i.e., experimental, correlational, survey) and qualitative (i.e., ethnographic, case study, historical) methodologies. Students will engage in the examination and selection of available instrumentation and appropriate analysis and interpretation of research findings.

Families, Communities, and Schools: Ethics and Educational Practices in a Diverse Society (3 credit hours)

In this course students delve into the roles, practices, and responsibilities of educators working with families and communities from the perspective of multicultures and diversity. Ethical and legal issues related to equity, services, advocacy, and professional behaviors of educators in multicultural settings are pondered.

Current Research in Human Development (3 credit hours)

This course engages students in the analysis of recent theoretical positions and research in human development. Selected research findings from the different domains (social-emotional, cognitive, language, and biological) are examined. Emphasis is placed on the educational applications/implications of developmental research, i.e., brain research, learning styles, multiple intelligences, and neo-Piagetian studies.

Evaluation and Assessment Practices (3 credit hours)

This course engages students in the analysis of critical issues and their relation to national/international trends in testing and legal and ethical issues in evaluation. Students will pursue a formal inquiry project that focuses on meaningful program effectiveness.

Teacher Leadership Institute: Action Research Project (3 credit hours)

The Teacher Leadership Institute is designed to provide opportunities for professional development that will enhance your leadership skills. One of the most powerful ways to deepen understanding of what you are studying is to conduct research in your own classroom. Learn how to design, implement, and evaluate an action research project using a topic that relates to what you have learned in the program and publish your research as a way to contribute to the knowledge base about practical applications of research on the brain and learning.

Admission Requirements

- completed admission application (including $50 nonrefundable application fee payable to Nova Southeastern University)
- earned graduate degree from a regionally accredited college, university, or administratively approved equivalent
- photocopy of highest-degree earned transcript
- official transcripts from all schools attended (required within 90 days of the starting term)

Tuition and Fees

For information on current tuition rates, fees and materials costs, visit *www.brainsmart.com.*

Instructional Delivery Systems

Participants use a combination of user-friendly distance education technologies and high-quality textbooks to complete the assignments in each of their courses. Online facilitators and peers provide a strong support network throughout the program of study. Students typically spend at least six hours per week completing assignments, readings, chats, and discussions.

Videos: Watch the BrainSMART authors bring cutting-edge research to life and model practical strategies with students in a variety of locations.

CD-ROMS: Discover important information about the brain and student achievement.

Texts: Gain a greater depth of knowledge about research on the brain and student achievement.

Online Threaded Discussions: Interact with students in the program from across North America. Many students report that they really benefit from this easy-to-use interactive technology.

Online Chats: Connect with other cohort members to learn more about topics being studied.

Get Started Now!

Bring the benefits of decades of brain research into your classroom and earn a graduate education degree with a BrainSMART specialization to advance your career in as little as 14 months of study. It's so easy. Here's how:

1. **Contact Us.**

   Call us at 866-SMART61 or (407) 740-8428, send an email to *edu@brainsmart.com*, or visit our Web site *www.brainsmart.com.*

2. **Apply.**

   Download the application form at *www.brainsmart.com.* Send the completed application, your $50 nonrefundable application fee (payable to Nova Southeastern University), and a copy of your highest-degree earned transcript to the address below:

BrainSMART/NSU Programs

127 W. Fairbanks, Suite 235
Winter Park, Florida 32789
P: 866-SMART61
F: 800-725-5508
www.brainsmart.com

Enrich Your Professional Development

Request a Visit by Dr. Donna Wilson or Marcus Conyers
Please Fax to 800-725-5508
Phone 866-SMART61 / 407-740-8095

Name: ______________________________

Address: ______________________________

City: ______________ State: ________ Zip: __________

Position: ______________________________

Phone: ______________________________

Fax: ______________________________

E. Mail: ______________________________

Date of Event: ______________________________

Approximate Number of Participants: ______________________________

Make Up of Audience: (Teachers, Administrators, Parents etc.) ______________________________

____

____

Length of Presentation: (One hour, half day, full day) ______________________________

____

Location for Event: ______________________________

____

Hours From Nearest Airport: ______________________________

Preferred Topic: ______________________________

____

____

____

____

____

____